BUSINESS RESEARCH METHODS

BUSINESS RESEARCH METHODS

T. Raju

(Formerly Regional Director of Research, Coffee Board, Government of India)
Professor and Head
Department of Management Studies
Coimbatore Institute of Engineering and Technology (Anna University)
Coimbatore, Tamil Nadu

R. Prabhu

Assistant Professor
Department of Business Administration
Government Arts College for Men
Krishnagiri, Tamil Nadu

MJP Publishers

MJP PUBLISHERS

© Publishers, 2024   New No. 5, Muthu Kalathy Street
All rights reserved   Triplicane
Chennai 600 005

PREFACE

There are many famous books on Research Methodology or Business Research authored by Indian as well as foreign researchers. But the students of MBA and other similar programmes neither have the inclination nor time to go through any detailed textbook. They are in need of a simple book to get through the research methodology paper. They also require a guide book to guide them in their research projects. This book is written in simple language with appropriate day-to-day examples keeping in view the students as the target beneficiaries.

This book covers the entire gamut of the research process, i.e., Defining the problem, Review of Literature, Formulation and Testing of Hypothesis, Research Design, Sampling Techniques, Collection and Processing of Data (including Measurement and Scaling), Data Analysis, Interpretation and Report Preparation. In addition how ANOVA and Chi-square tests could be applied to analyse the data collected through questionnaire/opinionnaire are also explained step by step. Writing of a research report with appropriate examples is detailed for the benefit of student-researchers.

As the authors are neither statisticians nor mathematicians but teaching research methodology over a decade, they have explained the research process without any statistical or mathematical complexities. They have not attempted to explain the rig morale of the cumbersome statistical procedures of multivariate analysis.

In a nutshell, it is a simple book for the students who do not have adequate knowledge in the research process or in statistical analysis.

T. Raju

R. Prabhu

CONTENTS

1

RESEARCH—AN OVERVIEW

The food we consume, the clothes we wear and the houses we live in are, by and large, the fruits of sustained research. But for human ingenuity in research, our civilization would have stagnated at the Stone Age or Iron Age level. We cannot imagine the ubiquitous TV sets, the multi-featured mobile handsets, the all-pervading tele-network, the computer highways, the fast and sleek cars, the high-speed bullet trains and the double-deck jumbo planes without systematic research. Life-saving drugs resulting in higher life expectancy, Green Revolution responsible for self-sufficiency in food grains, nuclear/thermal power to tide over energy crisis, etc. are the results of the untiring efforts of the research scientists. To put it in a nutshell, research is the lifeline of human civilization and development.

The changes brought in by research to improve the efficiency and effectiveness of the varied activities of humans are phenomenal; business is no exception. The enticing and scintillating advertisements which bombard us through print and electronic media, the concept of virtual office to accommodate high-flying professionals, the performance-based variable pay structure to boost the morale of exceptional performers, the Goleman's emotional intelligence to enhance interpersonal relationship and leadership style and the myriad management concepts and techniques influencing the functional areas of business, whether it is production, marketing, HRM, or finance are the results accrued from creative research in business.

Business research is applying the techniques and nuances of science to the art of management. All businesses operate in the world of uncertainty caused by the environmental factors, macro (demographic, economic, politico-legal, social, cultural, technological, or natural) or micro (competitors, internal/external customers, dealers, suppliers or substitutes) or both. There is no unique way to eliminate uncertainty entirely. But business research can minimize the degree of uncertainty.

WHAT IS RESEARCH?

In common parlance research connotes "search for more knowledge". But the real meaning of research goes beyond searching for knowledge.

Research is a systematic or scientific investigation

- to search for solutions to the existing and future problems
- to establish relationship, if any, among variables and
- to find something new to increase our knowledge

SEARCHING FOR SOLUTIONS TO PROBLEMS

Some examples of searching for solutions to problems are as follows:

- A medical scientist researching to invent/discover a medicine to cure cancer. Here, cancer is the problem and the new medicine is the solution.
- A horticulturist engaging in research to find a suitable chemical/method to improve the colour of the apple. In this case, dull colour is the problem and the new chemical/method is the solution.
- A design engineer in a car manufacturing company trying to modify the engine to reduce fuel consumption. Here, the problem is higher consumption of fuel and the solution is new engine design.
- The marketing team looking out for a new promotional programme to improve sales.

  Problem: Poor sales

  Solution: New promotional programme
- The personnel manager in a star hotel searching for appropriate incentives.

  Problem: Lack of motivation or low morale

  Solution: Appropriate incentive
- A financial analyst searching for a simple way of calculating VAT.

  Problem: Complex way of calculating VAT

  Solution: A simple procedure of calculating VAT

ESTABLISHING RELATIONSHIP AMONG VARIABLES

Some examples for establishing relationship among variables are as follows:

- Medical research undertaken to find out whether there is any true relationship between paan-chewing and mouth cancer, sweet-eating and diabetes or mental worries and baldness.

✿ Tea research station searching for correlations between shade pattern and yield of tea, sunshine and quality of tea or rainfall and fungal diseases.

✿ Marketing wings investigating the association between disposable income of middle income group and sales of four wheelers or educational background of housewives and demand for white goods.

✿ Production departments analysing the relationship between preventive maintenance and productivity, raw materials and product quality or training programmes and industrial accidents.

✿ HRD managers conducting surveys to find plausible association between absenteeism and supervisor's attitude, incentives and overtime work or frequency of strikes and grievances-handling mechanism.

RESEARCHING TO INCREASE KNOWLEDGE

Some examples for researching to increase knowledge are as follows:

✿ A clinical psychologist intensely observing how a HIV-positive person behaves in a group to add more information to group therapy.

✿ An agricultural scientist conducting a botanical survey to improve knowledge on plant diversity.

✿ Govt. of India sending teams of scientists to Antarctica to explore the possibility of any biological growth in freezing environment.

✿ Discovery channel deploying animal enthusiasts in African jungles to add more knowledge to animal behaviour.

✿ A personnel manager observing through a hidden video camera the behaviour of workers in the canteen, to improve his knowledge on off-the-job behaviour of workers.

✿ A marketing researcher posting himself in a corner of a departmental store to understand more about customer behaviours in customer relationship management.

OBJECTIVES OR PURPOSE OF RESEARCH

The objectives of research mostly depend on situational factors. The major objectives are

✿ to gain familiarity with a phenomenon (e.g., buying behaviour of rural population in respect of latest electronic gadgets)

✿ to analyse the characteristics of an individual, group or situation (e.g., understanding the leadership skills of a successful business magnate, the phenomenal expansion of a new company or the reasons for delinquency in low-income groups)

✿ to determine the frequency of occurrence of certain phenomena (e.g., fatal accidents in highways and railway crossings and alcoholism/absenteeism among workers)

- ✿ to test a causal relationship between variables (e.g., different age groups and their visits to beauty parlours or excess pocket money and students' absenteeism)
- ✿ to develop new techniques, concepts or theories (e.g., new advertisements through animation or promotional campaigns involving physically challenged persons) and
- ✿ to find solutions to problems (this could be the ultimate objective)

MOTIVES FOR RESEARCH

The motives in undertaking research vary from person to person and from situation to situation. The motives could be

- ✿ to derive satisfaction out of solving an unsolved problem (e.g., attempts made by Galileo, Newton, Franklin, Einstein and the like)
- ✿ to gain intellectual joy in creative work (e.g., the numerous inventions/discoveries made by Thomas Alva Edison and G.D.Naidu of Coimbatore)
- ✿ to serve various sections of the society (e.g., social scientists researching the habitats of tribal or functioning of self-help groups)
- ✿ to satisfy the needs of an organization/authority (e.g., sponsored research undertaken by scientists/scholars)
- ✿ to get a research degree (e.g., students of M.B.A., M.Phil., and Ph.D. programmes pursuing research)

CHARACTERISTICS OF A GOOD RESEARCH

To get qualified as a good research, the research must be

- ✿ *Rational* There is no place for rule of thumb or superstitious belief in research. There should be always a cause–effect relationship. The question of obtaining objects from thin air does not arise in a rational research. Dalton's time-tested theory "matter can neither be created nor destroyed and can only be transferred from one form to another" should be the underlying factor in rational research.
- ✿ *Systematic* There is order or methodology or logical sequence in conducting research. Here, the means are as important as the ends. Haphazard way of conducting a study is anathema to good research.
- ✿ *Scientific* There must be empirical evidence. That is, all results and inferences must be supported by data. All observations, attitude, opinions, etc. must be quantified for valid analysis and interpretation. For a good research, database is indispensable.
- ✿ *Objective* Judgements, i.e., inferences, must be made based on facts only without any personal prejudice or favour or external influence. A spade is always called a spade in objective research.

It is interesting to note that the term RESEARCH itself carries the quality of the good research. Further, the popular term "MOVIE" supplements "RESEARCH" in describing an ideal research.

R — *Rational ways of thinking*

E — *Expert treatment*

S — *Search for solutions*

E — *Exhaustive treatment*

A — *Analytical (Analysis of data)*

R — *Relationship between facts and theories*

C — *Constructive attitude, critical observation, condensed generalization and cautious/careful recording*

H — *Honesty and hard work*

M — *Mathematical precision/accuracy*

O — *Objectivity*

V — *Verifiability*

I — *Impartiality*

E — *Exactness*

- *Universal*   The results must be amenable for generalization and applicable for universal adaptation.
- *Increasing body of knowledge*   A research should enrich the existing knowledge. Additional data obtained must be valuable. Treading on beaten track is not a good research.
- *Verifiable*   Similar to universality, a good research must be amenable for verification. It should yield the same type of results under similar conditions. There could be exceptions as in the case of behavioural science.
- *Honesty*   Honesty is the backbone of research. The researcher must be honest and scrupulous in collection of data, analysis, interpretation and reporting of the results/ inference.

OBJECTIVITY IN RESEARCH

Objectivity means the willingness and ability to conduct research without any favour, fervour, or hatred. The conclusions drawn should not depend on personal beliefs, likes, dislikes or hopes. Collection of data, analysis and interpretation must be free from any sort of bias or prejudice. A good researcher should be impartial. That is why it is insisted that the researcher should formulate the null hypothesis (no effect, no difference or no relationship) first.

To make sure that research adopts a scientific procedure, the following aspects are taken into consideration seriously.

- clearly defining the purpose of the research
- describing the research process with all details
- following a thoroughly planned research design
- frankly revealing the limitations
- providing adequate/appropriate analysis
- presenting the findings unambiguously
- justifying the conclusions
- applying high ethical standards

FACTORS AFFECTING OBJECTIVITY

There are many factors which affect objectivity.

Personal prejudices and biases   Prejudices and biases originate from habits of thought, temperamental weakness, skeptical attitude, wishful thinking, vested interest, etc. These make one to believe in a particular aspect without considering the available evidence.

Value-related problems   Sometimes the researcher is influenced by his/her values, beliefs and attitudes towards persons, objects and happenings. Family background, upbringing during childhood or the community may also affect the outcome of the research.

Personal perception Even before initiating the research, the researcher may have his/her own perception or preconceived notions. These preconceived ideas/options are likely to distort the ultimate results or utility of research.

Ethical dilemmas These arise out of the researcher's relationship/acquaintance with others. More frequently the researcher may be biased in favour of sponsors of the research project or those who render help in collection of data. Sometimes personal interest or eagerness to satisfy the power-that-may-be creates ethical dilemma. In certain cases greediness for cheap popularity may make researchers unethical.

Social phenomena Customs, social beliefs and social status may also influence the interpretation/inference of research outcome.

WHY TO STUDY RESEARCH IN BUSINESS

The study of research methods provides the manager with the knowledge and skills needed to solve the problems and meet the challenges of a fast paced decision-making environment.

The factors that stimulate an interest in a scientific approach to decision-making are:

- increased need for more and better information
- availability of improved techniques/tools in collecting and analysing the data
- overload of information

The increasingly complex nature of business consequent to eventful changes in technology, competition, consumer behaviour, etc. is compelling the businessmen to bestow more attention on research. As an aid to economic policy, research has gained added importance, both for government and business organizations.

Systematic research provides the basis for nearly all business policies of the government and government's analysis of needs and desires of the people and revenue available to meet the expenditure rest on research.

Operational marketing and motivational research are crucial for taking strategic business decisions. Business and society are mutually dependent. Successful business relies on tracking the significant changes in the society. Research is a dependable tool to feel the pulse of the society.

Business research is a systematic inquiry that provides information to guide business decisions. The studies included in business research may be reporting, descriptive, explanatory or predictive.

The information needed and the interpretation essential in the different functional areas of research are overwhelming, and are as follows:

- *Marketing* Demand forecasting, consumer buying behaviour, measuring effectiveness of advertisement, media selection, test marketing, product positioning, new product potential, etc.
- *Production* What to produce, how much to produce, when to produce, for whom to produce, how to improve quality control or reduce inventory cost, etc.
- *Materials* Where to buy, how much to buy, when to buy and at what price to buy.
- *Finance* How to manage the working capital, how to juggle the debt–equity ratio or how to improve the accounting procedure.
- *HRD* Human resources planning, incentive schemes, employment trend, turnover, performance appraisal, etc.
- *Government* Budgets, planning, resource optimization, etc.

LIMITATIONS OF SCIENTIFIC RESEARCH IN BUSINESS

Certain limitations in business research make one skeptical about the "science" part of research in business. They include the following:

- *Uncertainty* All businesses operate in the world of uncertainty. It is a tall order to expect a direct cause–effect phenomenon in business research.
- *Unexplained principles* In spite of concerted efforts to explain most of the basic principles of management, there are certain grey areas, especially in the psychological and social aspects of human resources in management, where scientific explanation is inadequate.
- *Difficulties in replication* Scientific investigations are required to be repeated several times to draw valid conclusions. But in behavioural science which dominates human resource management, replication under similar conditions is a difficult process.
- *Complex human behaviour* Managing humans is the essence of management. The complex human behaviour eludes scientific explanation as no two persons behave in the same manner under similar conditions.
- *Controlling in scientific method* Scientific experiments demand controlling of extraneous factors. But in a live environment of business management, keeping all the extraneous factors is not an easy task.
- *Bias in observation/interpretation* There is every possibility that the investigator's own values/attitudes may influence both the observations and interpretations of data in management science.
- *Difficulties in measurement* The tools or techniques of measurement in social science (management) are not absolutely perfect. The techniques employed may bring in unexplained errors.

- ✷ *Lack of actionable results* Business/Management research can provide a number of facts or a set of guidelines but it rarely indicates actionable results.
- ✷ *Inadequacy* Some problems dodge scientific explanation, especially cause–effect phenomenon. A precise estimate of sales directly attributed to the expenditure on advertisement and promotional exercises generally baffles the marketing managers.
- ✷ *Manager's apathy* Business managers normally do not include research results in the overall decision-making. They mostly rely on intuition, experience or personal opinion.

RESEARCH METHOD VS RESEARCH METHODOLOGY

Student-researchers are likely to be confused with the terms research method and research methodology. Though the two terms appear to be similar, there is subtle difference between the two.

RESEARCH METHOD

Research methods are the techniques the researcher employs in conducting research. Techniques to collect data, statistical tools to analyse the data and the procedure used to evaluate and compare the results are known as research methods.

Non-participant direct observation, participant observation, mass observation, mail questionnaire, opinionnaire, interview schedule, personal interview, focused interview, telephonic interview and case study are the common techniques used to collect data.

The statistical techniques include correlation, regression, t-test, Z-test, Chi-square, ANOVA, non-parametric tests and the multivariate analyses (discriminant analysis, cluster analysis, factor analysis, etc.). Analyses of historical records/documents for comparison and evaluation of the current results constitute the evaluative techniques.

RESEARCH METHODOLOGY

Research methodology is the way a research problem is systematically solved employing the relevant research methods. Here, the various steps adopted and the logic in sequencing the steps are explained. In fact methodology decides the usage of various methods available. The scope of research methodology is wider than that of research method. It tries to answer why a research study is undertaken, how the research problem is defined, why a particular method is used and many more.

Research methods and methodology could be explained using the analogy of solving a mathematical problem. Addition, subtraction, multiplication and division are the methods and how these steps are used to solve a mathematical problem is the methodology.

TYPES OF RESEARCH

The type of research depends on the information needed, methods adopted and nature of population.

EXPLORATORY VS FORMAL RESEARCH

Exploratory   The objective is just to have a superficial idea of the problem without going deep into the subject. No attempt is made to solve the problem. This research helps in formulating a hypothesis. Scientists visiting Antarctica or the moon to collect data is an exploratory research.

Formal   Formal research is a full-fledged serious research with substantial structure of well-defined parameters. This involves testing of hypothesis to find a solution or to describe a situation. Generally a formal research is preceded by an exploratory research.

DESCRIPTIVE VS ANALYTICAL RESEARCH

Descriptive research   The purpose of descriptive research is to describe the existing or past state of affairs. In social science or business research, descriptive research is termed as Ex post facto analysis. The main characteristic of this research is that the researcher has no control over the variables and just describes what has happened or what is happening. For example, when an MBA student takes up a descriptive research on departmental stores in Coimbatore, he or she describes how many departmental stores are functioning in Coimbatore, where they are located, what types of goods are sold, how many persons are employed, what are the price structures, how many visit the stores, etc. The data may be obtained through surveys and presented in easily understandable format to have an idea about the state of affairs of departmental stores. Descriptive research attempts to answer the questions 'what', 'when', 'which' and 'where'.

Analytical research   Also called as diagnostic research, analytical research tries to find why a particular phenomenon has occurred or it is occurring presently. The questions 'why' and 'how' are answered in analytical research. Analytical research is always preceded by descriptive research. In the above example of study of departmental stores, the student, after describing the nature of the stores, shall try to reason out why people are visiting a particular store in large numbers or how it is possible for a particular store to price its goods at a cheaper rate.

QUALITATIVE VS QUANTITATIVE RESEARCH

Qualitative research   As the name suggests, qualitative research is concerned with the quality of phenomena which are not easily measured in quantitative terms. It is mostly used in behavioural science to understand why people behave differently. Studies on motivation, stress, perception, values, emotional intelligence, etc., are qualitative in nature. Word Association, Sentence Completion, Story Building and Rorschach Ink Blot tests are some of the commonly used techniques in qualitative research.

Quantitative research In quantitative research the observations are quantified and the results are expressed in terms of different units.

Conceptual vs Empirical Research

Conceptual research It is a qualitative research related to some abstract ideas defying clear explanations. Mostly followed by philosophers and thinkers, it is concerned with developing new concepts/ideas or reinterpreting the existing ones.

Empirical research It is data-based quantitative research amenable for verification. All scientific experiments are empirical in nature.

The following types of research could be descriptive, analytical, qualitative or empirical based on the objectives or purposes of research.

Longitudinal vs Cross-sectional Research

While longitudinal research is extended over a period of time, cross-sectional research is a one-time research confined to a single period time. Results in cross-sectional research are obtained within a short period while longitudinal research takes longer period to yield any result.

Field vs Lab/Simulation/Historical Research

Field research Field research involves conducting research in actual situations by collecting data through observation, questionnaire, interview, etc., from real population.

Lab/Simulation research Small group studies based on random behaviour, role plays and role analyses come under laboratory research. In simulation research, computers are extensively used to simulate (duplicate) the real situations. Crisis management in war fields or plane-crashes is researched employing simulation research.

Historical research It is confined to analysis and interpretation of historical records/documents. Secondary data (the data collected and compiled by other persons) are the base for historical research.

Conclusion-oriented vs Decision-oriented Research

Conclusion-oriented research In this type of research, the researcher is free to choose a problem and design the research as he/she wishes according to the objectives or situation.

Here, the researcher is the sole authority and is independent in formulating the research. An independent social worker investigating the aftermath of Tsunami in the coastal villages with his/her own funds/efforts is said to do a conclusion-oriented research. The researcher is not under any obligations to any authority.

Decision-oriented research In this type of research, the researcher conducts a research as per the requirements/direction of a decision-maker or authority. The topic and to some extent the research design are decided in advance by the authority. Here the researcher's freedom is restricted in choosing the topic, geographical areas, sample size, etc. A Management Professor undertaking a research project sponsored by a company to study the consumer behaviour with particular reference to the company's products/services is an example of a decision-oriented research.

Applied vs Fundamental Research

A research can be termed as applied or fundamental based on the objectives of the research.

Applied research It aims at finding a solution to the current or long-pending problem. Seeking a solution is the essence of applied research. Finding an easy cure for diabetes, formulating an effective drug to combat AIDS or cancer, developing a rice variety requiring less water, devising an advertisement capable of immediate attraction or retaining attention for longer period, inventing an incentive plan to motivate the employees, etc., are applied research. In applied research, the knowledge obtained in fundamental research is applied to seek a solution to the problem under investigation.

Fundamental research Termed as basic or pure research, fundamental research is concerned with throwing light on the basic aspects, theory or the intricacies of a phenomenon. Generally it does not seek solution to any problem. It is mostly related to gathering of knowledge for knowledge's sake. Studies on natural phenomena (thunder, lightning, cell division or atomic structure), pure mathematics or human behaviour with respect to age, gender, etc. are fundamental in nature.

Investigating the atomic structure and the characteristics of electrons, protons and neutrons is fundamental research. Utilizing the knowledge on atoms to generate nuclear power or to devise an atom bomb is applied research. Similarly, studying the behaviour of children at different ages is a fundamental research; utilizing these behavioural patterns to devise a programme for effective learning for children is applied research.

Which is more important, fundamental research or applied research? Both are equally important. There cannot be any applied research without understanding the fundamental aspects. At the same time, fundamental research will be an unproductive exercise unless the results are applied to find a solution to any problem. In essence, applied research derives its strength from fundamental or basic research and basic research is valuable when the results/ observations are applied to solve problems.

RESEARCH PROCESS

Research process, in essence, is the methodology or well-defined procedure of conducting a research.

- ✿ It is a rigorous and impersonal mode of procedure dictated by the demands of logic and objectives.
- ✿ It is systematic, logical, empirical and replicable.
- ✿ It involves various steps which are neither mutually exclusive nor separate or distinct.
- ✿ In brief, research process is a scientific enquiry.

Steps involved in a business research process are outlined in Figure 1.1.

Before attempting to go ahead with the process, it is a bygone conclusion that the researcher has already decided his/her area of research. Apart from selecting the major functional areas such as marketing, finance, human resource or production, specific areas are identified depending on the researcher's interest, inclination or scope.

Marketing Utility of products/services, consumer behaviour, advertisement and sales promotion, dealer network, market share, impact of competition, scope for improvement of products/services or new product/ service, features of products/services, awareness and scope of financial products/service, functioning of organizations in various industries, etc. are some of the major areas for investigation.

Finance Working capital management, financial performance, capital structure, equity or debt market, stock market, etc. are the commonly researched areas in finance.

Human resource The off-beaten tracks of organizational climate, quality of work life, labour welfare measures, compensations, training and development programmes, career planning and performance appraisal, motivational incentives, leadership styles, etc., continue to have wider scope in the ever-changing business environment.

Production The students with engineering background and a liking for technological improvement may delve into inventory management, logistics, cost of production, quality improvement, product development, etc.

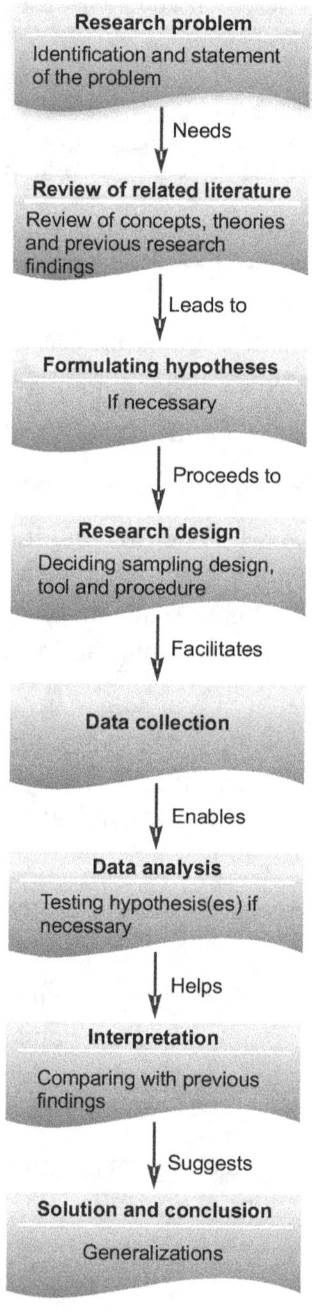

Figure 1.1   Flowchart of the research process

STEPS IN THE RESEARCH PROCESS

The steps involved in research process are detailed below.

Step 1   Defining the research problem

It is the process of identifying and pinpointing a specific problem which requires a detailed investigation. This helps the researcher to put himself/herself in the right track. The topic and primary objective depend on the well-defined research problem. Defining the problem without any ambiguity goes a long way in investigating the problem or finding an appropriate solution.

Step 2   Review of literature

For a first-time researcher, review of literature is an eye-opener. In fact, a review of relevant literature helps the researcher in fine-tuning the definition of a problem. Review includes collection of facts, details on concepts/theories and importantly the findings of earlier investigations/researches relevant to the problem in the process. Adequate information on the research methodology adopted by earlier workers, and limitations encountered by them would help in redefining the present research process. Better ideas are obtained in determining sample size and sampling technique, formulating hypotheses, selecting appropriate techniques in data collection, choosing relevant statistical tests of the collected data and even interpreting and drawing inferences from the analysed data. Academic/industrial journals, popular magazines, proceedings of seminars/workshops/symposia/conferences, reports of government organizations/NGOs, latest textbooks, etc. are the major sources of review. One source will, generally, lead to another. Nowadays, internet browsing has made things easier for the researcher in gathering adequate information.

Step 3   Formulating hypotheses

Hypothesis, which is a proposition, assumption or a tentative answer, is formulated to focus the research and to keep the researcher on the right track. Hypotheses (null hypothesis or alternative hypothesis) are either accepted or rejected based on the significance of statistical results. There is no need to frame hypothesis in exploratory research. In fact, exploratory research helps in formulation of hypothesis(es).

Step 4   Research design

It is the plan of actions to collect and analyse data aiming at combining the relevance of purpose of research and economy of execution. It is almost a blueprint of the research process. Depending on the nature of the problem, the research design could be exploratory, descriptive, diagnostic or experimental.

Research design includes:

- ✿ *Operational design*   Collection of data from entire population (census) or a sample.
- ✿ *Sampling design*   A definite plan for obtaining a sample from a given population.
- ✿ *Observation design*   Methods or tools such as interview schedule, questionnaire, personal/telephonic interview, participant/non-participant observations, etc. to collect information.
- ✿ *Statistical design*   Selection of appropriate statistical tests to analyse the data collected. The designs are flexible to accommodate the needs of various types of research.

Step 5   Data collection

Adequate and reliable data are collected employing appropriate technique (observation, interview, questionnaire, etc.). The data could be from the entire population (census method) or from a sample in the case of large population.

Step 6   Data processing and analysis

The original raw data is first condensed into a few meaningful and manageable groups and classified into purposeful and usable categories. Data processing includes editing, coding (if necessary) and tabulation. The tabulated data are analysed employing appropriate statistical tools (tests of significance). Statistical analysis determines whether the effects, relationships or differences are significant or not. Hypotheses are either accepted or rejected based on statistical analysis.

Step 7   Interpretation and inference

After testing the hypotheses through statistical analyses, the results are interpreted taking into consideration the past findings and present situations. An interpretation demands a thorough subject knowledge, analytical ability and common sense. Inferences are drawn from the interpreted data. Inferences are the final findings of the investigations.

Step 8   Solution and conclusion

Solutions are derived from interpretations/inferences. Solution is the answer to a problem in question.

Conclusions are arrived at based on the findings. It is generalization of the findings which is the essence of the whole study.

PILOT STUDY

Before embarking upon a full-fledged research involving considerable allocation of resources, both men and materials, it is advisable to conduct a pilot study. Pilot study is a mini-project or a "small-scale" replica of the main study. It is a miniature rehearsal of the main research.

A pilot study helps the researcher in a number of ways:

- fine-tuning the research problem and studying its various dimensions.
- reframing or refining the hypotheses, if necessary.
- selecting the appropriate target group for collection of data.
- deciding the adequacy and appropriateness of the sampling technique as well as the sample size.
- sorting out the problems associated with different methods of data collection and arriving at the best tool to collect relevant data.
- confirming the appropriate statistical tool to test the hypotheses.
- identifying the unforeseen practical problems.
- estimating the probable cost, time and resources needed.
- determining whether the problem requires an elaborate study/investigation.
- deciding ultimately, whether it is worth undertaking the main research.

The size, scope and design of the pilot study depend on the convenience, time and funds (including other resources) available at the disposal of the researcher.

ETHICS IN BUSINESS RESEARCH

- Ethics involves moral issues and choices.
- Ethics are norms and standards of behaviour.
- It guides people in their behaviour and in their relationship with others.
- Ethics refers to moral principles and values that determine whether the actions taken are right or wrong and the outcomes are good or bad.
- Ethical values determine "the right thing to do".
- The major objective of ethics in research is to ensure that no one is harmed or made to suffer due to the adverse consequences of research activities.

ETHICAL CONSIDERATIONS IN RESEARCH

Some of the ethical considerations to be taken care of in research are listed below:

- The rights of the respondents must be protected.
- The research must be conducted without favouring any individual or group.
- The research report should contain only the facts. There should not be any false report either for self-credit/benefit or for pleasing the interested parties.

- ☼ It is the responsibility of the principal investigator/researcher to ensure the safety of the research team members who conduct the research.
- ☼ The privacy of the respondents who take part in the research must be protected.
- ☼ The respondents must be explained as to why the research is conducted, how it is conducted and what are the benefits or consequences.
- ☼ No data/information should be gathered from the respondents on false promise.

REVIEW QUESTIONS

1. What is research? Explain with examples.
2. What are the objectives or purpose of research?
3. What are the motives for doing research?
4. Discuss the characteristics of a good research.
5. Analyse the term "objectivity" in research.
6. Why do we study research in business?
7. Discuss the limitations of scientific research in business.
8. Distinguish between research methods and research methodology.
9. What are the various types of research?
10. Discuss the various steps in the research process.
11. What is the importance of pilot study?
12. Discuss the relevance of ethics in research.

2

DEFINING THE RESEARCH PROBLEM

The research process starts with defining the problem. It is the base on which the entire edifice of research stands. It may be taken for granted that where there is no problem, there is no research.

The word "problem" originated from the Greek word *Probellein* meaning anything thrown forward, a question proposed for solution or a matter stated for examination.

A research problem, in general, refers to some difficulty experienced by a researcher in the context of either a theory or practical situation which requires a solution.

After deciding the area of research in management, i.e., marketing, human resource, finance, production or systems, the next logical step is identifying, selecting and properly defining (stating) the actual research problem. (It may be noted that exploratory/formulative research does not require any problem to be defined).

A problem usually exists under the following conditions:

i. *There must be an organization, a group of people or an individual experiencing some difficulties due to one reason or other* .

   In a manufacturing unit, the manager may encounter the problem of huge wastage, poor quality of products, high inventory cost or even frequent accidents. The HR manager may face the challenges of low morale of the workers, obsolete training/development programmes, inadequate performance appraisal mechanism, dissatisfaction with the compensation, etc. For a marketing manager, the problems could be poor sales, low market share, ineffective promotional programmes, the challenges posed by the core competence or competitive advantage of the competitors. The shortcomings experienced by the finance manager could be inadequate working capital, undesirable capital structure or poor financial performance as a whole.

In the real business world the problems are multifarious depending on the nature of business, PLC of the products, size of the business, type of management, composition of workers, management techniques adopted, leadership style, etc. In fact, to a researcher in management science or a management student going in for a research project there is no dearth of problems for every activity on earth comes under the ambit of management in one form or the other. Changes are inevitable and every change is challenged by a problem.

ii. *There must be some objectives, personal or organizational, to be attained. If one does not desire anything, there cannot be any problem.*

The objectives could be (in continuation of the examples cited above)

- to reduce wastage in processing of raw materials
- to improve quality of the products/services
- to bring down cost of inventory management
- to prevent accidents
- to boost employees' morale
- to introduce effective training programmes
- to streamline the performance appraisal mechanism
- to devise acceptable compensation package
- to overcome the unrest among the employees and enhance productivity
- to increase the sales
- to shore up market share of the products/services
- to invent attractive promotional campaigns
- to meet the challenges of the competitor's core competence or competitive advantage
- to fine-tune the working capital management
- to suggest an optimum combination in capital structure in tune with the financial environment
- to propose appropriate ways and means to prop up the financial performance of a firm as a whole.

iii. *There must be at least two ways to attaining the objective; if there is only one way, there is no confusion and hence no problem.*

With knowledge explosion and advent of sophisticated technologies, any managerial problem can be tackled from many angles. As many alternatives can be generated with concomitant advantages and limitations, a problem or dilemma always exists in selecting the best alternative.

In a remote village, if the only way through which an FMCG manufacturing company can reach the consumers is direct selling, there is no problem in selecting the best mode of access. The adman need not bother to experiment with the print media or the electronic media or the colour combination as the only way is direct selling which excludes any electronic or print media.

iv. *There must be some dilemma or confusion in selecting the best alternative to achieve objectives.*

In real business, due to changing environment there is no paucity of opportunities or alternatives to overcome any challenge. As the alternatives try to offer similar solutions, the researcher will be always in a state of confusion or dilemma to select the best alternative. Hence, there will be always a problem hanging around.

v. *There must be an environment which influences either the researcher or his/her ways.*

There is no certainty that the environment, whether macro or micro, will ever remain the same favouring the researcher or his/her method of conducting research. When the researcher is about to settle down for an appropriate solution, fresh problems may crop up due to changes in the macro-environmental factors such as government policies (legal/political), economic trend, technology or religious/social aspirations. The microclimate, viz., the unexpected game-plan of the competitors, ever changing "likes" and "dislikes" of customers, unjustified demands of dealers and suppliers or the resistance of employees to any change may pose many a problem compelling the researcher to re-do the process.

vi. *There must be some outcomes (results/findings) which may have positive or negative values.*

The research or investigations should finally bring out some meaningful or tangible results (solutions). If the results accrued are ambiguous and the question posed remains unanswered, then the entire process of research will be termed as a futile exercise; it can be concluded that there is no problem. Nothing is "impossible"; every problem should have a solution. But, by the quirk of nature, if there is no solution to a problem then the problem under reference is no more a problem. Prevention of death of living organisms is not at all a problem as there is no way of preventing death of any organism.

PROBLEM IDENTIFICATION AND SELECTION

Identifying and selecting a problem of topical interest will not be a difficult task for professionals like medical researchers, agricultural scientists, design engineers, production managers, service providers, marketing managers, HRM experts, system analysts or the financial wizards. But for a newcomer to research or for student-researchers, problem identification itself is a problem.

Problem identification and selection involve five aspects:

SOURCES FOR IDENTIFICATION OF PROBLEMS

The choice and identification of an appropriate problem, which is meaningful as well as interesting, is usually difficult because of one's limited knowledge or unpreparedness. In the case of a student-researcher of MBA programme, his/her inadequate knowledge in the area of specialization is the major limitation. As most of them are fresh from graduation, they do not have adequate experience to identify and choose a problem on their own.

The sources are the following.

Professional literature   Whether it is for the professional or the student-researcher, literature is an important source to identify a problem. Books, periodicals, research reports, dissertations, project reports, yearbooks or even weeklies and dailies will give directions or clues to choose a problem. A shrewd reader will pick up threads from the conclusions of others for further research. Many seasoned researchers deliberately include topics for future research. Review of literature is an eye-opener for further research.

Professional experience (self and others)   Apart from the problems encountered in one's own area of research, experience gained in participating in conferences, seminars and workshops could be a good source of identifying problems. Open discussion with colleagues and professionals in related fields may help in coming across new or novel ideas. Sharing of research reports may also lead to identification of unexplored areas of research.

In the case of student-researcher, self-reliance to identify a problem of importance or relevance may not yield much, excepting in cases where the students had some prior experience or possess an instinct for research. In many cases, professors with adequate theoretical knowledge in management sciences and the experienced professional managers in various industries will be dependable sources. The guidance of the knowledgeable professors or the experienced professional managers will go a long way right from defining the problem, through research process, to the final conclusion.

Inferences from theories and laws   In certain cases a deep probe into the established theories/laws may lead to new frontiers of knowledge.

The appropriateness or inappropriateness of motivational theories, leadership theories, attitude theories, etc. may be tested under varied conditions to generate new or supplementary theories. While research stalwarts may tap this type of resource, for ordinary students, it is beyond their scope.

JUSTIFICATION FOR SELECTING A PROBLEM

Once a problem is likely to be selected, one must satisfy himself/herself whether he/she is justified in selecting the problem.

Researcher's suitability The researcher must justify whether he/she has competence, capacity, courage and determination to complete the project and tolerance to face unforeseen or unexpected criticism/complaints. The researcher must make sure that timely guidance in the event of any confusion, and adequate finance are available.

In the case of a student-researcher (particularly MBAs), the question of justification does not arise because it is a requirement to get the degree. Nevertheless, the student-researchers must be cautious in selecting the appropriate area of research (production, marketing, human resource, finance or systems) and the organization/industry taking into consideration their aptitude, attitude and knowledge, competency of the guide, time available, source and adequacy of fund and above all the feasibility of completing the project in the specified period.

General rule The researcher must justify whether the research problem is relevant, important, interesting and significant. The research problem must possess creativity, originality and some utility value. The student should not select the problem just to fulfil the partial requirement for the award of the degree of MBA. The research problem must be self-satisfying. There should be some sort of mental fulfilment. The organization, industry or the public at large must get some benefit out of tackling a particular research problem. It may be a tall order for an ordinary student to solve any organizational or industrial problem. But the findings must add at least some additional information. If the students' projects are just run-of-the-mill stuff, then the industry will lose interest in allowing students for summer projects. It is always advisable if the research problem is on the lines of the suggestions/clues indicated by the organization or the industry.

CRITERIA FOR SELECTING A PROBLEM

There are certain criteria which govern the selection of a research problem, and are as follows:

- The problem must be related to a profession (in the case of an MBA student it must be related to a specific area of management function).
- The solution to be obtained should bring in some improvement in the existing status or at least some additional information which are new and useful.
- It must be feasible to find a solution to the problem before the time schedule. That is, the problem identified is amenable for a research process which could be completed in a definite time frame.
- It must suit the aptitude, attitude, interest, confidence and competency of the researcher.
- It must be practical. To find the influence of black money on Indian economy may be an interesting and useful research problem but estimating the amount of black money in circulation will be a Herculean task and not practical.
- The problem must possess creativity, novelty, originality and utility value.

- ✪ The research problem must be specific.
- ✪ The problem must be meaningful and realistic and there should not be any hunches or ambiguities.
- ✪ Controversial subjects should not be attempted by an average researcher or student-researcher.

DEFINING THE PROBLEM

A proper defining of the research problem enables the researcher to be on the right track. An ill-defined problem is likely to create confusion in finding a definite solution. Defining the problem involves the task of laying down boundaries within which the researcher should analyse the problem with pre-determined objectives.

Conditions to be satisfied to define a problem are as follows:

- ✪ The need to solve a problem must be felt by the researcher or the sponsor.
- ✪ The problem should have specific and achievable objectives.
- ✪ The defining of problem must help formulation of the hypotheses.

STATEMENT OF PROBLEM

Keeping in view some practical concerns and researcher's interest, the problem is stated in a broad general way initially. With the help of a pilot study or experts' guidance, the problem gets focused. But it is the responsibility of the researcher to narrow it down and phrase it in operational terms taking into consideration the possibility of a workable solution.

Problem delimitation   As a part of the statement of the problem, delimitation is the process of "fencing" or creating "boundaries" around a research problem. Whatever may be the problem, the scope of the study must be limited to the availability of time.

STEPS IN DEFINING A PROBLEM

- ✪ Stating the problem in a general way.
- ✪ Understanding the nature of the problem thoroughly.
- ✪ Surveying the literature to determine the dimensions of the problem.
- ✪ Developing ideas by discussing with guides and experts.
- ✪ Rephrasing the problem into a workable research problem.

Let us consider an example. A student-researcher is specializing in human resource management and desires to take up a research project in interpersonal relationship. Through literature survey (journals/magazines, reports, etc.), the student comes to know that attrition rate in a particular industry is high and it differs from firm to firm to a large extent.

The student understands that (by discussing with the knowledgeable professors and the experienced professional managers) the magnitude of attrition depends on many factors, the important one being the attitude of the line managers towards the workers. Going through the theories in organizational behaviour, the student is given to understand that emotional intelligence is an important factor influencing attitude. Now, as the problem is identified, the student may state the problem as, "Attrition rate of employees as influenced by emotional intelligence of line managers." In general, the problem is defined in the title of the research project itself. It is supplemented or complemented by the well-defined objectives.

REVIEW QUESTIONS

1. How is a research problem identified and selected?

2. What are the various sources of identifying problems?

3. How can you justify problem selection?

4. Analyse the criteria of problem selection.

5. How is a problem defined?

6. What is problem statement?

7. Discuss the steps in defining a problem.

3

REVIEW OF LITERATURE

Surveying and examining all available literature (information) concerning the research problem, right from the concepts/theory through methodology to the style of presentation of a report is known as review of literature. It is done not just for the sake of reading or for a casual reading like browsing through a novel or a comic. It is as serious and important as the research itself.

While reviewing, the researcher should note that

- ✣ review of literature is focused and directed towards specific purposes,
- ✣ it is selective, that is, related to the research topic and
- ✣ the preview starts with the areas of research defining the problem, continues though the details of various stages of the research process up to the finer points of the way of presenting the report.

SOURCES OF REVIEW OF LITERATURE

In the era of knowledge explosion, the information is increasing by leaps and bounds. Researchers in the academic line and industry, management thinkers and scholars pursuing higher studies contribute enormously to the world of management research. The number of publications on research is incredible. The researchers can gain adequate knowledge from the following sources.

Books   Encyclopaedias, yearbooks, textbooks and reference books.

Journals   A good number of journals are being published by professional associations, academic institutes and private entities in a definite format on a particular field in management or general management. Some examples are listed below.

- ✣ *The Academy of Management Journal*
- ✣ *Journal of Marketing Research*

- *Journal of Marketing*
- *The Journal of Finance*
- *Chartered Financial Analyst*
- *Banking and Finance*
- *Capital Market*
- *Journal of Entrepreneurship*
- *Journal of Industrial Relations*
- *Foreign Trade Review*
- *Finance India*
- *Journal of Retailing*

Journals are published at regular intervals (monthly, quarterly or half-yearly).

Publications like *Harvard Business Review* (Harvard School of Business), *Vikalpa* (Indian Institute of Management, Ahmedabad) *Decision* (IIM, Kolkata), *Journal of Social and Management Sciences* (National Institute of Bank Management), *Indian Management*, *Personnel Today*, etc., analyse issues of topical interest in management at greater depth.

Magazines These are the publications of various bodies released at short intervals (weekly, fortnightly or monthly) covering diversified areas in management. Policies, issues, performance of companies, etc. are analysed by professionals in an informal but informative and interesting styles (*Business Week, Business World, Business India, Business Today, Business Baron, Banking and Finance,* etc.)

Magazines like *Outlook, Frontline, The Week*, etc. also carry articles in management now and then.

Other sources

- Reports of committees/commissions or annual reports.
- Proceedings of conferences, symposia, seminars and workshops.
- Newspapers, audio-video tapes, microfilms or CDs.
- Internet—In the computerized world of business, almost all the information can be accessed through internet.

NEED AND PURPOSE OF REVIEW OF LITERATURE

The reasons why a researcher goes for a meaningful review of the information available and the benefits are many and are as follows:

1. Gaining preliminary orientation and background knowledge of the research topic.
2. Identifying and understanding the concepts related to the topic, the potential relationships, impact, etc.

3. Finding out the work already undertaken by others in the same line and to avoid duplication.

4. Studying how others have structured their research and tackled the issues.

5. Familiarizing with the research designs, methodology, techniques, style of report, etc.

6. Developing appropriate research designs.

7. Scouting for sources of supportive data and inferences for discussion.

8. Deciding on a reasonable sample size.

9. Formulation of hypothesis.

10. Updating the knowledge and searching for lacunae in the studies conducted earlier with the objective of justifying why a particular topic is selected for research.

HOW REVIEW IS CARRIED OUT

The style of reviewing literature may differ from researcher to researcher. The following procedure is suggested to a student-researcher.

1. Identify the sources of information (textbooks, reference books, reports, proceedings, journals, magazines, etc.). It is to be noted that for general topics such as job satisfaction, stress management, interpersonal relationship, performance appraisal, training programmes, consumer behaviour, advertising/promotional activities, dealers'/suppliers' opinion, customers' satisfaction, working capital, financial performances, capital structure, etc., the sources of data/information are plenty. But in the case of new areas (Emotional intelligence, spiritual intelligence, knowledge process outsourcing, BPOs in TIER II cities, MNCs' rural retailing, etc.) the data may be few and far between.

2. Decide the period of review. The period considered for review could be the least five years, ten years or even longer depending on the nature of the study and research problem.

3. Procure cards of convenient size ($8'' \times 5''$) available at stationery shops as reference or library cards. The number of reference cards could be 100 to 500 depending on the information available.

4. If a relevant information is come across in a journal, note down the names of the authors, title of the article, name of the journal, volume number, issue number, page numbers of the article and year of publication followed by a brief summary/abstract of the article. In the case of books, names of the authors (sometimes editors), title of the book, name of the publisher, place of publication, total number of pages and year of publication are noted down along with a summary of relevant points of interest.

5. The summary/abstract may be confined to two sides of the card. In the case of elaborate methodology or model, additional cards may be used.

6. Arrange the cards in chronological order under different heads depending on the research problem.

7. The summaries/abstracts are used in the chapters of introduction, review of literature, methodology, discussion or conclusion. The other details such as name of author, journal, etc. are necessary for inclusion in the section References/Bibliography.

8. Refer to the cards when the report is written.

9. Cross-check the details after completion of report writing.

HOW A REVIEW OF LITERATURE IS PRESENTED

After gathering sufficient information, they are grouped under relevant topics. The review is presented in **chronological** order (starting from the earliest work). Invariably the names of the authors are mentioned along with the year of publication. No initials or honours such as Mr., Ms., Dr. or Prof., are used. When there are two authors, both the names are mentioned. When the number of authors is more than two, only the name of the first author followed by "*et al.*" is mentioned.

EXAMPLE

Title of the project: "A critical analysis of HRD techniques adopted in the textile industry."

While discussing the industrialization strategies and industrial/human resources policies in Singapore, Malaysia, the Philippines and India, Kuruvilla (1996) contended that IS and IR/HR policy goals were closely intertwined and mutually reinforcing. On the deliberation on "partnership in HR functions" Pareek and Rao (1997) felt that it was necessary to integrate all the HR sub-functions both at the top and at bottom levels. Research by Oberg *et al.* (1999) showed that more than three-fourths of American companies have appraisal programmes to measure employee performance. While American companies use performance appraisal mainly to determine wage increases and promotions, Indian companies use it for training and development (Shetty, 2001; Rudrabasavaraj, 2002). In 2003, Bass *et al.*, identified three important factors that could necessitate training activity, viz., technological advances, organizational complexity and human relations. Davies in 2005 rightly remarked "it is advisable to use as many strategies as one can conveniently employ when evaluating training". McSherry (2006), while discussing team-building, observed that cohesiveness was the major factor. Mathis and Jackson (2007) expressed that the purpose of development programmes were to improve the intellectual and emotional abilities to handle greater responsibilities. According to French *et al.* (2008) successful organizations tend to match or fit the environments in which they operate with the type and context of management development programmes.

It is preferable and logical to present the review in a few sub-topics.

For example, in the case of "Organisational climate in XYZ Company", the review may be presented under the following subtopics:

- ✪ Management's attitude towards employees
- ✪ Interpersonal relationship among the employees
- ✪ Training and development programmes
- ✪ Performance appraisal system
- ✪ Compensation package

In each sub-topic, chronological order of works is maintained separately.

REVIEW QUESTIONS

1. What are the sources of research review?

2. What is the purpose or need for review?

3. How is a review of literature carried out?

4. How is a review presented?

4

FORMULATION AND TESTING OF HYPOTHESES

Excepting exploratory research or fact-finding investigation, hypotheses can be developed in all researches. Hypotheses are considered as the principal instruments in research. The main function of a hypothesis is to suggest new experiments, observations or surveys. In the case of experimental research, testing of hypotheses is the major objective. Decision-makers often encounter situations wherein they are forced to formulate hypotheses and take decisions based on test results. Testing of hypotheses is widely used in business for making decisions.

WHAT IS HYPOTHESIS

A hypothesis is always in a declarative form. A hypothesis could be defined by one of the following definitions.

- ✪ Hypothesis could be a statement to be verified by survey, observation or experiment.
- ✪ It could be a tentative solution to a problem of the researcher or a tentative answer to the researcher's question to be verified by appropriate means.
- ✪ It could be a tentative generalization or an assumption, a proposition or a shrewd guess to be proved.
- ✪ It could be a contextual statement of relation between two or more variables.

In short, hypothesis is an informal/shrewd guess, a supposition, a hunch, an assumption, a proposition or a tentative generalization of the existence of some facts, condition or relationship relative to some phenomena to guide the research to new truth.

There is a subtle difference between proposition and hypotheses. Proposition is a statement about concepts that may be judged as true or false if it refers to observable phenomena;

when a proposition is formulated for empirical testing (supported by data), it is known as hypothesis.

Hypotheses are statements in which variables are assigned to cases. A case is an entity or a thing the hypothesis talks about. The variable is the characteristic, trait or attribute that is imputed to the case in the hypotheses.

SOURCES OF HYPOTHESES

As in the case of defining a problem, there are a few sources which help researchers in formulating the hypotheses. The student can tap one or more of the following sources to formulate appropriate hypotheses in consonance with the research problem.

1. *Theory*   One can derive hypotheses from management theories. Take for example, Abraham Maslow's theory of hierarchy of needs in motivation. Maslow suggested that the higher need comes to play when the lower need is satisfied. A hypothesis can be formulated relative to this theory as "In spirituality-oriented people Maslow's hierarchy of needs does not hold water".

2. *Observations*   Routine observations of price movement in the market place, employees' behaviour on the job/off the job, the movement of sensex points, etc. may lead to new hypotheses (Example: The higher rate for organic produce is not related to lower production.)

3. *Intuition and personal experience*   In certain cases intuition or gut feelings help formulate hypotheses. But in many cases years of experience of the researcher in a particular field guides him/her to appropriate and meaningful hypotheses.

4. *Analogies (Comparison)*   Hypotheses can be formed based on the examples in other areas/ disciplines.

5. *Review of literature*   The habit of going through periodicals, abstracts, reviews, etc. will help locating hypotheses. As in the case of defining the problem, the role played by review of literature in forming hypotheses is significant.

6. *General culture*   The kaleidoscopic cultures seen in different strata of the society and the well-ingrained organizational cultures in various corporates throw light in locating hypotheses.

CHARACTERISTICS OF A GOOD HYPOTHESIS

As in the case of defining the problem, certain characteristics make a hypothesis get qualified as a good hypothesis. These characteristics include the following.

 ✣ A hypothesis must be expressed in simple language without any ambiguity in meaning.

 ✣ It must be specific and precise without creating any confusion.

 ✣ It must be amenable for testing with empirical data.

- It must be testable within reasonable time.
- It must be constructed with known facts and theory with specified scope.
- It must be able to predict/anticipate the previously unknown data.
- In the case of relationship hypotheses, the relationship between variables must be stated.
- It must provide an answer to the problem which necessitated the research enquiry.

FUNCTIONS OR ROLES OF HYPOTHESES

Hypotheses play many an important role in all disciplines of research; managerial research is not an exception.

A hypothesis provides a definite focus to the researcher and guides the study. Without a well-defined hypothesis the researcher may wander in the thick of data like a rudderless ship. It helps the researcher in the same way as a good navigator. With an unambiguous hypothesis, the chances of the researcher getting stranded are remote. The main functions of a hypothesis are the following.

- It specifies the sources of data which shall be collected, analysed and interpreted to answer a problem.
- It indicates the appropriate type of research as well as the research techniques.
- It may contribute to the development of theory. It links theory and investigation. A hypothesis may be deduced from a theory. When it is tested through studies and found true, it forms a part of the theory.

TYPES OF HYPOTHESES

Based on the nature of topic, objectives and research design, hypotheses are classified into a few categories.

DESCRIPTIVE HYPOTHESES

These are propositions that typically state the existence, size, form or distribution of some variable.

Examples

- Nearly 50% of current population of rural India is unemployed.
- In urban India the sale of white goods constitutes about 10% of total sales.
- In Indian IT industry 80% of the employees opt for stock as incentive.
- The capital structure in most of the Indian industries is not optimum.

- Not over 10% of the managers are aware of emotional intelligence as an effective tool in personnel management.
- In management institutes, the ratio of male to female faculty members is 50 : 50.
- In the manufacturing industry, working capital management is not appropriate.
- In MNCs, the average age of top-level managers is not more than 45 years.

RELATIONAL HYPOTHESES

These are statements that describe relationships among variables with respect to some case.

Examples

- The Americans perceive that Japanese cars are superior to American cars.
- Emotional intelligence quotient of managers in service industry is higher than that of manufacturing industry.
- Sale of white goods is more during Deepavali than during Pongal.

Relational hypotheses are further classified into two types:

i. Correlational relationship Here, the variables occur together in some specified manner without implying that one causes the other, that is, it cannot be claimed that one variable is influenced by another. The correlational relationship hypotheses simply state some relationship without specifying any cause–effect relationship.

Examples

- In the banking industry, employees over 40 years are less productive than those who are less than 40 years.
- Salesmen with good communication skills do better job than those who are poor in communication.
- Employees in IT industry prefer highly qualified managers than the employees in hotel industry.

ii. Explanatory or causal hypotheses These hypotheses claim that there is cause–effect relationship between variables, that is, one variable causes an effect on the other variable. Here, the variable which causes an effect on another variable is called independent variable and the variable which gets affected is known as dependent variable.

Examples

- An increase in family income leads to an increase in the percentage of expenditure on sight-seeing.
- Productivity increases as the quantum of incentives increases.

○ Loyalty to a particular departmental store increases the probability of purchasing the store's own brands.

In addition to the above hypotheses, some authors include the following types of hypotheses also:

COMMON-SENSE HYPOTHESES

These represent common-sense ideas of day-to-day observations.

Examples

○ frequent outings with family reduces tension in the family

○ all those who get good marks in the examinations need not be always intelligent

○ high-society consumers rarely patronize "discount-sale" outlets.

COMPLEX HYPOTHESES

These are abstract and not simple to be understood by ordinary people.

Examples

○ members of Asian minority groups in UK suffer from oppression psychosis.

○ excessive disposable income in nuclear families, where both husband and wife are employed, is the major cause for juvenile drug addiction.

All the hypotheses thus far discussed ultimately boil down to two practical hypotheses, viz., Null Hypothesis (N.H.), denoted by symbol Ho and Alternative Hypothesis (A.H.) denoted by Ha. The alternative hypothesis is further divided into non-directional (Ha_1) and directional (Ha_2).

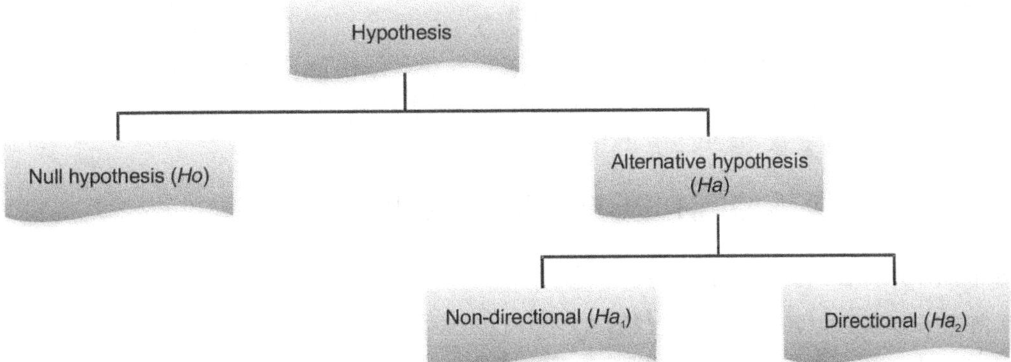

NULL HYPOTHESIS (N.H.)

A N.H. generally states that "There is no difference between X and Y," "There is no effect of X on Y," or "There is no association between X and Y," where X and Y are two different variables.

ALTERNATIVE HYPOTHESIS (A.H.)

An A.H. generally states that "There is difference between X and Y," "There is an effect of X on Y," or "There is association between as X and Y." It is also known as research hypothesis as most of the researchers are interested in A.H.s. While non-directional A.H. states that "there is difference" or "not equal to $(\mu_1 \neq \mu_2)$", directional A.H. states that "one is greater $(\mu_1 > \mu_2)$ or less than $(\mu_1 < \mu_2)$ the other" (μ_1 and μ_2 are the means of population 1 and 2 respectively).

Examples

i. *N.H. (Ho)*   There is no difference in the sales of Coke and Pepsi in Indian market. Symbolically it is represented as $\mu_1 = \mu_2$, where μ_1 is the mean sale of Coke and μ_2 is the mean sale of Pepsi.

   Non-directional A.H. (Ha)   There is difference in the sales of Coke and Pepsi in Indian market, i.e., $\mu_1 \neq \mu_2$.

   Directional A.H.

   Ha₁   Sale of Coke is greater than that of Pepsi, i.e., $\mu_1 > \mu_2$.

   Ha₂   Sale of Coke is lower than that of Pepsi, i.e., $\mu_1 < \mu_2$.

ii. *N.H. (Ho)*   Advertisements endorsed by cricketers have no influence on the sale of the product.

   A.H. (Ha)   Advertisements endorsed by cricketers influence the sale of the product.

   A.H. (Ha₁)   Advertisements endorsed by cricketers increase the sale of the product.

   A.H. (Ha₂)   Advertisements endorsed by cricketers decrease the sale of product.

iii. *N.H. (Ho)*   There is no association between compensation and productivity.

   A.H. (Ha)   There is association between compensation and productivity.

   A.H. (Ha₁)   Higher compensation increases productivity.

   A.H. (Ha₂)   Higher compensation decreases productivity.

BASIC CONCEPTS OF HYPOTHESIS TESTING

FORMULATION OF NULL HYPOTHESIS (*Ho*)
AND ALTERNATIVE HYPOTHESIS (*Ha*)

Based on the problem identified, null hypothesis and appropriate alternative hypothesis (non-directional or directional) are formulated.

The N.H. and A.H. are formed before the sample is drawn. Null hypothesis is the one, the researcher wishes to disprove and A.H. is usually the one which the researcher wishes to prove.

LEVEL OF SIGNIFICANCE

Testing of hypotheses depends on a test criterion. (Test criteria such as Z-test, t-test, F-test, etc. are discussed under "Tests of Significance"). A test-criterion is constructed to predict, in terms of probability, "how frequently" a difference of observed magnitude or more can arise purely due to "chance factors" and "chance factors" alone. Based on the magnitude of this probability, one is guided to decide whether the observed difference between two means, variances or proportions is genuine or is merely a chance difference. For instance, if the magnitude of this probability is considerable, the risk of being wrong in attributing the difference as genuine is also considerable; smaller the value of probability, smaller is the risk in taking decision. For example, if the chances are 10% that a difference of certain observed value is solely due to chance factors, the risk in concluding that it is a real difference is also 10%. On the other hand, if such a chance is less than 5%, the risk also is less than 5%. This level of risk is called the level of significance and its complement (i.e., 90% or 95%) is called the level of confidence, since the latter specifies the amount of confidence in making judgements.

It can also be said that the confidence with which an experimenter rejects or retains N.H. depends on the significance of level adopted. The level of significance (usually denoted by 'α') is generally specified before samples are drawn so that results obtained will not influence the choice of the researcher.

As pointed out above, the decision of the researcher in a given situation ultimately depends upon the choice of the level of significance, since it specifies the risk involved in such judgments. The moot question is *how small* the magnitude of the risk should be, before one concludes that the mean difference is produced by non-random effects. Should it be 10%, 5%, 1% or still less? The answer entirely depends on the amount of risk one is prepared to take. Based on practical consideration or scientific needs, the levels conventionally accepted are 5%, 1% or even less. It may be noted that the choice of the level of significance is purely arbitrary, but it may be guided by the need and nature of the problem. If the problem is one of the great theoretical values or if the decision involves heavy financial commitment, a more conservative level, 1% or 0.1%, may be chosen. If the study is of exploratory nature, it could be 5% or even 10%. In the absence of any such specific knowledge, the *rule of thumb* is to stick to 5%.

DECISION RULE (TESTING OF HYPOTHESES)

In testing of hypotheses N.H. and A.H. are formulated and observations/surveys are made or experiments are conducted. Based on the hypotheses, relevant statistical test (test of significance) is carried out. To decide whether the values obtained are significant or not, they are compared with the standards or the *table* values of the particular test. If the calculated value is less than the table value, the N.H. is accepted; that is, the evidence is not strong enough to reject the N.H. On the other hand if the calculated value is greater than the table value, the N.H. of"no difference", "no effect" or "no relationship" is rejected and A.H. of "there is difference", "there is effect" or "there is relationship" is accepted.

TWO-TAILED OR ONE-TAILED TESTS

In the context of decision-making, either accepting the N.H. or rejecting the N.H. based on the interpretation whether the calculated value is lower or higher than the table value, one must be sure whether it is a two-tailed or one-tailed test. It is the alternative hypothesis which decides whether a test is two-tailed or one-tailed. If the A.H. simply states that the means or variances or proportions are not equal, it is two-tailed; if the A.H. states either one is greater or lower than the other, it becomes a one-tailed test. Symbolically, it can be represented as below (in the case of comparing means).

Null hypothesis is $\mu_1 = \mu_2$.

If the A.H. is $\mu_1 \neq \mu_2$, it is a two-tailed test.

If the A.H. is $\mu_1 > \mu_2$ or $\mu_1 < \mu_2$, then it becomes a one-tailed test.

TYPES OF ERRORS

In testing of hypotheses there are chances that the researcher may reject the N.H. (*Ho*) when it is true or accepts the *Ho* when in fact it is not true. The former is known as Type-I error (α-error) and the latter Type-II error (β-error). In other words, Type-I error means rejection of hypothesis which should have been accepted and Type II error means accepting the hypothesis which should have been rejected. Type-I error or α-error is also called level of significance. The two types of error can be presented in a tabular form as shown in Table 4.1.

Table 4.1   Types of errors in hypothesis testing

Decision	Condition	
	Ho is true	*Ho* is false
Accept *Ho*	Correct decision	Type-II Error (β-error)
Reject *Ho*	Type-I error (α-error)	Correct decision

Which Error is More Serious, Type I or Type II

The answer could be illustrated with an analogy to our legal system. In the legal system an accused is presumed to be innocent unless there is a strong evidence to indict him. In the hypothesis testing this is the N.H., that is, there is no relation between the accused and the crime. The accused claims that he is innocent and he is not involved in the crime. The prosecution (police) claims that the accused is associated with the crime. This is the alternative hypothesis. The court of law maintains that there is no association between the accused and the crime until it is proved beyond doubt by the prosecution that the accused is involved in the crime. Based on the evidence produced by the prosecution, the court may either convict the accused or release him. If the evidence is strong enough the accused is convicted, that is, the N.H. (no association with the crime) is rejected and the A.H. (there is association) is accepted. Due to wrong interpretation there are chances that the court can unjustly convict an innocent person or can acquit a guilty person. One of two conditions exist—either the N.H. is true or A.H. is true. That is an accused person is innocent or guilty. When a Type-I error (α) is committed, a true N.H. is rejected; the innocent person is convicted. With a Type-II error (β) one fails to reject a false null hypothesis; the guilty person is acquitted. In the legal system it is more important to reduce the probability of convicting the innocent than acquitting the guilty. Similarly, in hypotheses testing more emphasis is placed on Type-I error than on Type-II. To cut the long story short, Type-I error is more serious than Type-II error.

Which Hypothesis is Taken for Testing, N.H. or A.H.

Testing and proving N.H. is more cumbersome and time-consuming. Drawing on the same analogy of our legal system, it will be a Herculean task for the accused to prove that there is no association between him and the crime. That is why the onus of proving that there is an association (A.H.) rests on the prosecution. When the prosecution is unable to provide strong evidence, the A.H. proposed is rejected and N.H. of no association is accepted resulting in the release of the accused. Similarly, the researcher as the prosecution has to prove the A.H. "there is association" with acceptable level of significance. If the researcher fails, the A.H. is rejected and N.H. is accepted.

STEPS IN HYPOTHESIS-TESTING

Step 1   State the null as well as the alternative hypotheses. Though the researcher is usually interested in testing hypotheses of change or difference, the N.H. is always used for statistical purpose.

Step 2   Choose the statistical test. An appropriate statistical test (Z, t, F, Chi-square or ANOVA) is selected depending on the problem.

Step 3 Select the desired level of significance. The exact level to choose is largely determined by how much risk one is prepared to take—0.10 (10%), 0.05 (5%), 0.025 (2.5%) or 0.01(1%). The most common level is 0.05 (5%).

Step 4 Compute the calculated value. Use the formula for the appropriate test of significance to obtain the calculated value.

Step 5 Obtain the critical test value. Look up the critical value in the appropriate table for the particular test. The critical value is the criterion that defines the region of rejection from the region of acceptance of the N.H.

Step 6 Make the decision. If the calculated value is larger than the critical value (table value) reject the N.H. and accept the A.H. If the calculated value is smaller than the critical value, accept the N.H. and reject the A.H.

REVIEW QUESTIONS

1. Define hypothesis.

2. What are the sources of hypothesis?

3. Discuss the characteristics of a good hypothesis.

4. What are the functions or roles of hypothesis?

5. Discuss the various types of hypothesis.

6. Analyse the basic concepts of hypothesis testing.

7. What are the types of errors in hypothesis testing?

8. Discuss the various steps in hypothesis testing.

5

RESEARCH DESIGN

Once the hypotheses are formulated the next step is to test the hypotheses for validity. To test the validity of hypotheses, observations, surveys and experiments are taken up based on the hypotheses. Collection of data through observations, surveys or experiments is done methodically for meaningful results. How the research is planned is detailed in a research design.

WHAT IS RESEARCH DESIGN

Research design is a logical and systematic plan to conduct a research study. The purpose of research design is indicated below:

- ✿ Research design specifies the objectives of the study and the methodology and techniques to be adopted to achieve the objectives.
- ✿ It is a plan deciding the types and sources of data.
- ✿ It is a program specifying the methods of collecting, analysing and interpreting the observations and data.
- ✿ It decides the allocation of resource and time frame.

In a nutshell, research design constitutes the blueprint of the research study similar to the blueprint of a building detailing all the relevant details.

A research design must answer the following questions unequivocably.

- ✿ What is the study about?
- ✿ Why is the study undertaken?
- ✿ Where will the study be carried out?
- ✿ What type of data is required?
- ✿ Where can the data be found?

- When can we conduct the study?
- What will be the sampling design?
- What techniques are to be used in collecting data?
- How will the data be analysed?
- What should be the style of report?

COMPONENTS OF RESEARCH DESIGN

Research design has four important components:

1. *Sampling design*   This deals with how a sample is selected (the question of sampling does not arise in studies based on census, i.e., collecting data from all the units of a population). It involves selection of an appropriate sampling technique. The various sampling techniques are discussed in the Chapter, "Sampling Techniques".

2. *Data collection design*   Data are collected through a number of means such as observation, interview or questionnaire. The design specifies the appropriate method of data collection. This component is discussed in the Chapter, "Collection and Processing of Data".

3. *Statistical design*   Data collected are subjected to statistical analysis for proper interpretation. This component deals with the statistical technique suitable for the particular type of data. The techniques generally employed are detailed in the Chapter, "Data Analysis (Tests of Significance)".

4. *Report design*   This component decides how the results or the research study as a whole are presented to the target audience. Type of report and the style of presentation of research report are outlined in the Chapter, "Interpretation and Report Preparation".

NEED FOR RESEARCH DESIGN

A well-planned research design goes a long way in helping the researcher carry out his/her study efficiently and effectively.

The purpose of the research design is

- to facilitate smooth running of the operations,
- to gain maximum information with minimum expenditure of efforts, time and money,
- to provide anchorage for the study to prevent it from straying aimlessly,
- to select appropriate methods/techniques to collect/analyse the data keeping in view the objectives of the study and availability of personnel, time and money, and
- to help the researcher in organizing his/her ideas to look for flaws/inadequacies/ limitations.

TYPES OF RESEARCH DESIGNS

Research designs are classified into various types based on the nature of the study and treatment given. The factors which influence the classification are the following.

i. The degree to which the objectives are clear (In a formal research such as descriptive and experimental research the objectives are clear, whereas in an exploratory or formulative research the objectives are hazy.)

ii. The method of data collection (Data may be collected through observations resulting in an observational study or through interviews resulting in a communication-based study.)

iii. The ability of the researcher to interfere (In action research or experimental research the researcher manipulates the independent variables or the causative factors; in other studies the researcher cannot interfere and report/analyse as it is.)

iv. The purpose of the study (In a descriptive study the researcher just describes the various parameters of a population and answers 'what', 'when', 'where' and 'which' but in a diagnostic/analytical study the researcher strives to answer the question 'why' and explain the relationship, if any, and reasons out why a particular phenomenon is occurring.)

v. Time dimension (To complete the study in a short time as in the case of a time-bound cross-sectional observation or to study the problem over an extended period as in a longitudinal study.)

vi. The depth of the study (In a case study, the subject as a whole is studied in depth, whereas in a statistical study only a sample is studied.)

vii. The research environment (Depending on the location and method, a study could be a historical study, a laboratory study, simulation study or a field study.)

Due to overlapping or similarity of some of the above-mentioned determinants, the research designs are categorized into four general types, viz., exploratory design, descriptive design, diagnostic (analytical) design and experimental design. Some authors bring the diagnostic/ analytical design under descriptive design. Observation study, communication-based study, cross-sectional or longitudinal study, case study, historical study, etc. are only different variants of descriptive design.

EXPLORATORY DESIGN

It is an unstructured design to gain familiarity with an unknown population or phenomenon. It seeks only general information to test the possibility of conducting a detailed research. It is similar to testing the water before one takes a plunge.

The purpose of an exploratory design is

- to generate new ideas
- to familiarize the researcher with the problem
- to make a precise formulation of the problem (formulation of hypotheses)
- to gather information for clarifying a concept
- to decide whether a particular study is feasible or not

This design does not aim at testing hypotheses. In fact, exploratory design is used to fine-tune the hypotheses to be tested in a formal research. It just attempts to see what is there in store for the researcher. No steps are taken either for a thorough description or for seeking association of variables.

Exploratory designs are particularly useful when researchers lack a clear idea of the problem. It helps researchers develop concepts more clearly, establish priorities, develop operational definitions and improve the final research design. It saves time and money. The possibility of continuing a research project in other areas may be decided with the help of an exploratory design.

The sampling technique employed is non-probability sampling techniques such as convenience or judgemental sampling.

Examples

- Space scientists exploring the possibility of existence of living organisms in other planets
- Zoologists/ecologists observing the behaviour of wild animals at close quarters in African jungles for "Animal Planet" channel
- A marketing researcher feeling the pulse of rural population to explore the possibility of large-scale retailing of micro-oven or computers
- An ad agency exploring the idea of figuring physically challenged persons in electronic media to popularize personal health care products
- A mobile restaurant introducing exotic cuisines for "budget" consumers
- A personnel manager introducing "performance-based variable pay structure" in one of the divisions to feel the reaction of the employees to the new system of compensation
- A management's trial to select managers based on emotional intelligence rather than work experience to improve interpersonal relationship
- A BPO company's attempt to improve the efficiency through "virtual office"

Sources of Exploratory Studies

Interaction with people, day-to-day happenings, freak incidents, etc. may help a vigilant researcher select topics for exploratory studies. The following are some of the common resources.

1. *Literature survey*   Going through periodicals, reports, surveys, etc. gives leads and clues to exploratory research.

2. *Experience survey*   Informal interviews with persons having experience will help researchers securing insights into the subject and related facts. People who might provide information include:

    i. Newcomers to the scene such as the employees recently transferred/promoted

    ii. Workers in isolated posts

    iii. Antagonistic workers or the workers in the most unproductive sections

    iv. Executives who do not fit well in the organization

    v. Employees who represent varied interests

3. *Focus groups*   A focus group is a panel of individuals led by a trained moderator. The moderator or facilitator uses principles of group dynamics to focus or guide the group in an exchange of ideas, feelings and experiences on a specific topic. The facilitator introduces the topic and encourages the group to discuss it among themselves without any inhibition. Typically the group consists of six to ten members.

4. *Analysis of insight-stimulating cases*   In an unexplored area of study, an intense probe into few selected cases may yield stimulating insights. Some examples are given below:

- In-depth interviewing using conversational method rather than structured interview
- Participant observation to have a first-hand perception of the participants
- Capturing the life of the group under study through films, videotapes, photographs, etc. for detailed observation
- Employing projective techniques and psychological tests (Thematic Apperception Test, Games, Role-plays, etc.)
- Street ethnography to understand how a group behaves at the street level
- Elite interviewing with influential and well-informed people
- Usage of proxemics and kinesics to study space and body motion communication

Exploratory vs Formal Design

In contrast to exploratory studies, formal studies are structured with clearly stated hypotheses or investigative questions. Formal research studies try to answer a variety of objectives that are as follows:

- Descriptions of phenomena or characteristics associated with populations
- Estimates of proportions of populations
- Discovery of associations among different variables
- Establishing cause-and-effect relationships among variables, if any

DESCRIPTIVE DESIGN

As the name suggests descriptive design describes an organization, industry, people, situation, phenomenon, etc. It covers size distribution, proportions, etc. of populations. Tangibles as well as intangibles are described. Employees' opinion/attitude on management, interpersonal relationship, performance appraisal, training and development programmes, etc. come under descriptive design. An in-depth investigation/description of an individual/ organization over a period of time results in a case study. Some of the characteristics of descriptive design are given below:

- Descriptive design is more specific than exploratory design as it focuses on specific aspects/dimensions of the problem.
- Descriptive design aims at identifying the various characteristics of a community, an institution or a problem.
- It is used in fact-finding investigation to gather detailed information.
- The data are presented as ranges, means, percentages or proportions.
- Descriptive design may be simple or complex.
- The objective of a descriptive design is to answer the questions 'who', 'what', 'when', 'which' or 'where' of the problem.
- Collection of data through descriptive design is a pre-requisite for diagnostic/analytical design.
- The simplest descriptive study is concerned with hypotheses to state something about the size, form, distribution or existence of a variable.

The population can be studied or described by census or sampling. If the population is small and manageable, census (collecting data from each and every unit of the population) is appropriate. In the case of a large population, a representative sample is taken for the study.

The sampling technique chosen to take sample from a population for descriptive study depends on the nature of population. If the population is finite (where all the units of the population are identifiable), probability sampling technique (simple random sampling, systematic sampling, stratified sampling, cluster sampling or multi-stage sampling) is selected. If it is an infinite population (where some of the units are not identifiable), non-probability sampling (convenience sampling, judgemental sampling, quota sampling or snow-balling technique) is chosen.

Examples

- To study the market share of a company's product or services vis-à-vis that of the competitors to devise a strategic plan for further expansion
- To describe the dealers' network of a company in respect of their size, turnover, products, infrastructure facilities, workforce, etc. for effective management of company–dealer relationship
- To observe the consumers' behaviour towards a particular service for further refinement of the service
- To gauge the opinion/attitudes of the employees on the existing HRD techniques in an organization/industry for introduction of new technique
- To find out the satisfaction level of workers on the statutory/non-statutory welfare measures and social security in an organization/industry
- To learn the types of stress experienced by employees in different functional areas of a company
- To test the emotional intelligence of people of different age groups, educational background, income, status, etc.
- To compile the financial and non-financial incentives practised in various industries
- To study the capital structure, working capital or financial performance of various types of companies
- To analyse the sensex movement of BSE and Nifty companies in different periods

DIAGNOSTIC DESIGN

While descriptive design is solely concerned with "what is existing/happening?" diagnostic design throws light to answer the question "why is it existing/happening?" Some authors consider diagnostic design as a part of descriptive design. But in many cases, the researchers are more particular about answering the 'why' part of a problem. The usefulness of diagnostic design are as follows:

- Diagnostic design tries to find out the relationships, if any, among the various variables, dimensions or parameters.
- It aims at identifying the causes of a problem to enable the researcher search for a solution.
- It helps in testing of hypotheses.

Examples

- To study the reasons for the low/high market share of a particular product/service
- To find out why the dealers' interest in a particular product/company is on the decline

- To understand why the consumers behave in a particular way towards a particular service/product

- To know why the employees have a negative attitude towards the particular HRD technique of a company

- To point out why the workers are not satisfied with welfare measures provided in a company

- To learn why employees in particular operational areas are more stressed than employees in other areas

- To test why emotional intelligence varies among different groups of employees and find the relationship between emotional intelligence quotient and productivity

- To elicit the relationship between incentives and productivity.

ANALYTICAL DESIGN

This design is a part of diagnostic design. It is presumed that analysis is a prerequisite for diagnosis. In medical profession, the physician subjects the patient to a number of tests (analyses) such as measurement of blood pressure, blood/urine sugar, haemoglobin, cholesterol, etc. for diagnosis of the ailment. Similarly, a researcher in the field of finance analyses various financial ratios (liquidity ratios, leverage ratios, activity ratios, profitability ratios and growth ratios) to diagnose the reasons as to why a particular company's financial performance is exemplary or poor. Generally, research problems related to finance are brought under analytical design.

Examples

- To compare the financial performances of firms in an organization and to seek reasons for the variance

- To analyse the working capital management and its impact on revenues/profit

- To investigate the capital structures of companies in an industry and their influence on the performance of the companies

- To study the factors related to volatility of sensex

- To find out why there is no relationship between price-index and inflation rate in India.

EXPERIMENTAL DESIGN

In Ex-post facto/descriptive study the researcher interviews respondents and observes what is happening or what has happened. Diagnostic/analytical study has the potential of discovering association or causality. In these studies, the researcher accepts the world as it is found. He/she cannot manipulate. But in experimental study, the experimenter is able to alter the variables of interest and observe the after-effect. Experiments are studies involving intervention by the experimenter. The usual type of intervention is to manipulate the setting/situation through independent variables.

In experimental study there are three basic requirements: First, there must be at least one independent variable and a dependent variable. Secondly, beyond the relationship of independent and dependent variables, time order of the occurrence of the variables is important. That is, the dependent variable should not precede the independent variable, but they can occur almost simultaneously. Thirdly, the experimenter must be sure that other extraneous factors do not influence the dependent variable.

Examples

✧ A physician administering different medicines on groups of patients to find out the most curative medicine

✧ An agricultural scientist applying various types of fertilizers in the field to choose the best fertilizer for improvement of yield of a crop

✧ An ad-specialist trying a few models of advertisement to select the most attractive one to make a product more popular

✧ A HRD manager introducing a few new methods of motivation to decide the most important motivating factor to improve productivity

✧ A marketing manager arranging several promotional activities to finalize the cheap and effective activity

✧ A management professor employing some unconventional methods of teaching to settle down for the most appropriate method of MBAs.

Experimental design refers to the framework or structure of an experiment. There are several experimental designs. As these designs originated from agricultural research mostly agricultural terms such as treatment, plot, block, etc. are used in business context also.

Treatment   Treatments are different conditions imposed by the experimenter.

Plots   Plots are small experimental areas/groups (A group of plants, animals, people, etc.).

Blocks   Block is a group of plots.

Experimental designs are classified into two broad categories, viz., informal and formal designs. While informal designs employ simple forms of analyses, formal designs rely more on control and precise/sophisticated statistical techniques for analysis.

Informal Experimental Designs

i. Before and after without control   In this simple design a group/area is earmarked for experimentation. The dependent variable (effect) is measured before and after introduction of the independent variable (treatment) and the difference noticed in the dependent variable indicates the effect of the treatment.

Example

An MBA professor is interested in finding out the effect of a new method of teaching of case study developed by her on the performance of students in analysing cases. The new method is the treatment, i.e., independent variable, and the performance of the students is the effect, i.e., dependent variable. The professor measures the performance of the students before introducing the new method. Let it be X. Let the performance of the students after introduction of the new method be Y. Then the effect of the new teaching method (called treatment effect) is $Y - X$.

The major limitation of this experiment is that with passage of time extraneous factors may interfere.

ii. After-only with control Here, two groups or areas (plots), one as experimental plot and other as control plot, are earmarked and the treatment is effected only in the experimental plot (test plot). Then the effect is measured in both the plots at the same time. The difference in effect shows the treatment effect.

Example

In this design a professor selects two groups of students or divides the class into two sections. To one group of students or section he teaches the new method. This group is the experimental group (plot). To the other group/section known as control group (plot) he does not teach the new method of teaching. Let the performance of students in the experimental plot be Y and that of control plot Z. Then the effect of the new method is the difference between Y and Z $(Y - Z)$.

In this method it is assumed that before the treatment is effected, both the groups are identical to exclude the influence of any extraneous factor.

iii. Before and after with control This design similar to the above, also selects two groups (plots). One is designated as experimental plot and the other control plot. The presumed dependent variable is measured in both the plots before the treatment is effected. Then the treatment is effected only in the experimental plot. After effecting the treatment, the dependent variable is measured in both the plots. The treatment effect is calculated as the difference in the changes of the dependent variable in the treated and control plots.

Example

When the professor in the example already discussed chooses this design, she selects two groups of students. One group she designates as a control and the other as experimental plot. The performance of the students is measured in both the plots. Let it be A in the control plot and X in the experimental plot. Then the new method is taught to the experimental group and the performance is measured in both the groups. Let it be Z in the control plot and Y in the experimental plot. Treatment effect is $(Y - X) - (Z - A)$.

This design excludes the extraneous influence resulting from the passage of time as well as from heterogeneity of the plots.

BASIC PRINCIPLES IN EXPERIMENTAL DESIGN

Principle of randomization Assigning the treatments or factors to be tested to experimental units according to definite law of probability is technically known as randomization. The advantages of randomization are shown below:

- Randomization guarantees the elimination of systematic error.
- Every experimental unit will have the same chance of receiving any treatment.
- It provides protection against the effects of extraneous factors.
- The variations caused by extraneous factors can be combined under "chance factors".
  (In the case of experiment to test different fertilizers, the treatment yielding the highest could be due to the inherent fertility of the particular plot, more soil organic matter or absence of pests/diseases in addition to the effect of the fertilizer).

Principle of replication Replication is the repetition of an experiment under identical conditions; it is not a mere repetition. In replication, experimental materials and all procedures, sequence, time interval, etc. will be the same. The need for replication are given below:

- Replication is essential for estimating the error influence.
- It is introduced to increase the precision of a study.
- Replication with randomization alone will provide a basis for estimating the error variance.
- If randomization ensures the elimination of systematic error, replication keeps the random error at a low level.

Examples

- In deciding which medicine is superior, the physician has to administer the various medicines not on only one group but many different groups over a period of time. That is, he has to repeat his treatments many times.
- The agricultural scientist has to apply the different types of fertilizers on a number of plots over many climatic seasons before coming to a conclusion as to which fertilizer is the best. That is, repeating the field trials on different agro-climatic conditions.
- The management professor who wants to select the best method of teaching among lecture method, case analyses, group discussions, self-motivated presentations, assignments, mini-projects, etc. has to take classes in different semesters/trimesters over a period of time (that is, replicating many a time) before arriving at a conclusion.

The number of replications to be decided in any experiment depends on many factors, like the homogeneity or heterogeneity of the experimental material, the number of treatments, the degree of precision required, etc. It is suffix to mention that the number of replications in a design should provide at least 10–15df (degrees of freedom) for computing the experimental error mean square. If the number of treatments is 2, there should be 6–7 replications, for 3 treatments 4 to 5 replications and for 4 treatments 3 to 4 replications.

Principle of local control Local control means control of all factors except the ones under investigation. Like replication, it is another device to reduce or control the variation due to extraneous factors and increase the precision of an experiment. For instance, if an experimental field is heterogeneous with soil fertility then the field is divided into smaller blocks so that plots within each block tend to be more homogeneous. In testing the new methods of teaching, the IQ of the students in the class must be uniform. In the case of varying IQs, the students with almost same IQs are grouped separately and the methods tried.

This kind of homogeneity of plots (experimental plots) ensures an unbiased comparison of treatment means as otherwise it would be difficult to attribute the difference between two means, solely due to the difference between treatments, when the plot differences also persist.

Provision of "control plots" (Plots not receiving any treatment) as mentioned in the informal experimental design is another way of excluding the error variance due to heterogeneity.

Formal Experimental Designs

Completely randomized design (CRD) In this design, the treatments are allocated to the experimental plots completely at random. This design ensures that any experimental plot will receive any treatment. For instance, if four methods of teaching, viz., lecture method, seminars, assignments and case study are to be compared for their efficacy and if it is decided to replicate the experiment five times there will be 20 (4 × 5) experimental plots (groups of students). The four treatments (methods of teaching) are allotted to the experimental plots completely at random, so that every plot will have the same chance of receiving any of the four treatments.

The unrestricted type of random allocation of treatments to different experimental units presupposes all the experimental units to be as alike as possible so that the differences observed in the responses are attributable to the differences in the treatments rather than differences in the experimental plots. But this may not be possible in all the cases as the experimental plots tend to vary in one way or the other. This design permits partitioning of total variability present in the observations into two components—one attributable to the experimental error (chance factors) and the other due to treatment differences.

One-way ANOVA is used to find out the significance of differences among the treatments.

Advantages

- ☼ It is completely flexible and many number of treatments and replications may be used.
- ☼ Statistical analysis (ANOVA) is easy and straightforward.
- ☼ The layout of the design is simple. Only random allocation of treatments should be strictly adhered to.
- ☼ The number of degrees of freedom for estimating the experimental error will be high.

Limitation

The major limitation is that since the design presumes homogeneity of experimental units, it may not be efficient when the number of treatments and replications is fairly large.

Randomized complete block design (RCBD)   To overcome the main limitation of CRD (assumption of homogeneity of experimental plots) Randomized complete block design (RCBD) is adopted. When agricultural scientists experiment with different varieties they cannot make sure that all the plots are uniform in soil fertility. Similarly, the MBA professor while experimenting with various teaching methods, cannot take for granted that the IQ of all the experimental groups of students is same. In such cases, RCBD is employed where the main objective is to control, remove or reduce variability due to heterogeneity in the experimental plots.

In this design, the experimental plots are divided into separate homogeneous plots known as blocks. In the case of the varietal trial, the plots are divided into blocks of less soil fertility, medium soil fertility or high soil fertility. Similarly, the MBA professor divides the experimental groups into low IQ, moderate IQ and high IQ. Each block consists of experimental plots exactly as many in number as there are treatments. If there are four methods of teaching these will be four groups (experimental plots) in each block. Each block is viewed as a complete replication since all the treatments are tried once in each block. The only requirement, the essential one in the formation of blocks, is that within each block the experimental units should be as homogeneous as possible and at the same time the blocks be as heterogeneous as possible between one another. Within each block the treatments are allocated at random.

In RCBD, two-way ANOVA is used where the sources of variability are the blocks (replications) and the treatments.

Advantages

- ☼ Even when the experimental plots are heterogeneous, a large number of blocks (replications) may be arranged.
- ☼ As the experimental plots are placed in compact homogeneous blocks, it helps to reduce the component of experimental error.
- ☼ The design has the advantage of having blocks not necessarily contiguous in their location.

Limitations

- It is less efficient when the number of treatments is fairly large.
- When the heterogeneity persists in many directions, this design removes the variability due to heterogeneity only in one direction.

Latin square design (LSD) If all the experimental units (plots) are almost uniform, CRD is used. If the variation is in one direction (one dimension) RCBD is used. When the variation is in two directions (two dimensions) Latin Square Design (LSD) is employed. That is, the blocking concept is one-dimensional in RCBD but two-dimensional in LSD.

Restrictive features of LSD

- The experimental layout should be a square with as many columns and rows as there are treatments.
- Every column and every row will have all the treatments tried once.

Example

Allocation of four treatments with four replications may be as follows in CRD, RCBD and LSD.

A	C	B	A
D	C	A	B
C	D	C	D
D	A	B	B

CRD

A	C	B	D
C	B	A	D
B	D	A	C
D	A	B	C

RCBD

D	B	A	C
A	C	B	D
B	D	C	A
C	A	D	B

LSD

In the CRD layout of the given example, any treatment can take any plot. In RCBD, each row will have all the four treatments. But in LSD, all the four treatments are seen in each column as well as in each row.

Factorial design When the experimenter desires to study the effect of more than one factor simultaneously, a factorial design is selected. Factorial designs are of two types, simple and complex factorial design. In simple factorial design, the effect of not more than two factors are tested. Two factors at two levels is a 2×2 factorial design. In complex factorial design, experiments with more than two factors at a time are involved. If there are three treatments at two levels then it becomes $2 \times 2 \times 2$ factorial design. Other experimental designs such as confounded designs, lattice designs, etc. are also available to try complex problems.

CASE STUDY METHOD

A case study is an in-depth and thorough study of an organization, a group of people, an industry, an individual or a phenomenon. It is a sort of descriptive design. When reasons are sought for the happenings, it becomes a descriptive-cum-diagnostic design. Some of the characteristics of case study method are given below:

- Case study describes the peculiarities of a case.
- It probes uncommon, unique, extreme or even typical cases whose features are not studied by usual methods.
- It provides a wealth of information for intensive analysis of specific details.
- It examines the complex factors to understand the causative variables.
- It is a long-term process.

In short, a case study focuses on everything about something rather than something about everything. A biography or an autobiography is a typical case study.

A case study has its own merits/limitations.

Merits

- All methods of data collection are useful.
- Any dimension of any topic can be studied.
- It may be conducted in any kind of setting.
- It gives a wider range of insights.
- It is more useful to study groups or processes.

Limitations

- Generalization of the findings is not possible or is very limited.
- It is more time-consuming.
- It is inadequate to study macro-problems.
- Researcher's bias is likely to be more.

Examples

- To study the phenomenal growth of a company like Reliance Industries
- To analyse the astounding success of corporate giants like Azim Premji and Narayana Murthy in IT industry
- To understand how Tatas and Birlas are able to manage their take-over spree in foreign land
- To appreciate the reasons for overflow of Indian forex kitty consequent to liberalization and globalization

✿ To find out why highway accidents are on the increase despite better roads and awareness of fatal incidents

LONGITUDINAL VS CROSS-SECTIONAL STUDY

Both longitudinal study and cross-sectional study come under descriptive /diagnostic design. While longitudinal study is conducted with a section of population over a period of time, cross-sectional study deals with cross sections of the population in a short time.

When a behavioural scientist desires to study how physically handicapped girls behave at different ages, he/she has the option of selecting a few girls and observing their behaviour from the 1st year through a period of time (up to 18 years) or select girls of different age groups (from 1 to 18 years) and observing their behaviour in a single year. The former is a longitudinal study and the latter is a cross-sectional study.

In marketing research, when the researcher studies the same panel of consumers to report consumption data over a period of time it is longitudinal study; when he/she studies different panels of consumers at one point of time it is cross-sectional study.

The main differences between exploratory/formulative design and descriptive/diagnostic design are highlighted in Table 5.1.

Table 5.1   Summary of exploratory/formulative design vs. descriptive/diagnostic design

Component	Type of design	
	Exploratory/formulative	Descriptive/diagnostic
Sampling design	Only non-probability	Probability or non-probability depending on nature of the population
Observational design	Unstructured instruments to collect data	Structured instruments
Statistical design	No pre-planned design	Pre-planned design
Operational design	No fixed procedure	Advance decision on procedures
Overall design	Flexible	Rigid

REVIEW QUESTIONS

1. What is research design?
2. What are the components of a research design?
3. What is the need for research design?
4. Discuss the different types of research design.
5. What is case study?
6. Differentiate longitudinal study from cross-sectional study.

6

SAMPLING TECHNIQUES

After deciding what research design is to be adopted, the next step is collection of data. The need for adequate and reliable data in any study is of paramount importance. There are two ways to collect the required information or data: census and sampling.

CENSUS METHOD

It is also known as complete enumeration survey method. In this method, data are collected from each and every unit of the population or universe (student, household, college, shop, customer, firm, etc.). Population or Universe is the complete set of items which are of interest to the researcher/study. The most popular example is the population census undertaken by Government of India periodically. Here, information/data are collected from each and every household.

Advantages of census method

✿ Information can be collected from each and every unit of the population when individual data are the essence of the study. Examples are recruitment of personnel, preparation of voters' list or income tax assessment of individuals.

✿ The results of a complete enumeration are expected to be more accurate than sample method.

Disadvantages

✿ Census need not necessarily provide accurate information as evidenced by the experience of a number of enumerators. The errors in a complete enumeration survey arise mainly from incomplete coverage and inadequate observation due to the difficulties encountered in organizing a survey on a large scale and lack of sufficient number of trained personnel to conduct the survey.

- ○ The effort, money and time required for carrying out complete enumeration will be, generally, extremely large or prohibitive.

- ○ When the units of population get damaged or distorted while testing or collecting data, census cannot be adopted. For instance, when the organizer of a party orders for cakes and desires to check the quality of cakes he cannot adopt a census method as he cannot afford to taste each and every cake. In this case sampling is the alternative. This method, where the units get damaged while testing, is known as destructive sampling.

SAMPLING METHOD

In the sampling method instead of every unit of the population, only a part of the population is studied and conclusions are based on the data/information collected from that part of the population.

Though the theory of sampling acquired much importance only in the recent past, the idea of sampling is age-old practice. A housewife examining a few grains of boiling rice to know whether the pot of rice is cooked or not, a doctor examining a few drops of blood to know about the blood constitution of the whole body, a soil chemist testing a small soil sample to know about the fertility of the entire field, a shopkeeper placing orders for materials by examining a small sample of the materials, a professor questioning a few students to understand whether the entire class has followed what has been taught, a cup-taster taking only a few sips of brewed coffee to evaluate the entire coffee lot, etc. are common scenes of sampling. In fact sampling is used in every field either consciously or unconsciously.

PRINCIPLES OF SAMPLING

There are two important principles which govern the theory of sampling.

1. *Principle of statistical regularity* This principle is based on the mathematical theory of probability. The law of statistical regularity states that "a moderately large number of items chosen at random from a large group, are almost sure on the average to possess the characteristics of the large group". This principle points out that if a sample is taken at random from a population it is likely to possess almost the same characteristics as that of the population. This principle emphasizes the need for choosing sample at random.

2. *Principle of "inertia of large numbers"* It states that, other things being equal, larger the size of the sample, more accurate the results are likely to be. This points out to the fact that conclusion drawn based on a larger sample is more reliable than that based on a smaller sample.

TERMS USED IN SAMPLING

Population   A population is the total collection of elements/units about which some inferences are drawn. It is also known as universe. All the cancer patients in a city for medical research, all the mango trees in an orchard for a horticultural research, all the customers of a store for a CRM study, all the students in a class for a teaching method study, all the bolts/nuts manufactured for a quality control research or all the rice grains in a bag are examples of populations.

Finite population   If the number of elements/units in a population is limited and accessible to the researcher for data collection, it is known as a finite population (car manufacturers in a country, exclusive dealers of a popular brand of white goods, students in a class, employees in an organization or the exporting units in SEZ).

Infinite population   If the researcher has no definite idea of the total number of units of a population, and accessibility to all the units is not easy for data collection, it is an infinite population (TV viewers, bicycle owners, black money launderers, drug addicts, cell phone users in a city, income tax evaders, customers of a departmental store or consumers of pizza).

Target population   It is part of the total population about which the study is concentrated (users of a particular network among the mobile phone owners, students with commerce degree among the MBA students, computer-savvy employees in an organization or post-graduates among the call centre employees).

Element/Unit   It is a member of the population and the subject on which information is collected or measurement is made.

Census   It is the study or collection of information/data from all the units/elements of a population.

Sample   A sample is the portion of the population which is supposed to truly represent the population. Some of the cancer patients in the medical research, few of the mango trees in an orchard for the horticultural research, a group of customers of a store in the CRM study, a section of the students in a class in the teaching method study, a small number of bolts/nuts in the quality control research or a handful of rice grains from a bagful of rice constitute a sample.

Sampling   It is the process of selection of a sample (a part of the population) with a view to obtain information or draw inference about a population.

Sampling technique/Design   It is the procedure adopted to select a sample (probability or non-probability).

Sampling frame   It is a list containing all sampling units from which the sample is to be drawn. In finding out the satisfaction level of customers of BSNL in Coimbatore, the Coimbatore Telephone Directory is the sampling frame. In studying the performance level of a particular brand of car the list of buyers maintained by the dealer is the sampling frame. For the study on income tax payers, the list of IT payers maintained at IT office is the sampling frame.

Parameters vs statistics   A parameter is a characteristic of a population, whereas a statistic is a characteristic of a sample.

Parameters are characteristics which describe a population. Statistics are characteristics which describe a sample. Mean, variance, S.D., etc. are the characteristics to describe a population or sample (Table 6.1).

Table 6.1   Parameters vs statistics

Characteristics	Symbols	
	Population parameters	Sample statistics
Size (No. of units)	N	n
Mean	μ	$\bar{x}$
Variance	σ^2	s^2
Standard deviation	σ	s

NEED FOR SAMPLE/SAMPLING

- Sampling reduces the time and cost of research. Study of a small portion of the population (sample) is certainly cost-effective and saves time.

- Sampling saves labour. The requirement of human resources to collect data/information from a sample is always less than that of a population.

- Sampling improves quality of research. As more attention/concentration can be bestowed on a sample, supervision and processing of data would be better than that of census. In census, the researcher may lose the focus due to tiredness and boredom of collecting data from a large volume of units.

- Sampling provides quick results. Studying a sample consisting of a fewer units is quicker than studying more units in a population.

- Sampling is the only way out in certain situations. When the units get damaged while testing (finding the breaking strength of pencils or testing of rasagollas) only sampling helps to know about the population. And also when the population is infinite (TV viewers, drug addicts or pizza eaters) sampling is the only course.

However, when the population is small or heterogeneous, census will be better than sampling.

LIMITATIONS OF SAMPLE/SAMPLING

✿ Sampling must be carefully planned and executed. It demands a thorough knowledge of sampling methods; otherwise the results obtained may be inaccurate or misleading.

✿ When the population is heterogeneous or the characteristic to be measured occurs rarely in the population, a large sample is required. A large sample has all the drawbacks of a census.

✿ A complicated sampling technique may require more labour and the services of experts.

CHARACTERISTICS OF A GOOD SAMPLING DESIGN

A good sampling design must

✿ yield a truly representative sample

✿ result in a small sampling error

✿ be viable when funds are limited

✿ control systematic bias in a better way

✿ be applicable universally with reasonable level of confidence.

A good sampling design helps in collecting a sample which is representative of the population, and which is accurate, precise and of appropriate size.

SAMPLING AND NON-SAMPLING ERRORS

The term "error" refers to the difference between the value of a "statistic" and that of the corresponding "parameter", that is, the difference between a population value and sample value (e.g., difference between population mean μ and sample mean $\bar{x}$). Various forces combine to produce the error and they are grouped into sampling error and non-sampling error.

SAMPLING ERROR

Even if utmost care is taken in selecting a sample, the results derived from the sample may not be representative of the population from which it is drawn because samples are seldom perfect miniatures of the population. The non-representativeness of the sample and inadequacy of sample size leads to sampling error. Sampling errors arise due to the following reasons.

✿ The sampling is done by a non-random method.

✿ The sampling frame is incomplete or inaccurate.

✿ Some sections of the population are not available, or they refuse to cooperate.

✿ The sample size is too small.

A large sample selected using random method reduces this error to a great extent.

NON-SAMPLING ERRORS

These are errors caused by sources other than sampling and are as follows:

- ✿ *Errors of observation* Data collected through the method of observation/ interviewing and the physical procedures of observation/interviewing are subject to imperfection which causes errors.
- ✿ *Measurement errors* These errors arise due to faulty processing and analysis of data.
- ✿ *Errors of response* These include incorrect responses of the respondents, mistakes in noting their responses, etc.

While census suffers from non-sampling errors, sampling suffers from both sampling error and non-sampling error.

SAMPLING DESIGNS (SAMPLING TECHNIQUES OR SAMPLING METHODS)

The different types or methods of sampling are governed by two factors—basis of representation and technique of selection of the units.

Basis of representation The sample may be a probability sample or a non-probability sample. In probability or random sample, each unit of the population has an equal chance to get into the sample. In probability sample the units getting into the sample depend on chance factor or judgement of the researcher.

Technique of selection of units The sampling may be either unrestricted or restricted. When the samples are drawn from the entire population without any segmentation, it is unrestricted sampling. When the population is segmented into different segments and the sample consists of units from the different segments, it is restricted sampling.

The various sampling methods are shown in Table 6.2.

Table 6.2 Sampling methods

Selection method of units	Basis of representation	
	Probability sampling	Non-probability sampling
Unrestricted	Simple random sampling	Convenience or haphazard sampling
Restricted	Complex random sampling	Purposive or deliberate sampling
	Systematic sampling	Judgement sampling
	Stratified sampling	Quota sampling
	Cluster sampling	Snowballing sampling
	Multistage sampling	

PROBABILITY SAMPLING

SIMPLE RANDOM SAMPLING

This refers to the sampling technique in which each and every item of the population is given an equal chance of being included in the sample. The selection is thus free from personal bias as the investigator does not exercise his/her discretion of preference. If the sample is chosen at random and the size of the sample is sufficiently large, it will represent all the units in the population. That is why, random sampling is sometimes referred to as representative sampling.

The term "random" in random sampling should not be mistaken for the literal meaning "without definite aim, direction, rule or method."

Methods of obtaining simple random samples   Any of the following methods may be adopted depending on the size of the population.

Lottery method   This is a popular method when the population is of manageable size. In this method all the units/elements/items of the population are numbered or named on separate slips of paper of identical size, colour and shape. These slips are folded and mixed up thoroughly in a container. From this a blind-fold selection is made of the number of slips required to constitute the desired size of the sample.

For instance, when an MBA student wants to select a sample of 200 respondents from 700 workers in a factory, all he/she has to do is, write the names or identity roll numbers of all the 700 workers on separate slips, fold them and shuffle them in a convenient container and take 200 slips one after another. The selection of respondents depends entirely on chance.

Here also there are two alternatives:

i. *Sampling with replacement*   After drawing one slip, the name or number is noted and the slip is put back into the container. The process is continued till the desired size is selected. If the same slip reappears, it is ignored and put back. This procedure guarantees each unit the same probability of getting included in the sample.

ii. *Sampling without replacement*   In this procedure, the drawn unit is not put back into the container. Here, the probability is not uniform.

Though sampling with replacement appears to be a little difficult, it is ideal compared to the sampling without replacement.

Using table of random numbers   When the size of the population is large, the lottery method is cumbersome. The convenient method is using table of random numbers such as Tippett's table of random numbers, Fisher and Yates numbers or Kendall and Balington Smith given in any standard book on statistics.

Using computer As an alternative to random numbers, now using the computer to print out the desired number of random numbers has become popular. State lotteries generally employ computers to select the lucky winners.

Suitability of simple random sampling This sampling technique is suitable when the units/items in a population are almost uniform. When the population is heterogeneous, there are chances that only a particular group may get into the sample and the observation/ data from this particular group cannot represent the entire population. For instance, when the student-researcher selects a sample of 100 respondents from among 1000 employees comprising 300 unskilled workers, 300 skilled workers, 200 diploma-technicians and 200 engineer-technicians, there is a probability that only the unskilled workers may get into the sample. The opinion expressed or data collected from the unskilled workers cannot adequately represent the entire population of the employees. When the population is finite but heterogeneous, stratified sampling is more effective.

The use of random sampling necessitates a complete list of the items of population. But it is often difficult to have a list of all the items of population as in the case of many marketing research projects. When the population is finite and homogeneous, simple random sampling technique ensures an unbiased, representative sample.

Merits

- ✪ All the elements/items of the population have equal chances of being included in the sample.
- ✪ It is simple to adopt and understand.
- ✪ The quantum of sampling error can easily be computed.

Limitations

- ✪ It is often impractical, because of non-availability of population list or difficulty in enumerating the population.
- ✪ It does not ensure proportionate representation to various groups constituting the population.
- ✪ It takes more time and money.

SYSTEMATIC SAMPLING

As in the case of simple random sampling, this method is used in those cases where a complete list of the population is available. This method involves selection of every kth item from the list where k refers to the sampling interval. k is calculated by dividing the size of the population (N) with sample size (n). The starting point or the 1st item between the first and kth item is selected at random.

For example, a student wants to select a sample of 200 respondents from 1000 workers in a factory. Here, the sampling interval is 5 (1000/200) and only eve ry 5th item is selected.

The first item between one and 5 is selected at random. Suppose this item happens to be the 3rd then the following items will be 8th (3+5), 13th (8+5), 18th (13+5) and so on.

As the interval between sample units is fixed, it is also known as fixed-interval method.

Merits

✧ It is more convenient to adopt than random or stratified sampling technique.

✧ Time and work involved are smaller.

✧ In the absence of any periodic features, the results obtained are found to be quite satisfactory.

✧ Sample is spread evenly over the entire population.

✧ It is more efficient than simple random sampling when population elements are arranged in chronological order or by size.

Limitations

✧ It ignores all the elements between the two kth elements. Further, except the first element the rest of the elements are not chosen at random. In the strict sense, this method cannot be considered as complete random sampling.

✧ Excepting the elements present in the 1st interval, other elements do not have equal chance to get into the sample.

✧ Systematic sampling becomes less representative when there is hidden periodicity in the population. For instance, when a researcher studies the amount of traffic once a week for one year on a main road where a church is located, and if the 1st day selected at random happens to be a Sunday, he/she has to study the traffic only on Sundays for 52 weeks. Since Sunday has more traffic near churches the observation will not be representative for the whole year.

STRATIFIED SAMPLING

Simple random or systematic sampling procedure will be effective when the population is homogeneous, that is, when the units of the population are uniform. When the population is not homogeneous, but finite, then stratified sampling is more effective. For instance, if a researcher desires to take a sample of 100 respondents from the employees of an organization comprising 150 engineering graduates, 200 diploma holders and 300 skilled workers, there are possibilities that the entire sample of 100 units may come from only engineering graduates or only diploma holders or only skilled workers when simple random sampling method is used. If this is so, then the sample will not represent the entire population. In a heterogeneous population when each group wants to get represented, stratified sampling is more appropriate.

In this method, the heterogeneous population is divided into smaller homogeneous groups or strata and from each stratum, random sample is drawn. The sub-samples drawn from each stratum are combined to form a composite sample. The sub-samples can be taken from each stratum by three methods.

1. *Equal method*   An equal number of units is taken at random from each stratum irrespective of the size of the individual stratum. In the said example, the sample will consist of 25 engineering graduates, 25 diploma holders, 25 skilled workers and 25 unskilled workers.

2. *Proportionate method*   The number of units to be taken is proportionate to the size of the stratum. In the said example the number of engineering graduates will be 15(100 × 150/1000), diploma holders 20(100 × 200/1000), skilled workers 30(100 × 300/1000) and unskilled workers 35(100 × 350/1000).

3. *Optimum method*   In cases where there is heterogeneity within the strata, the number of units from higher variable stratum will be higher than the stratum with lower variability. The researcher shall decide the number of units from each stratum depending on the degree of variability within the strata.

Among the three methods, the proportionate method is preferable. Though proportionate method enhances the representativeness of the sample by providing proper representation to all the sub-groups in a population, a prior knowledge of the composition of the population and the distribution of the population characteristics are required to adopt this method. The identification of the strata might lead to classification errors resulting in the inclusion of some units into the wrong strata. Improper classification of the strata may vitiate the interpretation of results.

CLUSTER SAMPLING

Simple random sampling or stratified random sampling method is used when the population is concentrated in a smaller area and is easily accessible as in the case of an organization or a small market place. But when the units/elements of a population are scattered over a larger area and accessibility is expensive and time-consuming, cluster sampling is more appropriate.

In this technique the units of population are divided into a number of groups or clusters and each cluster will be considered as a sample unit. Thus the large numbers of units are reduced to a manageable cluster. In many cases, clusters exist in populations.

For example, the Government of India wants to study the impact of the IRDP on the farming community. A simple random sampling may be adopted as the number of households engaged in farming are available in the census record. But it will be time-consuming and costly. Instead, the villages will be considered as sample units and a few villages are selected through random sampling. All the farming households in the chosen villages are approached to collect data. Here each village is a cluster.

The cluster may be an institution, a geographical area or a group depending on the nature of survey.

The number of elements in a cluster is the cluster size. The clusters in most populations are of unequal size (e.g., villages, districts, organizations, households, etc.). Clusters of equal size are often the result of planned conditions such as number of matchboxes in a bundle or number of bottles in a crate.

Cluster samples usually give less precise estimates than simple random samples of the same size. But it is economically more efficient in terms of time and cost and more convenient in large geographical areas.

Limitations

✿ The cluster sizes may vary resulting in a biased sample.

✿ The sampling error is greater; thus it is statistically less efficient than other probability sampling methods.

✿ Adjacent clusters of study (e.g., villages in one state) tend to have more similarity than clusters distantly apart. This influences the 'representativeness' of the sample.

The major differences between cluster and stratified sampling are presented in Table 6.3.

Table 6.3 Differences between cluster and stratified sampling

Cluster sampling	Stratified sampling
The sampling unit is a cluster, i.e., a sub-group of population units.	The population unit itself is the sampling unit.
The population is divided into many clusters or sub-groups.	The population is divided into a few sub-groups or strata.
Clusters tend to be homogeneous, and within the cluster, the units may be heterogeneous.	Strata tend to be heterogeneous and within each stratum the units may be uniform.
Clusters are selected using random sampling technique.	Elements with the strata are chosen based on random sampling method.
Sampling error may be more.	Sampling error may be less.

Area sampling In large field surveys, clusters of geographical areas like districts, taluks or villages are selected by random sampling. As geographical areas are chosen as sampling units the method of sampling is called area sampling. It is not a separate method of sampling but forms a part of cluster sampling.

MULTI-STAGE SAMPLING

As the name suggests this method refers to a sampling method which is carried out in several stages. The population is regarded as made up of a number of first-stage sampling units, each of which is made of a number of second-stage units and so on. At first, the first-stage units are sampled by random sampling. Then a sample of second-stage units is selected from each of the selected first-stage units again by random sampling. Further stages may be added as required.

Example

To find out the effectiveness of rural banking in India, it is possible to go in for simple random sampling as the number of rural banks is available in records. But accessing the banks selected through random sampling would be time-consuming and expensive. Under the multistage sampling, the first-stage sampling units are the states. Among the various states a few are taken at random. The second-stage sampling units are the districts. Among the selected states a few districts are taken at random. The third-stage sampling units are the villages. From the chosen districts a few villages are drawn at random. The fourth and last stage of sampling units are the banks. A few banks are selected from the chosen villages to collect data.

MULTI-STAGE VS MULTI-PHASE SAMPLING

In multi-stage sampling, the sampling units are of different types at different stages such as states, districts, villages and banks. But in multi-phase sampling, the different phases of observation relate to sample units of same type. It is also known as sequential sampling.

NON-PROBABILITY SAMPLING

CONVENIENCE SAMPLING

It is also known as incidental or haphazard sampling. Some experts call it a chunk. A chunk is a fraction of population taken for investigation because of its convenient availability. Here, the sample is selected neither by probability nor by judgement but by convenience.

It is also sometimes called accidental sampling, because those units entering into the sample enter by accident; they just happen to be at the right place and at the right time, that is, where and when the information for the study is being collected.

A sample obtained from readily available lists such as telephone directories or automobile registrations is a convenient sample even though the sample is drawn at random from the available lists.

In a study on customers' satisfaction on mobile network, the student is likely to collect data from the mobile-phone users whom he/she comes across at bus-stops, railway stations, college campuses, etc. It is a typical convenience sampling technique.

Convenient sampling is useful in making pilot studies.

Advantages

- It is the cheapest and simplest method.
- It does not require the list of population.
- No statistical expertise is needed.

Limitations

- Its results are generally biased and unsatisfactory.
- Researchers' subjectivity influences sample collection.
- It can hardly be representative of the population.
- There is no way of estimating the representativeness of the sample.
- The findings cannot be generalized.
- It is the least reliable sampling method.

In most of the marketing research, where the customers/consumers cannot be enumerated adequately, convenience sampling is a deliberate choice. That is, when a population cannot be defined easily or the list of units in a population is not available, convenience sampling is inevitable.

Judgement Sampling (Deliberate or Purposive Sampling)

In this method the population units getting into the sample depend exclusively on the judgement of the researcher. Sometimes researchers can take the opinion of experts in the field. In other words, the researchers exercise their judgement in the choice of sample units and include those units in the sample which think are most typical of the population with regard to the characteristics under investigation.

For instance, when the student-researcher wants to study to what extent a particular brand of a car, say, Swift, compares with other models such as Getz, Tata-Indigo or Santro, he/she can certainly get the list of Swift owners from the local dealer and collect information. But there is no point in collecting data from all the owners of Swift because many of the Swift owners may not be aware of the features of other models. The researcher must deliberately select the Swift owners, who in his/her judgement are familiar with the features of other cars also to give a comparative opinion.

Similarly when social researchers desire to study how far IRDP is appreciated by the farmers in a particular village, they have to go in for a judgement sampling, though they can very well get a random sample. Because all the farmers may not be aware of the IRDP they have to deliberately contact the farmers who are aware of or are familiar with IRDP (Integrated Rural Development Programme). If the researchers take a random sample there are chances that the sample may contain farmers who are not aware of IRDP and collecting information from the farmers ignorant of IRDP does not serve any purpose.

Advantages

Though the principles of sampling theory are not applicable to judgement sampling, this method is often used in solving many types of economic and business problems.

- ✪ Judgement sampling is used when size of the sample is small. In such a case simple random sample may miss the more important elements, whereas judgement selection would certainly include them in the sample.
- ✪ In solving business problems and making public policy decisions the investigators pressed hard for time, cannot wait for a detailed random sampling. In such cases judgement sampling is the only practical method.
- ✪ This technique may also be used in pilot studies.

Caution The success of judgement sampling depends on the excellence or reliability of judgement. If the researcher is knowledgeable about the population and good in judgement/decision-making, the resulting sample may be representative; otherwise, the inferences based on the sample may be erroneous.

Quota Sampling

It is a type of judgement or convenient sampling technique. In a quota sample, quotas (proportions) are set up and within each quota the sample units are selected according to the convenience or judgement of the researcher. The basic design is similar to stratified sampling. While stratified sampling is used when the population is finite and the strata contain known number of units, quota sampling is for infinite population where the number of units in each quota is not known. In stratified sampling, within the stratum, sample units are selected using simple random sampling method, whereas in quota sampling the sample units within the stratum are selected based on the researcher's judgement or convenience.

Suppose a researcher wants to study the utility aspects of a particular brand of scooter among women in a particular city, all the women who use the particular brand constitute the target population. As the precise number or identity of these women is not readily available, the researcher goes for non-probability sampling. As in the case of stratified sampling the women scooter riders are differentiated into different groups (quotas), viz., housewives, working women, professionals and college girls. From each group, sample units are taken at the convenience or judgement of the researcher. The size of the sub-sample from each group depends on the approximate size or importance of the group.

In opinion poll, readership survey, etc., quota sampling is commonly used because of its simplicity. In a heterogeneous infinite population where precise results are not warranted and only a general opinion is aimed at in the shortest notice, quota sampling is appropriate.

The merits/demerits of quota sampling are almost similar to convenient/judgement sampling.

SNOWBALL SAMPLING

It is a technique of "building up" a list or a sample of a special population by using an initial set of sample units or members as indicators/informants.

For example, a researcher wants to study the challenges of life being experienced by Indians in Gulf countries. It is assumed that the researcher does not have the list or the locations of the respondents. In the first instance the researcher contacts one or two respondents through neighbours, relatives or acquaintances. These initial respondents may give the names/locations of a few other Indians in the Gulf. This process continues till the researcher is able to attain a desired size of the sample.

As a small snowball becomes bigger and bigger when it rolls down from the top of a snow-clad mountain, in snowball sampling technique, the initial small sample becomes bigger due to right leads and contacts.

This technique is beset with similar limitations encountered in convenience/judgement sampling.

SAMPLE SIZE

Once the sampling technique to be adopted is decided, the next logical question is what should be the size of the sample. But there is no fixed number of units or percentage of population that determines the optimum size of a sample. The so-called "thumb-rule" of 10% of the population is not based on any scientific proof. The size of the sample depends on many factors.

DETERMINANTS OF SAMPLE SIZE

i. *Nature of the population*   If the variation within the population is almost nil, i.e., if it is a homogeneous population, a smaller sample is sufficient. If the variation is substantial, i.e., if it is a heterogeneous population, then a larger sample is needed.

To know whether rice is cooked properly or not, testing just a single rice grain will tell whether the rice in the entire pot is cooked or not. But to know whether the 'avial' (a popular Kerala dish containing different types of vegetables) is cooked, a big spoonful is to be tested because of the variation in the vegetables.

To know how MBA students in a particular class perform, a small sample is sufficient as it is assumed that all the students have almost same environment. But to study the performance of students in a particular region, a larger sample representing different colleges is required.

ii. *Nature of the study*   If the units/elements are to be studied, the sample may be small. For a general survey, a large sample is necessary.

To know how the management schools function in India a large number of schools are taken for collecting data. But to know why some are doing exceptionally well and some are abnormally poor, a few schools are chosen in various categories and studied thoroughly.

iii. *Type of sampling*   In the case of random sampling (probability sampling) a small sample is sufficient. But in the case of convenience or quota sampling (non-probability) a larger sample is necessary.

iv. *Level of accuracy*   If it is decided to have the accuracy or precision at higher level, sample size must be large to reduce the error.

v. *Availability of target population*   If the number of units available in the target population itself is low then getting a larger sample is difficult. In the case of studying the mental health of drug addicts among students it is difficult to get a larger sample as the number of drug addicts will be very few.

vi. *Type of measuring techniques*   If the duration of an experiment in the experimental design is long or the questionnaire /schedule is long then only a small sample is feasible.

vii. *Time*   If the study is to be completed in a short duration as in the case of an emergency investigation, then only a small sample is possible.

viii. *Availability of resources*   If finance and personnel to collect and analyse data are not a constraint then a large sample can be taken.

APPROACHES TO DETERMINE THE SIZE OF SAMPLE

There are two alternative methods to find the size of the sample. One method is based on precision rate and confidence level. The other method is based on Bayesian statistics to weigh the *cost* of additional information against the *value* of the additional information.

1. Method based on precision and accuracy   This method is capable of giving a mathematical solution. It does not analyse the cost of gathering information and also the expected value of information.

    i.   *When the population is infinite*   When the total number of units in the population is not known, the sample size (n) is decided by using the formula

$$n = \frac{Z^2 \sigma^2}{e^2}$$

where,

Z = The table value of Z at certain confidence level (1.65 at 90%, 1.96 at 95% and 2.58 at 99%)

s = Standard deviation of the population (equivalent to SD of a large sample)

e = The acceptable range of error ± 1 or ± 2 or ± 3

n = Sample size

Example In a study on the IQ of students in a college, the researcher likes to estimate the mean of population with an accuracy of ± 3 with 95% level of confidence. Find out the size of the sample to be taken.

If the S.D. of the population found by a trial sample is assumed as 4.8 then

$$n = \frac{1.96^2 \times 4.8^2}{3^2} = 10$$

where 1.96 is the table Z-value at 95% level of confidence, 4.8 is the S.D. of the population based on a trial sample and 3 is the accepted level of error.

ii. *When the sample size is finite* When the number units of a population (N) is known, the sample size n is calculated using the formula

$$n = \frac{Z^2 \cdot N \cdot \sigma^2}{(N-1)e^2 + Z^2 \sigma^2}$$

where, N = total number of units in the population. Other connotations remain the same.

Example Determine the size of the sample for estimating the true confidence level of girl students numbering 5000 at 99% confidence level and within an error range of 0.8.

The S.D. has already been found to be 2.

$$n = \frac{Z^2 \cdot N \cdot \sigma^2}{(N-1)e^2 + Z^2 \sigma^2}$$

$$= \frac{(2.58)^2 (5000)(2)^2}{(5000-1)(0.8)^2 + (2.58)^2 (2)^2} = 41$$

where 2.58 is the table Z-value at 99% level of confidence.

2. Method based on Bayesian statistics This intricate method is beyond the scope of this book.

REVIEW QUESTION

1. Distinguish between census and sampling.

2. Discuss the principles of sampling.

3. What is the need for sampling?

4. Analyse the limitations of sampling.

5. What are the characteristics of a good sampling design?

6. Differentiate sampling error from non-sampling error.

7. Discuss the various probability and non-probability sampling techniques.

8. How is sample size fixed?

7

MEASUREMENT AND SCALING

After deciding the type of sampling technique as well as sample size but before heading for collection of information/data it is necessary to have a practical knowledge on measurement and scaling technique which will be useful in selection of appropriate tools for data collection.

In management science, particularly in marketing and HR, the investigator or researcher encounters various social and psychological variables. The measurement of these variables is inevitable. Further, measurement of psychological variables is not an easy task.

MEASUREMENT

Measurement is defined as assignment of numerals to objects/events according to rules or to represent amounts or degrees of a property possessed by all of the objects.

In a research process it is to be noted that it is the properties of objects which are measured and not the objects themselves. Abstract properties like intelligence, attitude, motivation, etc. cannot be measured directly. Inference is drawn based on the presumed indicants of properties. For instance, the intelligence of a child cannot be measured directly. Only the score in an intelligent test will indicate whether the child is intelligent or not. Similarly employee satisfaction cannot be measured directly. It is inferred only through the opinion of employees on various determinants such as compensation, training/development programmes, social security measures, management's attitude, etc.

NEED FOR MEASUREMENT

Measurement serves several purposes such as the following.

✲ Facilitates empirical description of social and psychological dimensions

✲ Renders data amenable for statistical analysis

- ✪ Helps in testing of theories and hypotheses
- ✪ Enables researchers to differentiate among people/objects based on specific properties.

POSTULATES OF MEASUREMENT

There are three postulates basic to measurement:

1. *Order* Numbers are ordered. One number may be greater than, less than or equal to another ($a > b$ or $a < b$ or $a = b$).

   If $a = b$ and $b = c$ then $a = c$; if $a = x$ and $b = y$, then $a + b = x + y$.

2. *Distance* Difference between numbers is ordered. The difference between any pair of numbers may be greater than, less than or equal to the difference between any other pair of numbers.

3. *Origin* The number series will have a unique origin indicated by the number zero.

LEVELS OF MEASUREMENT

Based on the combination of the above three characteristics, viz., order, distance and origin or absence of any of these characteristics, four levels of measurement are identified. The characteristics are summarized in Table 7.1.

Table 7.1 Levels of measurement

Levels	Characteristics	Utility
Nominal	No order, distance or origin	Determination of equality
Ordinal	Order but no distance or origin	Determination of less than or more than value
Interval	Both order and distance but no origin	Determination of equality of intervals/differences
Ratio	Order, distance and origin	Determination of equality of ratios

NOMINAL MEASUREMENT

- ✪ It is the simplest and lowest level of measurement.
- ✪ It includes the classification of variables into several subclasses by assigning numerals or any other symbols to mutually exclusive subclasses. For example, gender is classified into male and female and the numeral 1 may be assigned to male and 2 to female. In the case of religion, Hindus may be assigned the numeral 1, Muslims 2, Christians 3, Sikhs 4,

Jains 5 and others 6. Here, the numerals 1, 2, 3, etc. are just labels and have no quantitative value.

- It indicates no order or distance relationship and has no arithmetic origin.
- The only quantification possible is counting the number of units in each sub-class or category.
- It is the least power of the four levels.
- For statistical analysis, only mode, chi-square and coefficient of contingency can be employed.
- It is generally used for categorizing population, personal variables, types of organizations, work groups, etc.

ORDINAL MEASUREMENT

- In this measurement, objects/persons are placed in order by assigning ranks in ascending or descending order as 1st, 2nd, 3rd, etc.
- The numbers indicate only rank order. They indicate that the intervals between them are neither equal nor absolute quantities. The real difference between ranks 1 and 2 may be more or less than the difference between ranks 2 and 3. For instance the student in plus 2 exam getting the highest mark, say 1175 out of 1200 is ranked 1st. The next highest mark 1174 gets 2nd rank. The 3rd highest (1170) gets 3rd rank. But the difference between 1st and 2nd rank (1175 and 1174 marks) is not equal to the difference between 2nd and 3rd rank (1174 and 1170 marks). That is the interval between consecutive numbers is not same.
- The statistical techniques that could be used are median, percentile/quartile measure, rank order coefficients and non-parametric methods as tests of significance.

INTERVAL MEASUREMENT

- In addition to the features of nominal and ordinal levels, interval measurement has the concept of equality of interval.
- But the numbers on an interval scale cannot be multiplied or divided because the scale does not have a true zero; it has only an arbitrary zero.
- Centigrade or Fahrenheit thermometer is a typical example of interval level of measurement. 40°C is 10 degrees warmer than 30°C or 10 degrees cooler than 50°C but 40°C cannot be considered as 4 times warmer than 10°C. Other examples are watches, altimeter (to measure altitude based on sea level) and calendar years.
- Though interval scales are easier to use, it is difficult to use them for socio-economic and psychological variables.
- Statistical techniques that could be used are arithmetic mean, standard deviation, Product moment technique and *t*- and *F*-tests.

RATIO MEASUREMENT

- ✲ This is the highest and most ideal level of measurement. Foot-scale is the typical example. Those properties which have natural or absolute zero, such as weight, height, distance, area, money value, population, rate of return, etc. can be measured. As there is absolute zero, all arithmetic operations, viz., addition, division, multiplication and subtraction, are possible.

- ✲ Apart from the statistical tools that can be used at nominal, ordinal and interval levels, geometric and harmonic means and coefficient of variation can also be used in ratio measurement.

CHARACTERISTICS OF SOUND MEASUREMENT

The measurement to be qualified as a good measurement should have three important characteristics, viz., validity, reliability and practical.

TEST OF VALIDITY

It refers to the extent to which a test measures what is actually meant to be measured. It is the effectiveness (or success) of a test in measuring the specific property intended to be measured.

Measuring parameters such as height, weight, length, etc. does not pose any problem to the investigator as standardized measuring devices such as weighing machines and foot-scales are available. But measuring abstract properties such as opinion, attitude, belief, values, morale, motivation, etc. is not an easy task as these cannot be measured directly. They can be assessed only through carefully designed logical questions through questionnaire, interview, etc.

Validity is further classified into three types, viz., content validity, criterion-related validity and construct validity.

Content validity   It is the extent to which a measuring instrument provides adequate coverage of the study. There are again two forms of validity—face validity and sampling validity.

Face validity is a logical type depending on the investigator's subjective evaluation. For example, the investigator may prepare an inventory consisting of 15 statements to know individuals' opinion on globalization. The investigator then, evaluates each statement to assess whether the statements can really extract the opinion on globalization and may also get it confirmed from a specialist. It is a poor way of determining validity.

Sampling validity refers to the represented character of the content of the instrument. It is an appropriate sample and sampling technique to represent adequately the content of the population.

Many a time, the methods used may not adequately measure the real content. Assume that a marketing researcher desires to know which TV serial is most popular to insert his/her company's advertisement and may attach a device to the TV sets of the respondents to record which serials are mostly viewed by the respondents. Based on the record the researcher may prefer a particular popular serial for the company's commercial. But the researcher must remember that there are many people who switch over to other serials/programmes whenever the commercials appear on the screen thus nullifying the results of observation. That is, the serial may be observed to be popular but there is no guarantee that all those who view the serial would pay attention to the advertisement also.

Criterion-related validity It relates to the ability to predict some outcome or estimate the existence of some current condition. If the instrument is capable of predicting future performance, it can be said that it has predictive validity; if it is able to relate to other measures of known validity it is concurrent validity.

For example, if there is a significant correlation between the scores in the admission test and the performance (grades obtained) in the first semester then it can be concluded that the admission test has predictive validity. However, the statistical association between predicted outcome and subsequent outcome exhibited need not be a conclusive proof of the instrument's predictive validity; because the exhibited performance may be influenced by extraneous factors. In the present example, the students who scored low in the admission tests may get better grades in the semester examinations because of their hard work or special tuition.

Construct validity It is the degree to which scores on a test can be accounted for by explanatory constructs of a theory. There are procedures to test construct validity.

Known group methods In this method the instrument (a questionnaire) is administered on people with 'known' characteristics. The instrument discriminates the group if it is valid. For instance, if the scores obtained by communists, naxalites and democrats on political attitude are significantly different, then the instrument has construct validity because the political ideals of these groups are well-known.

Multipart–multimethod matrix method In this method, convergent–discriminant conception of validity is involved. In convergence, different methods of measurement of a particular property should yield similar results. In discriminability the same or a similar instrument should reveal different measurements with different properties. This method should measure at least two properties and each property is measured at least by two different methods. The intercorrelations among variables within and between methods are computed. Correlation coefficients among scores of a given property measured by different methods must be higher than correlations among different properties measured by different instruments.

Factor analysis It is the most powerful method of construct validation. This is a statistical technique designed to determine the basic components of a measure. It is explained under the Chapter "Tests of significance".

It is to be borne in mind that all the three types of validity must be taken into account in selecting an instrument.

TEST OF RELIABILITY

Reliability is the ability of an instrument (a questionnaire) to measure accurately with consistent results. A reliable instrument should be like a good weighing machine which indicates the same weight of an object when it is weighed several times. Reliability has two aspects; one is stability, i.e., an instrument is considered stable if it gives consistent results with repeated measurements of the same object; the other is equivalence. While stability is concerned with personal and situational fluctuations from one time to another, non-equivalence or non-variability is concerned with variations at one point in time among investigators and samples. For instance, when a structured observation elicits the same type of observations when repeated several times by the same investigator, then the instrument (structured observation) is said to be stable. When the same information is obtained by several investigators with several samples at one point of time using the same instrument then it is accepted that the instrument has equivalence.

Perspectives on reliability are stability, equivalence and internal consistency.

Stability A measure is said to be stable when one can secure consistent results with repeated measurements of the same person with the same instrument.

Equivalence It is concerned with how much error may be introduced by different investigators (in observation) or different samples of items being studied.

Internal consistency This is related to consistency or homogeneity among the items.

In opinion surveys or attitude measurement, formulation of reliable instrument (questionnaire, inventory or observation method) is a difficult task as the information given by the individuals over a period of time is likely to vary. Various factors such as problem of memory or recall, personal characteristics of the respondents, environmental factors, ambiguous instruments, etc. may cause variable errors.

Methods of estimating reliability

Test-retest method In this method a measuring instrument such as a questionnaire is administered on a group of people at two different times and coefficient of correlation is computed between the two sets of scores. It can be inferred that higher the correlation value, higher the degree of reliability.

This method has two limitations. First, the respondents may remember how they responded the first time and may respond the same way the second time. This may yield a high correlation but it will be an over-estimation of reliability. Secondly, as human attributes such as opinion, attitude, etc. are subject to change, it is possible that changes may have occurred in the measured attribute during the measurement interval, thus resulting in lowering of the reliability.

Parallel forms technique   Here, two forms of the same instrument containing different but relevant items are administered on the same group of people. The correlation coefficient is calculated between the two sets of scores. If the instrument is reliable, the correlation will be significantly higher.

Split half method   It can be used when the measuring tool has many similar questions or statements to which the subject can respond. After administering the instrument, the results are separated by items into even and odd numbers or into randomly selected halves. If the results of correlation are high the instrument is supposed to possess high reliability in terms of internal consistency. Spearman–Brown correction formula is used to adjust for the effect of test length and to estimate reliability of the whole test.

Cronbach's alpha   In addition to the above, Cronbach's Alpha can also be used to test the internal reliability of a questionnaire.

Validity vs reliability

The salient differences between validity and reliability are indicated below:

- A reliable instrument (questionnaire) does contribute to validity but a reliable instrument need not be a valid instrument.
- An instrument that is valid is always reliable but an instrument that is not valid may or may not be reliable.
- A reliable instrument need not be valid but a non-reliable instrument is never valid because a necessary condition for validity is reliability.
- While reliability is more directly tested using statistical method, validity is often inferred by a comparison of predicted and/or measured behaviour.
- Validity is more important than reliability.

TEST OF PRACTICALITY

The measuring instrument must be economical, convenient and interpretable.

Economy   A good research generally costs more. But there must be a trade-off between ideal research project and budget allowed. The instrument must be selected in such a way that reasonably good results must be obtained with reasonable cost. Economy depends on the length of the instrument, interview/observation time, number of respondents/items (sample size), etc.

Convenience   The measuring instrument must be easy to administer by paying more attention to the layout of the instrument. It must be clear without any ambiguity.

Interpretability   The instrument must be devised in such a way that whoever uses the instrument, other than the designer of the instrument, must be able to interpret the result easily. Detailed instruction for administering the test, providing keys and proper guidelines will help in improving the interpretability of an instrument.

SCALING

When the object to be measured is concrete and the measuring instrument is a standardized one (as in the case of measuring the length of table using a measuring tape), there will not be any problem in measurement. But if we measure the length of the table with our forearm the measurement will not be accurate. The situation gets worse when the item to be measured is abstract (not concrete) and no standardized measuring instrument is available as in the case of researchers attempting to measure the attitude or opinion of respondents on certain phenomena using a questionnaire which is not standardized (questions about attitude). In such cases the test scores fail to reflect the true scores. A good measurement should reduce the gap between the true scores (real attitude) and the test scores (revealed attitude). Constructing measurement scales is scaling. In this section scaling is concerned with measuring abstract concepts such as attitudes and opinions.

Scaling is a procedure to assign numbers (or symbols) to a property of objects to impart some of the characteristics of numbers to the properties in question.

For instance, when we want to measure the temperature of air, we cannot measure it directly. We can measure it only indirectly through expansion or contraction of materials such as mercury. We use a thermometer to measure the temperature. It is indicated by the rise and fall of the mercury column in the thermometer. Similarly, the durability of paint can be determined by scrapping a particular thickness of the paint using a scrub brush with pre-determined pressure. The number of scrubs required to wear through the particular thickness of paint indicates the durability of the paint.

SELECTION OF AN APPROPRIATE SCALE

This requires decisions in six key areas:

i. Study objective   A scale may be designed to (i) measure the characteristics of the respondents who complete it or (ii) use respondents as judges of the objects or stimuli presented to them. For example, we may present students with a scale on the college's various extracurricular activities to obtain their opinion. If the respondents themselves are interested in the extra curricular activities we may combine each student's answers to form an indicator about the activities. Here the emphasis is on measuring differences in opinion among the students. In the second case, the same data are used to find out the opinion of the students on the various extracurricular activities.

ii. Response scales   Scales may be either rating or ranking.

Rating scales 'known' as category scales are used when respondents give scores on object/ attitude without making a direct comparison to another object or attitude. For example, the students as respondents may be asked to rate the teaching method on a 5-point scale, i.e., quite effective, effective, average, ineffective and quite ineffective.

Ranking scales are used to make comparisons among two or more objects. For example, the respondents may be asked to select the car, "Swift" or "Santro Zing", which has more attractive styling. They may be asked to rank or order the importance of comfort, ergonomics, price, maintenance cost, pickup and mileage.

iii. Degree of preference   In preference measurement the respondents are asked to choose the object or solution each prefers. In non-preference evaluation, the respondents are asked to judge an object without any personal preference towards objects or solutions.

iv. Scale properties   Scaling approaches are viewed in terms of the properties possessed by each scale (nominal, ordinal, interval or ratio).

v. Number of dimensions

One-dimensional scale   In this scale the researcher seeks to measure only one attribute of the respondent or object, e.g., employee potential as promotability.

Multidimensional scale   Here, the object is better described with many dimensions rather than one, e.g., Instead of measuring potential just with a simple dimension, promotability, it can be expressed by three distinct dimensions, viz., managerial performance, technical performance and team work.

vi. Scale construction   Scales may be classified by the methods to build them. There are five approaches to design a scale, viz., arbitrary, consensus, time analysis, cumulative and factor scale.

RESPONSE METHODS

To measure concepts, attitudes or opinions, questioning is a widely used method. When a manager is asked his views on a particular employee, the response could be "a good worker", "a troublemaker", "a union activist", "reliable", "a fast worker" or "always a latecomer". But this type of response is of limited value to the researcher. To improve the usefulness of such replies quantification is necessary. To quantify dimensions that are essentially qualitative, rating scales or ranking sales are used.

RATING SCALES

Rating scales are used to judge properties of objects without reference to other similar objects. The ratings may be "like–dislike", "good–average–bad", "always–often–sometimes–rarely" or "strongly agree–agree–no idea–disagree–strongly disagree". There is no conclusive support for choosing a three-point scale over scales with five or more points. The most widely used scales range from three to seven points.

Simple category scale   This scale has two response choices. The choices could be 'yes' or 'no', 'important' or 'unimportant', 'agree' or 'disagree', etc. The scale is particularly useful for demographic questions or where a dichotomous response is adequate. This produces nominal data.

Example

"I plan to join only a premier management institute": Say 'Yes' or 'No'.

Multiple choice – single response scale   This scale is appropriate when there are multiple options available for the respondent and only one answer is sought.

Example   "Which magazine do you read often for business news?" Tick (✓) any one

Business India	Business Today	Business Week
Business World	Business Standard	Other (Specify)

Similar to simple category scale, this also produces only nominal data.

Multiple choice – multiple response scale   As a variation of the above scale, this scale allows the respondent to select one or several alternatives.

Example   Check any of the following books you consulted to prepare for organizational Behaviour examination.

O.B. by Fred Luthans

O.B. by Keith Davis

O.B. by Stephen.P. Robbins

O.B. by McShane

O.B. by L.M. Prasad

Other (Specify).

It is possible that the six sources would have been consulted. This presents a problem for reporting when the readers expect the responses to add up to 100%. This scale also produces only nominal data.

Likert scale   It is the most frequently used variation of summated rating scale. Summated scales consist of statements that express either a favourable or unfavourable attitude towards the object. The respondent is asked to agree or disagree with each statement. Each response is given numeral score to reflect its degree of attitude of favourableness and the scores are totalled to measure the attitude of the respondent.

Example   "Assignment is the best way of measuring management students' potential"

Strongly agree	Agree	No idea	disagree	Strongly disagree
5	4	3	2	1

In the above example, the respondent chooses one of the five levels of agreement. The numbers indicate the value to be assigned to each possible answer with 1 the least favourable opinion and 5, the most favourable opinion.

Between 20–25 properly constructed questions about an attitude/opinion would be required for a reliable Likert scale. The scale can be used to compare one respondent's score with that of others. This scale produces interval data.

Semantic differential scale   This scale measures the psychological meanings of an attitude. It is used for brand image, organization image, political issues, etc. It is based on the proposition that an object can have several dimensions of connotative meaning which are located in a multidimensional property space called semantic space. The scale consists of a set of bipolar ratings, usually with seven points.

Example   The semantic differential scale items for analysing candidates for leadership position are shown below.

Successful	3	2	1	0	−1	−2	−3	Unsuccessful
Progressive	3	2	1	0	−1	−2	−3	Regressive
Strong	3	2	1	0	−1	−2	−3	Weak
Active	3	2	1	0	−1	−2	−3	Passive
Fast	3	2	1	0	−1	−2	−3	Slow
True	3	2	1	0	−1	−2	−3	False
Sociable	3	2	1	0	−1	−2	−3	Unsociable

Advantages

✿ It produces interval data

✿ It is an efficient and easy way to find out attitudes from a large sample

✿ The attitudes may be measured in both direction and intensity

- ✲ It is a standardized technique that can be easily repeated
- ✲ The total set of responses provides a comprehensive picture of the meaning of an object and a measure of the respondent doing the rating.

Numerical scales   They have equal intervals. The extreme points are labelled by verbal anchors. Numeric scales are often 5-point scales.

Example   Performance appraisal can be done on a numerical scale.

Extremely favourable   5   4   3   2   1   Extremely unfavourable

A number of favourable statements like co-operation as team members, knowledge of task, planning effectiveness, ability to attend to minute details, presentation, etc. are included and the panelists are to indicate their numbers for each component. The scale provides both an absolute measure of importance and a relative measure (ranking) of the various items rated.

Multiple rating lists   It is similar to numerical scale, but differs in two aspects; one, it accepts a circled response from the respondent and second, the layout allows visualization of the results.

Example   To find out the relative importance of the various characteristics of the after-sales service of a two-wheeler manufacturer, the scale could be as follows:

"Please indicate how important or unimportant each service characteristic is"

Fast and reliable repair	Important	7	6	5	4	3	2	1	Unimportant
Service at customers' place	Important	7	6	5	4	3	2	1	Unimportant
Knowledge and skill of technicians	Important	7	6	5	4	3	2	1	Unimportant
Genuineness of spares	Important	7	6	5	4	3	2	1	Unimportant
Repair charges	Important	7	6	5	4	3	2	1	Unimportant

Fixed sum scale   This scale helps the researcher to find out proportions. The proportions of different categories must sum up to 100. Though up to ten categories can be used, the precision and patience of the respondents suffer when too many categories are proportioned and summed. The scale is used to record attitudes, behaviour and behavioural intent.

Example   Preference given to various dimensions of a product (body spray) by a respondent

Price	Brand	Size	Smell	Shape	Total
30%	15%	15%	30%	10%	100%

Staple scale   It is used as an alternative to semantic, differential scale when it is difficult to find desired bipolar adjectives.

Example To find out the corporate image, five attributes may be used and the opinion on these attributes may be obtained on staple scale as follows:

+5	+5	+5	+5	+5
+4	+4	+4	+4	+4
+3	+3	+3	+3	+3
+2	+2	+2	+2	+2
+1	+1	+1	+1	+1
(Customer friendly)	(Technology leader)	(Exciting products)	(World-class reputation)	(Socially responsible)
−1	−1	−1	−1	−1
−2	−2	−2	−2	−2
−3	−3	−3	−3	−3
−4	−4	−4	−4	−4
−5	−5	−5	−5	−5

Graphic rating scale

- It was created to enable researchers to find out the fine differences in the attitude/opinion of respondent.
- Theoretically an infinite number of ratings is possible as there is no fixed interval.
- The respondent marks his/her response at any point along a continuum.
- Usually the score is a measure of length (in mm) from either end point.
- Coding and analysis are difficult as there are no pre-determined categories.

Example "How likely are you to recommend your College/Institute to others seeking admission for MBA programs?"

Very Likely ———————————————————————————— Very Unlikely

Putting an 'X' at any position along the line reflects the respondent's suggestion.

Problems of rating scales Successful measurement using rating scales depends on the assumption that a respondent is able to make good judgements. But the respondents tend to make errors and the most common errors are leniency, central tendency and halo effect.

Leniency The error of leniency occurs when a respondent is either an "easy rater" or a "hard rater". The raters are inclined to give higher score when they know the respondents well and where the acquaintances are lower the scores will be less.

Central tendency   When the raters are reluctant to give extreme judgement, scores will be near the centre of the scale resulting in the error known as central tendency. To overcome this in a rating scale like Likert's type of scale, the mid-score is avoided to make the raters mark either positively or negatively (Instead of having a 5-point scale such as strongly agree, agree, no idea, disagree and strongly disagree, there can be a 4-point scale, i.e., strongly agree, agree, disagree and strongly disagree, by removing the midpoint.)

Halo effect   It is a systematic bias the rater introduces by carrying a generalized impression from one rating to another. For instance, when an examiner of answer scripts is impressed with the answer to the first question, he/she carries the impression that the subsequent answers are also good resulting in the student scoring better grades even though the other answers are not as good as first question's answer.

RANKING SCALES

In ranking scales, the respondent directly compares two or more objects and makes choices among them.

Paired-comparison scale   In this scale the respondent can express attitudes/opinions unambiguously by choosing between two objects. The number of judgements required in paired comparison is $n(n-1)/2$ where n is the number of objects or stimuli.

Example   Assume that an MBA student for her summer project "Functioning of departmental stores in Coimbatore" interviews 200 customers on their preferences of five departmental stores A, B, C, D and E. The customers are requested to compare only two stores at a time. Their preferences are tabulated as follows:

It is concluded that store B is most preferred and store D is least preferred.

Preference of departmental stores (The figures indicate the number of customers)

	A	B	C	D	E
A	–	164*	138	50	70
B	36	–	54	14	30
C	62	146	–	32	50
D	150	186	168	–	118
E	130	170	150	82	–
Total	378	666	510	178	268
Rank	3	1	2	5	4

*   This is interpreted as 164 out of 200 preferred Store B (column) to store A (row).

Forced ranking scale In this scale the respondents are asked to rank the attributes/objects relative to each other. For instance, if the marketing researcher desires to know which attribute is to be given preference in a new car model he/she may ask the consumers to rank the attributes such as price, safety, style, colour, mileage, size, etc. relative to each other attribute. This method is faster than the paired comparisons and is usually easier and more motivating to the respondent. With 5 items, it takes 10 paired comparisons to complete the task but in the simple forced ranking it requires ranking just 5 items. Here, there is no transitivity problem where A is preferred to B and B to C but C is preferred to A. The major drawback is that when the number of items/objects/ stimuli is high [>10], the respondents may get tired of ranking resulting in careless comparisons. Further, rank ordering produces ordinal data as the interval between preferences is not known.

Comparative scale In this scale the respondents are required to compare the items/objects/ stimuli against a standard. It is ideal for comparison of programmes, processes, brands, points of sale, people, etc. if the respondents are familiar with the standard. Suppose the Principal of a college wants to compare his college with others, he may ask the PG students to compare the ambience of the present college with their previous college as "superior–same–inferior".

SCALE CONSTRUCTION TECHNIQUES

In social science studies as well as in many of the management research projects, the opinions or attitudes of the respondents are obtained using questionnaire, opinionnaire or inventory. This approach uses a number of questions/statements relevant to the topic and the respondents are required to express their agreement or disagreement. The statements/questions are formulated in such a way that they are able to elicit responses which are psychologically related to the attitude being measured and discriminate not only the extremes of attitude but also among individuals who differ slightly.

Inferring attitude from the recorded responses has several limitations:

- Respondents may conceal their attitude and express socially acceptable attitudes/ opinions.
- They may not really know how they feel about the issue under investigation.
- They may not be aware of their attitude about an abstract situation.
- They may not be able to predict their reaction until confronted with a real solution.
- At times, behaviour itself will not be a true indication of attitude.

Despite these limitations psychologists and sociologists developed several scale construction techniques.

The scale construction techniques employed and scales developed are shown in Table 7.2.

Table 7.2 Scales developed employing various scale construction techniques

Scale construction techniques	Scale developed
Arbitrary	Arbitrary scales
Consensus	Differentiated scales such as Thurstone differential scale
Item analysis	Summated scales such as Likert scale
Cumulative	Cumulative scales such as Guttmann's scalogram
Factor analysis	Factor scales such as Osgood's semantic differential scale and multi-dimensional scale

ARBITRARY SCALES

These scales are developed on ad hoc basis. The designs of the scales largely depend on the researcher's own subjective selection of items.

- ✪ The researcher collects several items/dimensions which are believed to be unambiguous and appropriate to a given topic.
- ✪ Some of the items are selected and included in the instrument.

Illustration Assume that the researcher is interested in studying the image of a company compared to other companies. The researcher may decide to consider a few dimensions, viz., place of work, social responsibility, compensation, equal opportunity employer and innovation to assess the image of the company. A 5-point scale may be constructed taking into consideration the relevant dimensions.

As a place to work	Bad	-	-	-	-	-	Good
As a socially responsible Co.	Bad	-	-	-	-	-	Good
As an ideal compensator	Bad	-	-	-	-	-	Good
As an equal opportunity employer	Bad	-	-	-	-	-	Good
As an innovating company	Bad	-	-	-	-	-	Good

The respondents are required to score each of the items from 1 to 5 depending on the degree of favourableness.

The results are studied in several ways:

- ✿ Totals may be made by individual items, by company or by companies as places to work, as socially responsible company, etc.
- ✿ Totals for each company or for individual respondents are calculated to determine how they compare.

Advantages

- ✿ Easy to develop, inexpensive and can be designed to be highly specific.
- ✿ They provide useful information and are adequate if developed skillfully.

Limitations

- ✿ The approach is subjective.
- ✿ The researcher's insight and ability offer the only assurance that the items chosen are representative of the universe.
- ✿ There is no evidence that the respondents will view all the items with the same frame of reference.

CONSENSUS SCALING

In this technique the items to be included in the questionnaire are selected by a panel of judges. The judges evaluate the items based on relevance to the topic, potential for ambiguity and level of the attitude they represent.

A popular consensus scale is Thurstone equal appearing interval scale (Thurstone scale).

Developing Thurstone scale

- ✿ A large number of statements, usually more than 20 are written on cards expressing various views toward the object, institution or idea under study.
- ✿ There is only one statement per card.
- ✿ The cards are submitted to a panel of judges (more than 50).
- ✿ Each of the judges arranges the statements in 11 piles or groups ranging from one extreme opinion/attitude to another in position.
- ✿ In case of marked disagreement among the judges in assigning a position to an item, that item is discarded.
- ✿ Three of the 11 piles are labelled as "favourable" and "unfavourable" at the extremes and 'neutral' at the midpoint.
- ✿ The eight intermediate piles are unlabelled to create the impression of equal-appearing intervals between the three labelled positions.

✿ The statements whose median scores are spread evenly from one extreme to other are considered for inclusion in the final scale.

Thurstone scale is rarely used in management research because of its high cost, time and staff requirement.

ITEM ANALYSIS

It is a procedure for evaluating an object, group, institution, etc. based on how well it discriminates between those persons whose total score is high and those whose total score is low. The most popular scale using item analysis is the summated or popularly known Likert scale.

Developing Likert-type scale

✿ A large number of statements relevant to the topic is prepared and shown to a group of people similar to those who are going to be studied.

✿ They are asked to read the statements and indicate the level of their agreement in the 5-point scale (5—Strongly agree; 4—Agree; 3—Undecided; 2—Disagree and 1—Strongly disagree)

✿ Each person's scores are added to find out the individual total score.

✿ The top 25% and the bottom 25% of the scores are selected and the respective means are calculated.

✿ For each statement, t-value is found out for the low mean score and high mean score (using t-test to compare two means).

✿ The statements whose t-values are more than 1.75 are selected for inclusion in the scale.

Advantages of Likert scale

✿ It is easy and quick to construct.

✿ Each item that is included has met an empirical test for discriminating ability.

✿ Since respondents answer each item, it is more reliable and provides a greater volume of data than other scales.

CUMULATIVE SCALES

An important scale of cumulative scales is the scalogram. Scalogram analysis is a procedure to determine whether a set of items forms a one-dimensional scale. A scale is unidimensional if the responses fall into a pattern in which agreeing of the item reflecting the extreme position results also in agreeing to all items that are less extreme.

For example, assume that the researcher is gathering opinion regarding a new body spray X. A preference scale is developed of four items.

✿ The body spray **X** is good looking.

✿ I will insist on body spray **X** next time.

✿ The appearance of body spray **X** is acceptable to me.

✿ I prefer the body spray **X** to other sprays.

Respondents indicate whether they agree or disagree. If these items form a one-dimensional scale, the response patterns will resemble the ideal configuration as shown Table 7.3.

Table 7.3   Ideal scalogram response pattern

Item				Respondent score
2	4	1	3	–
X	X	X	X	4
–	X	X	X	3
–	–	X	X	2
–	–	–	X	1
–	–	–	–	0

X: Agree   –: Disagree

A score of 4 indicates all statements are agreed to and represents the most favourable attitude. Persons with a score of 3 disagree with item 2 but agree with all others. These types of scales are useful for assessing behaviours that are highly structured. Though they have potential for managerial application, it is used less often.

FACTOR SCALES (SEMANTIC DIFFERENTIAL SCALE AND MULTIDIMENSIONAL SCALING)

Factor scales are developed through factor analysis or on the basis of inter-correlations of items which indicate that a common factor accounts for the relationship between items. Two important scales based on factor analysis are semantic differential scale and multidimensional scaling.

Semantic differential scale   Developed by Charles E. Osgood *et al*. S.D. scale is an attempt to measure the psychological meanings of an object to an individual. They produced a long list of adjective pairs useful for attitude research. According to them, three factors contributed most to meaningful judgements by respondents, viz., evaluation, potency and activity.

Steps in S.D. scale construction

✧ Selection of concepts—nouns, noun phrases, or visual sketches chosen by personal judgement.

✧ Selection of scale (at least three scales)

✧ Panel of judges is used to rate the various stimuli (or objects) on the various selected scales and the responses of all judges would then be combined to determine the composite scaling.

Example   S.D. scale for analysing candidates for an industry leadership position.

1.	Sociable	3	2	1	0	−1	−2	−3	Unsociable
2.	Strong	3	2	1	0	−1	−2	−3	Weak
3.	Active	3	2	1	0	−1	−2	−3	Passive
4.	Progressive	3	2	1	0	−1	−2	−3	Regressive
5.	Tenacious	3	2	1	0	−1	−2	−3	Yielding
6.	Fast	3	2	1	0	−1	−2	−3	Slow
7.	True	3	2	1	0	−1	−2	−3	False
8.	Heavy	3	2	1	0	−1	−2	−3	Light
9.	Hot	3	2	1	0	−1	−2	−3	Cold
10.	Successful	3	2	1	0	−1	−2	−3	Unsuccessful

Items 1, 4, 7 and 10 indicate "evaluation", items 2, 5 and 8 "Potency" and items 3, 6 and 9 "Activity" dimensions.

Multidimensional scaling [MDS]

It is also known as perceptual mapping. This technique is commonly used to identify the product attributes that are important to the customers. It is also, employed to measure the product's relative importance.

MDS is useful in answering questions such as the following:

i. What are the major attributes considered by customers while choosing a product/service?

ii. Which attributes do customers compare to evaluate different brands?

iii. Which is the ideal combination of attributes according to customers?

iv. Which type of advertising message is compatible with the customer's brand perception?

Example   Perceptual mapping of five baby care products, A, B, C, D and E on two dimensions, viz., price and nature of product.

Data on the perception of the customers about the products based on two-dimensional, i.e., low-priced or high-priced and organic or synthetic are collected. The resulting map may look like the following:

[Actual calculation for mapping are beyond the scope of this book]

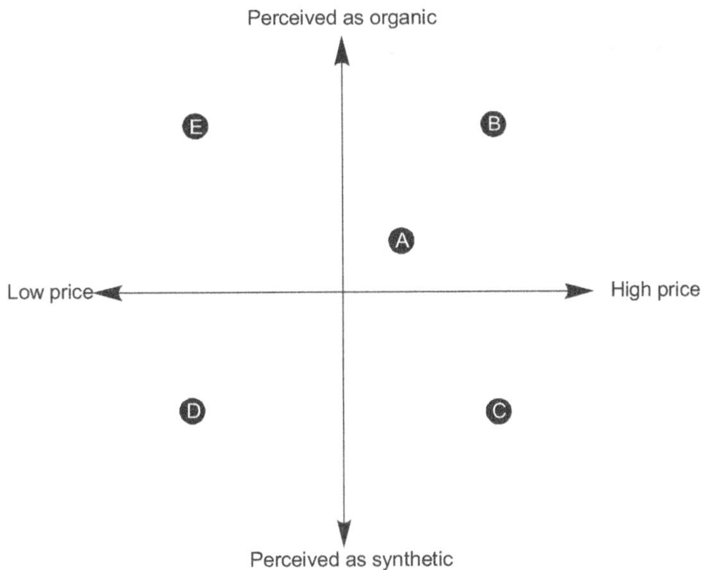

Perceptual mapping of baby care products

Interpretation

- ✿ Product E is relatively more organic and low-priced.
- ✿ Product D is relatively low-priced but perceived as more of synthetic.
- ✿ Product C is perceived as synthetic as well as high-priced.
- ✿ Product B is perceived as organic but high-priced.
- ✿ Product A is perceived as moderately priced and it is considered as neither synthetic nor organic.

REVIEW QUESTIONS

1. What is measurement?

2. What are the levels of scales of measurement?

3. Discuss the characteristics of a good measurement.

4. What is scaling?

5. Discuss the various rating scales.

6. What are ranking scales?

7. Analyse the various scale construction techniques.

8

COLLECTION AND PROCESSING OF DATA

Data constitute the foundation of any scientific analysis and interpretation. Data can be obtained from three important sources: (i) Secondary source (ii) Internal records and (iii) Primary source. Depending on the source, the data will be secondary, internal or primary.

KINDS OF DATA

SECONDARY DATA

When an investigator (the student researcher) uses the data which have already been collected by others, such data are called secondary data. Secondary data can be obtained from journals, reports, government publications, publications of organizations, professional bodies, project reports, etc.

Before using the secondary data, the investigator must examine the following aspects:

- Whether the data are suitable for the purpose of investigation
- Whether the data are adequate for the investigation
- Whether the data are reliable.

Features of secondary sources of data

- Ready-made and readily available
- Consist of data over which the researcher has no control
- Do not require the direct involvement of the researcher

Advantages

- ✿ Secured quickly and cheaply
- ✿ Wider geographical area and longer reference period may be covered without much cost
- ✿ Database broadened can be from which scientific generalizations can be made
- ✿ Enables a researcher to verify the findings of primary data.

Limitations

- ✿ The data may not meet the specific requirements of the investigation
- ✿ The data may not be accurate as desired
- ✿ Because of time lag, the data may become obsolete.

INTERNAL DATA

These data are generally available in the routine business in various departments like finance, production, personnel, sales, R & D department, etc.

Data on employees' salary from payroll, sales amounts from sales journal, raw materials from stock registers, labour and manufacturing expenses from production records and cash receipts from cash books are internal data. Data seen in balance sheet and profit–loss account are the major internal data available for projects in finance.

In many instances internal data are also considered as secondary data.

PRIMARY DATA

Primary data are collected directly by the researcher from the original sources. In primary data collection the researcher can collect the required data according to his/her research needs. The researchers can collect them when they want and in the form they need. Of course, primary data collection is costly and time-consuming. But in several cases, secondary data may not be available necessitating collection of primary data.

METHODS OF PRIMARY DATA COLLECTION

The important methods are observation, interviewing, mail survey, experimentation, simulation and projective techniques.

OBSERVATION

Observation may be defined as a systematic viewing of a specific phenomenon in its proper setting for the purpose of gathering data for a particular study. Observation is not only seeing and hearing, it includes perceiving as well.

Observation becomes scientific when it serves a formulated research purpose.

- ○ It is planned deliberately.
- ○ It is recorded systematically.
- ○ It is subjected to checks and controls on validity and reliability.

Characteristics   Observation as a method of data collection, has certain characteristics:

- ○ It is both a physical and a mental activity.
- ○ It is selective.
- ○ It is purposive, not casual.
- ○ It captures the natural context.
- ○ It grasps the significant events and occurrences.

TYPES OF OBSERVATION

Observations are classified in different ways:

- ○ Depending on the investigator's role, it may be participant observation or non-participant observation.
- ○ In terms of the mode of observation, it could be direct observation or indirect observation.
- ○ Considering the rigour of the system adopted, it could be controlled observation or uncontrolled observation.

i. Participant observation   Here, the observer is a part of the phenomenon or group which is observed and acts as both an observer and a participant. For example, the investigator who wants to study how the BPO workers relieve their stress in week-end outings may join as a BPO worker. The BPO workers who are observed should not be aware of the investigator's purpose; only then will their behaviour in the outings be "natural".

Advantages

- ○ The observer as an investigator can understand the emotional reactions of the observed group and get a deeper insight of their experiences.
- ○ The investigator will be able to record context which gives meaning to the observed behaviour and heard statements.

Disadvantages

- ○ The scope or range of observation of the participant observer is narrow as the observation is confined to a limited group.
- ○ The investigation will not be objective if the investigator has emotional participation.
- ○ The dual demand of recording and participation may result in inadequate observation.

ii. Non-participant observation   In this observation the observer stands aloof and records his/her observation without actually participating in the phenomenon. This method calls for skill in recording observations without getting noticed.

iii. Direct observation   The investigator observes the phenomenon personally when it takes place. This method is flexible enabling the observer record subtle aspects of events and behaviours as they occur. The major disadvantage is that the investigator may not be able to cover all relevant events when things happen quickly.

iv. Indirect observation   Here, the physical presence of the observer is not required and the recording is done by mechanical, photographic or electronic devices. Though this method is less flexible than direct observation, the bias and error in recording will be less. It provides a permanent record.

v. Controlled observation   In this method the observational techniques are standardized with maximum control over extrinsic and intrinsic variables by adopting experimental design and recording the observations systematically. In a typical controlled observation the decisions on what, how and when to observe will be explicit and clear. It is primarily used for inferring causality and testing causal hypothesis.

vi. Uncontrolled observation   This method does not involve control over extrinsic and intrinsic variables. It is primarily used for descriptive research.

Advantages of observation methods

- It is possible to study behaviour as it occurs. There is no need to ask the respondents about their opinion, attitude, etc.
- The data describe the observed phenomena as they occur in their natural settings.
- It is the only method of studying subjects who are unable to articulate meaningfully (children, tribals, low-level workers, etc.).
- Contextual background of behaviour can be analysed, i.e., what one says and behaves can be compared.
- The investigator does not trouble the respondents to collect information.
- For continuous observations over longer periods, mechanical devices can be used.

Limitations of observation methods

- Past events or activities cannot be studied.
- It is not suitable to study opinions and attitudes of the respondents.
- The investigator has to wait for the event to occur.
- Direct presence of the investigator for observation may not be possible in all cases.
- Observation method is a slow and expensive process.

EXPERIMENTATION

It is a research process used to study the causal relationship between variables. It aims at studying the effect of an independent variable on a dependent variable keeping other extraneous variables under control. Experimentation is described in Chapter 5.

SIMULATION

It is a process of conducting experiments on a symbolic model representing a phenomenon.

TYPES OF SIMULATION

Man simulation   It is a game played by people in a laboratory setting to simulate people in real life.

Computer simulation   This is an operational model programmed to generate a sequence of interactions. This type of simulation requires precise definitions, storing of large amounts of data on the system to be analysed and programming of the analysis.

Man-computer simulation   In this type, persons play the role of decision-makers while the computer is responsive to the players' activities. In this game, the computer is provided with a script.

Simulation can be employed in behavioural problems, social problems, political problems, economic problems, war strategies, business problems, etc.

In the case of business problems such as determination of proper order quantities, production scheduling, designing complex distribution systems, waiting line problems in transport services, maintenance scheduling in factories, airline and bus service, assembly line scheduling, consumer behaviour prediction, financial forecasting, introduction of new products, control system, etc., simulation can be employed.

INTERVIEWING

It is defined as a two-way systematic conversation between the researcher and the respondent, initiated for obtaining information relevant to a specific study.

- ✪ Interview is a prominent method of data collection. It involves not only conversation but also learning from the respondents' gestures, facial expressions, etc. It requires face-to-face contact or contact over phone (nowadays videoconferencing) and demands special skills.

- ✪ It may be structured or unstructured and may be used either as a main method or as a supplementary one in studies of persons.

- It is the only suitable method for gathering information from illiterate or less educated respondents.
- Interviewing is useful for collecting a wide range of data from factual demographic data to highly personal and intimate information relating to the respondents' opinions attitudes, values, beliefs, past experience and future intentions.
- It is inevitable where probing is necessary.
- It is superior to other data-gathering models as people are usually more willing to talk than to write.
- It adds flesh to statistical information.
- It permits the investigator to seek clarifications.

Advantages

- With a well-conceived schedule, personal interview can obtain a great deal of information.
- Personal interview improves the percentage of response and the quality of information received.
- The interviewer can gather supplement information like the living conditions and environment of the respondents.
- The interviewer can use special scoring device to improve the quality of interviewing.
- The accuracy and dependability of the responses of the respondents can be checked by observation and probing.
- Interview is flexible and adaptable to individual situations.

Limitations

- It is costly in terms of both money and time.
- It may be adversely affected by the interviewer's mode of questioning/interactions and incorrect reading.
- Respondents' faulty perception/memory and inability to articulate may influence the interview.
- In the face-to-face interview, the respondents may be reluctant to divulge information on personal matters and financial aspects.
- Recording information may be a distraction to both the respondent and interviewer affecting the thread of conversation.
- Interviewing is a highly skilled job and training of interviewers is a long and costly process.

TYPES OF INTERVIEW

i. Structured or directive interview

- It is made with a detailed standardized schedule.
- Same questions are put to all the respondents in the same order.
- Each question is asked in the same way in each interview to promote measurement reliability.
- It is used for large-scale formalized surveys.

Advantages

- Data from one interview to the next one are easily comparable.
- Greater precision is achieved.
- Attention is not diverted to extraneous, irrelevant or time-consuming conversation.

Limitations

- It tends to lose the spontaneity of natural conversation.
- Investigators' own biases may override the respondents' views.
- The scope of exploration is limited.

ii. Unstructured or non-directive interview

- The interviewee is encouraged to talk freely with a minimum of prompting or guiding.
- Instead of a detailed pre-planned interview, only a broad interview guide is used.
- The interviewer avoids channelizing the interview direction.
- It is more useful in case studies rather than in surveys.
- It is particularly useful in exploratory research where the lines of investigation are not clearly defined.
- It is more useful to gather information on sensitive topics.
- It provides opportunity to explore the various aspects of the problem in an unrestricted manner.
- The advantages are the spontaneity of natural conversation and less influence of interviewers' bias.

Limitations

- Data obtained may not be comparable and hence not suitable for surveys.
- Time may be wasted in unproductive conversation.
- Coding and classifying of responses requires more time.
- It calls for greater skill than the formal survey interview.

iii. Focused interview

- It is a semi-structured interview where the investigator attempts to focus the discussion on the actual effects of a given experience to which the respondents have been exposed.
- The focus is on the subjective experiences of the respondents such as their attitudes, emotional responses, etc. to particular situations.
- The situation is analysed prior to the interview and an interview guide related to the research hypothesis is used.

iv. Clinical interview   It is similar to the focused interview but with a subtle difference. While the focused interview is concerned with the effects of a specific objective, clinical interview is concerned with broad underlying feelings, motivations or life experiences.

v. Depth interview

- It is an intensive and searching interview aiming at studying the respondents' opinion, emotions or convictions.
- It deliberately aims to elicit unconscious as well as extremely personal feelings and emotions.
- It is generally a lengthy procedure designed to encourage free expression of one's feelings.
- It requires real probing questions.
- The interviewer should totally avoid advising or showing disagreement. Instead he/she should use encouraging expressions to motivate the respondent to continue discussion.
- This interview requires much more training in interpersonal skills than structured interview.

vi. Telephonic interview

It is useful when

- the population is composed of persons whose names are listed in the telephone directory
- the study requires responses to 5 or 6 simple questions
- the study is to be completed in a short period
- the study is interesting or important to the respondents
- the respondents are geographically widespread (reside in far-away places)
- the respondents cannot afford to spend more time in answering a questionnaire

Advantages

- Telephone interviewing is less expensive.
- Time taken is short.
- As there is no face-to-face contact, interviewer's bias is reduced resulting in quality response.
- It is less demanding on the interviewer.

Disadvantages

- As the population is restricted to persons in the telephone directory, the study may be incomplete.
- The responses cannot be elaborative.
- Respondents' body language cannot be assessed.
- Establishing rapport will not be easy.
- As the identity of the interviewer is not confirmed, there may be suspicion resulting in poor response.

MAIL SURVEY (POSTAL/E-MAIL)

This method involves mailing the questionnaires to the respondents to get their responses.

Advantages

- Mail survey is less costly than personal interview.
- It can cover extensive geographical areas.
- It is useful in contacting busy executives who generally avoid interviews.
- The respondents can fill up the questionnaire leisurely.
- Due to anonymity responses may be free from inhibition.
- As there is no personal contact, interviewer's bias is absent.

Disadvantages

- It is limited only to literate population.
- Response rate is generally low and hence the sample may not be representative.
- The causes for inadequate or non-responses cannot be explained.
- If the questionnaire is incomplete, it cannot be rectified.

TOOLS FOR DATA COLLECTION

The various methods of data collection involve the use of appropriate tools or instruments. These tools/instruments facilitate data collection.

i. Observation schedule or observationnaire

- This is a form used to record the observations.
- The items to be observed are determined in advance and grouped into appropriate categories.
- The items are structured with possible alternatives.
- Space is provided against each unit observation.

ii. Interview guide

✧ It is used for non-directive and depth interviews.

✧ It contains only the broad topics or areas to be covered in the interview.

✧ It serves as a suggestive reference or prompter during interview.

✧ It aids in focusing attention on salient points relating to the study.

✧ It helps in securing comparable data in different interviews by the same or different interviewers.

iii. Interview schedule and mailed questionnaire

✧ Both these tools are widely used in surveys.

✧ Both contain lists of questions to be answered by the respondents.

✧ While schedule is filled out by the interviewer, questionnaire is completed by the respondent.

iv. Opinionaire

It is similar to interview schedule/mailed questionnaire. It is used for studying opinions of people. Wording of statements may differ.

v. Inventory

It is essentially a list that the respondent is asked to mark or check in a particular way regarding personal qualities.

CONSTRUCTION OF QUESTIONNAIRE OR SCHEDULE

A questionnaire/schedule should have provision to collect personal information of the respondents apart from the information on the study under reference. The personal information generally pertain to (i) Gender (ii) Age group (iii) Marital status (iv) Educational background (v) Occupation (vi) Salary/Income (vii) Experience, etc., depending on the nature of study. This information is essential to differentiate the opinion based on gender, age, income, etc. of the respondents.

When surveys are conducted among businessmen/business houses, the data on the type of business, turnover, number of employees, dealers' network, etc. are collected.

The questions included may be open-ended, closed-end questions, dichotomous, multiple-choice questions or declarative ones.

i. Open-ended questions   These are unstructured ones providing free scope to the respondents to reply with their own choice of words and ideas.

Example   What is your opinion on the present trend in HR? What are your comments on the Government's initiatives in improving FDI?

Open-ended questions are helpful in initiating discussion or for an in-depth investigation. The major limitation is that it is difficult for compilation, classification and for analysis of the responses.

ii. Closed-end questions These are structured ones with two or more alternative responses for the respondent to choose. They generally contain standardized answers. They are simple to administer and easy to compile and analyse. As the alternatives are designed with reference to the requirements of the study, the chances of securing relevant answers are better. The limitations are:

- The response is forced in terms of the investigator rather than that of the respondent.
- The respondent is led to choose a response even when he/she has no knowledge of it.
- The limited alternatives may not cover all the viewpoints.
- Different respondents may interpret the same words and statements differently.

iii. Dichotomous or two-choice questions A dichotomous question can be answered either as "yes" or "no". Here, there is no choice for the respondent to say "undecided", "do not know", "sometimes" or "partially".

iv. Multiple choice questions These questions contain more than two alternatives.

Example Why do you prefer a particular brand of mobile hand-set?

- Price is reasonable
- Handy
- Sleek
- More features
- Others (please specify)

As the alternatives may not be all-inclusive, "others (please specify)" is included to provide for any other option.

v. Declarative questions It is a type of multiple choice questions in which a series of statements are given and the respondent is asked to select the one which represents his/her view.

A few model questionnaries are included in the *Appendix II*.

CHARACTERISTICS OF A GOOD QUESTIONNAIRE

- *Questions must be short and simple*   The questions must be short, simple and easy to understand. It should convey the purpose without any ambiguity. Unless the respondents are technical persons, technical terms and jargon must be avoided.

- *The number of questions must be as few as possible*   Though the precise number of questions to be included in a questionnaire depends on the objective and scope of the investigation, 15 to 25 may be regarded as a fair number. If a lengthy questionnaire is unavoidable, it should be preferably divided into two or more parts.

- *Questions should be logically arranged*   To elicit a natural and spontaneous reply, the questions are arranged in a logical sequence. For example, asking a woman respondent how many children she has before knowing whether she is married or not is undesirable. Similarly, it is illogical to know the salary of a respondent before knowing whether he/she is employed or not.

- *Questions should be capable of getting objective answers*   Depending on the type of study the questions can be dichotomous or multiple-choice. Open-ended or free-answer questions must be placed at the end.

- *Cross-checks*   One or more questions may be repeated in different formats to cross-check whether the respondent answers the questions sincerely and carefully.

QUESTIONS TO BE AVOIDED

Questions requiring calculations   Questions should not require calculations to be made. Asking daily wage earners their annual income or percentage/ratios of spending on provisions, clothes, luxuries, etc. must be avoided as they involve calculations. Wherever calculations are involved, the general tendency is to avoid the question or give a wrong answer.

Questions of sensitive nature   As far as possible, questions of a personal and pecuniary (related to finance) nature should be avoided. People in the higher echeleon generally avoid questions related to personal opinion on their income.

Leading questions   A leading question is one that is worded in such a way as to influence the respondent to give a certain answer. It must be avoided as it does not elicit the correct viewpoint.

Examples

- Would you like to specialize in HR which has a large scope?
- BPO jobs are monotonous. Is it not?

Loaded questions   A "loaded" question is one that contains words which are emotionally charged and suggests an automatic feeling of the approval.

Examples

- Should not the terrorists be hanged on the spot?
- Corrupt officials must be dismissed summarily. Is it not ?

Ambiguous questions   These are the questions which do not convey clear meaning.

Examples

- Do you prefer a small or a big house?
- How small is "small" or how big is "big" depends on the social status of the respondent.

Double-barrelled questions   These questions contain two or more different ideas/suggestions/ references.

Example

Do you favour or oppose "increased job security" and "productivity-linked" wage system?

Long questions   Long, complex or compound questions may be ambiguous or confusing.

Questions with double negatives   As in the case of long questions, double-negative questions such as, "Are not the incomes of rural doctors not comparable with urban doctors" may also lead to confusion.

PRETESTING OF QUESTIONNAIRE

A researcher should not expect that the first draft of his/her efforts would result in a usable/accepted questionnaire. It is the respondents who judge whether a particular questionnaire is effective or not. To make the questions serve the purpose of eliciting the right response, pretesting the questionnaire is of vital importance. Pretesting a questionnaire is similar to test marketing of a new product. As test marketing of a product provides the real test of customer reactions, pretesting of a questionnaire testifies whether it is effective or not in getting the required information from the respondents.

For pretesting the questionnaire, it is desirable to cover a cross section of the target population. The draft questionnaire is administered on a few respondents personally and the valid suggestions/corrections made by the respondents are incorporated, thus making the questionnaire a complete one.

PROCESSING OF DATA

Prior to any sort of statistical analysis for interpretation, the data collected from experiments, observations and surveys, etc. are processed. Data processing includes identification of variables, hypothetical relationship, if any, among the variables and tentative research hypothesis.

Steps in Data Processing

The important steps in data processing are:

- Identifying the types of information
- Editing the data
- Coding of data in the case of large volume of data and where secrecy is to be maintained
- Classifying and tabulation of data

i. Identifying the types of information   The information collected is identified whether they are quantitative and qualitative in nature. All the qualitative information is converted into quantitative data. For instance, the opinion collected in respect of overall job satisfaction of employees on a 5-point Likert type scale is quantified appropriately ("Strongly Agree" gets 5 points, "Agree"—4 points, "No idea"—3 points, "Disagree"—2 points and "Strongly Disagree"— 1 point).

ii. Editing   Editing is the process of detecting and correcting of errors and omissions. Editing is mainly done to check for completeness, accuracy and uniformity.

Completeness   The information gathered is scrutinized and whether all the questions in a questionnaire/opinionaire/inventory are answered is checked. In the case of observation it is checked whether all the relevant observations are made by the researcher as per the predetermined structure. In the case of minor omissions the researcher/editor can fill it up based on the available data. If the missing information is of vital importance to the study, the respondents are contacted again. In experimental designs, "missing plot technique" is employed to find out the missing data.

Accuracy   A random check may be helpful to verify the accuracy of data. Along with accuracy, consistency in responses can also be ascertained. Irresponsible responses are deleted. One way of checking the accuracy/consistency is to repeat the question in different formats, either as a negative or positive statement.

Uniformity   To elicit meaningful responses and uniform interpretation, the questions formulated should be unambiguous. In the case of opinionaire or inventory, the statements must be either only positive or only negative. If positive and negative statements are mixed up "reverse scoring" is resorted to during analysis. In the positive statement the opinions, Strongly Agree, Agree, No idea, Disagree or Strongly Disagree get points 5, 4, 3, 2 and 1 respectively. In the case of negative statement the points will be 1,2,3,4 and 5 accordingly.

iii. Coding of data   In comparatively small research projects, such as MBA summer project, where the number of respondents in a survey is around 200–250 or the number of companies or the number of financial years taken is few, coding is not necessary. But when the number of variables and respondents are many, coding is done. Further, coding is essential when the researcher feels that some sort of secrecy is required when the data are subjected to analysis. The coding could be numeric or alphabetic.

Example

Gender　　　　Male may be codified as M or 1 and Female as F or 2

Occupation　　Salaried as S or 1

　　　　　　　Business as B or 2

　　　　　　　Professional as P or 3

　　　　　　　Retired as R or 4

　　　　　　　Others as O or 5

iv. Classification and tabulation　Classification must be appropriate depending on the available data in relation to the objectives of the study. Suppose the researcher desires to know the satisfaction level of the different age groups of employees, then the employees are classified as young (<30 years) middle aged (31 to 45 years) and old (> 45 years). In the survey, where the age difference is not perceptible as in the case of BPO organization, classification based on age becomes irrelevant.

Classification should be exhaustive, i.e., all the categories are taken into consideration. When the researcher wants to classify the respondents based on marital status generally they are classified as married, or unmarried. Here, the widower, widow or separated cannot find a place. To overcome this category "others" is included.

The categories must be mutually exhaustive. For example, while classifying the respondents based on income it could be <₹10,000, ₹10001–20000, ₹20001–30000 and more than ₹ 30000. It should not be < ₹10000, ₹10000–20000 and 20000–30000, which is not mutually exclusive.

TABULATION

Tabulation is the process of summarizing raw data into meaningful categories and presenting them for a quick understanding. Tabulation is a pre-requisite for statistical analysis.

COMPONENTS OF A TABLE

- ✿ Heading—table number, title of the table and designation of units
- ✿ Body—Stub-head (headings of all rows or blocks of sub-items)
- ✿ Body head—headings of all columns or main captions and sub-captions
- ✿ Field/body—cells in rows and columns
- ✿ Notations—footnotes and sources wherever applicable

TYPES OF TABLES

Based on the number of dimensions or variables there would be one-way table, two-way table, three-way table, etc.

One-way table   It is classification of respondents/distributions based on a single dimension or variable such as gender, age or income.

Example

Classification of the employees based on age is shown in the following table.

Classification of respondents based on age

Sl. No.	Age group	No. of respondents	Percentage
1.	< 20 years	25	10
2.	21–40 years	125	50
3.	> 40 years	100	40
	Total	250	100

Two-way tables   It is classification of respondents/distributions based on two dimensions/variables.

Example

Classification of the employees based on gender and qualification is given in following table.

Classification of the respondents based on gender and qualification

Sl. No.	Gender	Qualifications			Total
		Matriculates	Graduates	Postgraduates	
1.	Male	30	75	45	150(60)
2.	Female	20	50	30	100(40)
	Total	50(20)	125(50)	75(30)	250(100)

* The figures within the parentheses are the respective percentages.

GUIDELINES FOR CONSTRUCTION OF TABLES

- All the tables must be numbered for easy reference. It could be in a consecutive serial order such as Table 1, Table 2, Table 3, etc. or chapterwise as 1.1., 1.2, 1.3 … for the tables in chapter 1 and 2.1, 2.2, 2.3… for the Tables in Chapter 2.
- Every table should have a title or caption which is clear and concise to give a clear description of the contents.
- The units of measurement must always be indicated.
- If any symbols or abbreviations are used due to lack of space, they must be identified in the footnotes below the table.
- If the data presented are not original, the sources of data must be indicated below the table.
- There should be proper alignment of columns, figures, decimal points, plus or minus signs, etc.
- Miscellaneous and exceptional items are placed in the last row(s).
- While discussing, tables are referred to only by number and not "as table given above" or "the following table".
- Tables wider than the size of the report are placed in landscape format so that the title is near the margin or binding side.
- Tables should be made as logical, clear, concise and simple as possible.

REVIEW QUESTIONS

1. Distinguish between primary and secondary data.
2. Discuss the various methods of primary data collection.
3. How is a questionnaire or interview schedule constructed?
4. Analyse the characteristics of a good questionnaire.
5. How is a questionnaire pretested?
6. What is data processing?
7. What are the different types of tabulation?

9

DATA ANALYSIS
(Tests of Significance)

The purchase manager in a star hotel places order with a supplier for supply of 1000 apples for a party and insists that the mean weight of apples should be 200 g. The supplier supplies 1000 apples and claims that the mean weight is 200 g. Before making payment the manager wants to confirm the mean weight but he neither has the time nor the device to verify the weight of all the 1000 apples. He decides to verify a sample of 20 apples. He finds that the mean weight of the sample is only 195 g. Now, he is in a dilemma whether to accept the lot of 1000 apples or reject it.

On another occasion, not only the manager insists on the mean weight of 200 g, he demands that the variation in weights among the apples should not be more than 10 g. He again takes a sample of 20 apples and finds that the variation ranges from 8 to 12 g. Now also he is in a dilemma whether to accept the whole lot or not.

An agricultural scientist tests three chemicals and finds that chemical A increases the yield of paddy by 1.2 t/ha, chemical B by 1.9 t/ha and chemical C by 1.5 t/ha. The manufacturer of chemical A contests that the yield increase in the plots tested with chemicals B and C are not due to the inherent capacity of the chemicals B and C but only due to higher soil fertility and claims that his chemical A is on par with B and C. What does the scientist do? Does he decide that chemical B (1.9 t/ha increase in yield) is superior to A and C based on the numerical data? How can he answer the query of the manufacturer of chemical A?

These types of dilemmas are not uncommon and to overcome these piquant situations, tests of significance come to one's rescue.

In common parlance, test of significance is a technique to find out whether or not observed means, percentages, proportions, variances, etc. differ significantly. The solution is to formulate a test criterion on which to base one's judgement, whether an observed difference between means, variances, percentages or proportions is a chance difference due to extraneous factors or the difference is genuine.

PARAMETRIC VS NON-PARAMETRIC TESTS

The tests of significance, in general, are grouped as parametric and non-parametric (distribution-free) tests. As the terms indicate, in parametric tests such as Z-test, t-test, F-test, ANOVA, etc., relevant parameters of the population such as total number of units or size of the population (N), mean of the population (μ) and variance (σ^2) or standard deviation (σ) are known. In the case of non-parametric tests the population parameters are inadequate.

Assumptions of parametric tests include the following:

- The observations must be independent (The selection of any one unit should not affect the chances of any other unit to be included in the sample).
- The observations should be drawn from normally distributed populations.
- The populations should have equal variances.
- The measurement scales should be at least intervals so that arithmetic operations can be used with them.

There are many non-parametric tests such as sign test, Mann–Whitney U-test, Kruscal–Wallis test, etc. Chi-square as a test of independence and to test goodness of fit is a non-parametric test.

There are specific tests available to find out the significance of differences between means, variances, percentages, proportions, etc.

Univariate and Bivariate Analyses

- When the mean, variance, standard deviation or proportion of a sample are to be compared with that of the population concerned, it is a univariate analysis, i.e., only a single sample is involved.
- When the means, variances, standard deviations or proportions of two samples (i.e., two populations) are to be compared for their differences, it is a bivariate analysis.

SUMMARY OF COMMONLY USED SIMPLE TESTS AND THEIR APPLICATIONS

Table 9.1 gives a summary of simple tests of significance and their applications.

Table 9.1   Types of tests, objectives and formulae

Type of test	Objectives	Formulae
Z-test	i. To find the significance of difference between mean of population and mean of sample when the sample size is large (> 30 units)	$Z = \dfrac{\bar{x} - \mu}{\sigma / \sqrt{n}}$
	ii. To find the significance of difference between the means of two large samples	$Z = \dfrac{\bar{x}_1 - \bar{x}_2}{\sqrt{\dfrac{\sigma x_1^2}{n_1} + \dfrac{\sigma x_2^2}{n_2}}}$
	iii. To find the significance of difference between population proportion and sample proportion	$Z = \dfrac{\hat{p} - p}{\sqrt{\dfrac{p \cdot q}{n}}}$
	iv. To find the significance of difference between two sample proportions (In the case of percentages, they are converted into proportion, e.g., 60% as 0.6)	$Z = \dfrac{\hat{p}_1 - \hat{p}_2}{\sqrt{\dfrac{\hat{p}_1 \cdot \hat{q}_1}{n_1} + \dfrac{\hat{p}_2 \cdot \hat{q}_2}{n_2}}}$
t-test	i. To find the significance of difference between mean of population and mean of sample when the same size is small (<30 units)	$t = \dfrac{\bar{x} - \mu}{s / \sqrt{n}}$
	ii. To find the significance of difference between means of two small samples	$t = \dfrac{\bar{x} - \bar{y}}{s \sqrt{\dfrac{1}{n_1} + \dfrac{1}{n_2}}}$ where $s = \sqrt{\dfrac{(n_1 - 1)s_x^2 + (n_2 - 1)s_y^2}{n_1 + n_2 - 2}}$
Paired *t*-test	To find out the significance of difference of values in the same sample (before and after treatment)	$t = \dfrac{\bar{d} \cdot \sqrt{n}}{s}$ where $\bar{d} = \dfrac{\sum d}{n}$ d = deviation and $s = \sqrt{\dfrac{\sum d^2 - n(\bar{d})^2}{n-1}}$

(Contd.)

Table 9.1 (Continued)

Type of test	Objectives	Formulae
Chi-square test as a parametric test	To find out the significance of difference between population variance and sample variance	$\chi^2 = \dfrac{s^2(n-1)}{\sigma^2}$
F-test	To find out the significance of difference between variances of two samples	$F = \dfrac{s_1^2}{s_2^2}$ $s_1^2 =$ Higher variance $s_2^2 =$ Lower variance
ANOVA	To find out the significance of difference between means of two or more samples (Z-test and t-test are applied when the samples are only two)	$F = \dfrac{\text{MSS of treatment}}{\text{MSS of error}}$
Correlation	To find out the relationship between two different sets of variables	$r = \dfrac{N\sum XY - (\sum X)(\sum Y)}{\sqrt{\{N\sum X^2 - (\sum X)^2\}\{N\sum Y^2 - (\sum Y)^2\}}}$
Chi-square test as a non-parametric test	i. To find out the significance of difference between observed and expected values (Goodness of Fit test)	$\chi^2 = \sum \dfrac{(O-E)^2}{E}$
	ii. To find out whether there is any association between two variables [independent and dependent]. It is known as test of independence.	$\chi^2 = \sum \dfrac{(O-E)^2}{E}$
Rank correlation	To find out the significance of association between ranks	$R = 1 - \dfrac{6\sum D^2}{N^3 - N}$

Notes:

N = Size of population (No. of units in the population)

n = Size of sample (No. of units in the sample)

n_1 = Size of sample 1

n_2	=	Size of sample 2
μ	=	Mean of population
$\bar{x}$	=	Mean of sample
$\bar{x}_1$	=	Mean of sample 1
$\bar{x}_2$	=	Mean of sample 2
σ^2	=	Variance of population
σ	=	Standard deviation of population
s^2	=	Variance of sample
s	=	Standard deviation of sample or combined S.D.s of two samples or S.D. of differences
s_1^2	=	Variance of sample 1
s_2^2	=	Variance of sample 2
s_1	=	Standard deviation of sample 1
s_2	=	Standard deviation of sample 2
d	=	Difference of value in the same sample unit (before and after treatment)
$\bar{d}$	=	Mean of differences
p	=	Proportion in population
q	=	$1 - p$
q_1	=	$1 - p_1$
q_2	=	$1 - p_2$
$\hat{p}$	=	Proportion in sample ($\hat{p}$ is read as p hat)
$\hat{q}$	=	$1 - \hat{p}$ ($\hat{q}$ is read as q hat)
$\hat{p}_1$	=	Proportion in sample 1
$\hat{p}_2$	=	Proportion in sample 2
$\hat{q}_1$	=	$1 - \hat{p}_1$
$\hat{q}_2$	=	$1 - \hat{p}_2$
r	=	Correlation coefficient
D	=	Difference in rankings

STEPS IN TESTS OF SIGNIFICANCE

Step 1   Formulate the null hypothesis (*Ho*), such as "there is no difference" or "no effect" or "no association/correlation".

Step 2   Formulate the alternative hypothesis (*Ha*) such as "there is difference" (or, one is greater or less than the other), "there is effect" or "there is association/correlation".

Step 3   Write down all the given data using appropriate symbols.

Step 4   Based on the given data, select the appropriate test criterion.

Step 5   Calculate the test value using the appropriate formula.

Step 6   Find out the table value of the appropriate test at the desired level of significance (1%, 5% or 10% level of significance) and for relevant degrees of freedom wherever applicable.

Step 7   *Interpretation*   Compare the calculated value with the table value. If the calculated value is less than the table value, accept the null hypothesis and reject the alternative hypothesis; if the calculated value is greater than the table value, reject the null hypothesis and accept the alternative hypothesis.

Step 8   Based on the interpretation, draw appropriate inference relevant to the problem.

Z-TEST

TO TEST THE SIGNIFICANCE OF DIFFERENCE BETWEEN POPULATION MEAN AND SAMPLE MEAN (WHEN SAMPLE SIZE IS LARGE AND POPULATION VARIANCE IS KNOWN)

Example 1

A particular variety of wheat plants has shown a mean height of 82.63 cm and standard deviation of 3.89 cm. From this population of plants, 50 plants are selected at random and each plant is inoculated with a chemical which claims to increase the height of plants. After inoculation the mean of the height of 50 plants is found to be 83.66 cm. On the basis of this evidence can it now be concluded that the chemical has a beneficial effect on the growth of plants at 5% level of significance?

There is a numerical difference of 1.03 cm (83.66 − 82.63 cm) in the means. Now the question is, "Is the difference significant?" ($\mu = \bar{x}$).

Solution

Null hypothesis (Ho)   The chemical has no effect on the growth of wheat plants. That is, the mean height of the sample 83.66 cm does not differ significantly from the population mean of 82.63 cm.

The increase in height of 1.03 cm is only due to chance factor and not due to the chemical.

Alternative hypothesis (Ha)   The chemical has a positive effect on the growth of wheat plants and the mean height of the sample 83.66 cm significantly differs from the population mean of 82.63 cm. The increase in height of 1.03 cm is due to the effect of chemical and not due to chance factor.

Given data m = 82.63 cm, $\bar{x}$ = 83.66 cm, n = 50, S.D. = 3.89

Test criterion   Here, the sample mean is to be compared with population mean. As S.D. of population is known and the sample size is large (>30), Z-test is used.

Calculated Z-value

$$Z = \frac{\bar{x} - \mu}{\sigma/\sqrt{n}} = \frac{83.66 - 82.63}{3.89/\sqrt{50}} = 1.87$$

Table Z-value   Table Z-value at 5% level of significance is 1.96 (As finding the table Z-value at different levels of significance is a little difficult it is better to remember the table Z-values for the commonly used levels of significance. Table Z-value at 10% level is 1.65; at 5% level, 1.96 and at 1% level, 2.58.)

Interpretation   As the calculated Z-value (1.87) is less than the table Z-value of 1.96, the null hypothesis is accepted.

Inference   Though there is an increase in the height of wheat plants consequent to the application of the chemical, the increase is not statistically significant. That is, the observed increase of 1.03 cm is mostly due to chance factor and not entirely due to the chemical. Therefore, it is inferred that the chemical has no effect in increasing the height of wheat plants.

Example 2

Overweight women taking brisk walks in the Race Course in Coimbatore, had a mean weight of 87 kg two years ago. Now, a sample of 40 women is taken at random and the mean weight is found to be 72 kg. Variance is found to be 25 kg. Test at 1% level of significance whether brisk walk is effective in reducing weight.

Solution

Null hypothesis (Ho)   Brisk walk has no effect in reducing weight ($\mu = \bar{x}$) where μ is the mean weight of women two years ago and $\bar{x}$ is the mean weight of 40 ladies after two years of walking.

Alternative hypothesis (Ha)   Brisk walk reduces body weight.

Given data $\mu = 87$ kg, $\bar{x} = 72$kg, $\sigma^2 = 25$kg, S.D $= \sqrt{\sigma^2} = \sqrt{25} = 5$; $n = 40$

Test criterion   Here, the sample mean is to be compared with the population mean. As S.D. of population is known and the sample size is large (>30), Z-test is used.

Calculated Z-value

$$Z = \frac{\bar{X} - \mu}{\sigma/\sqrt{n}} = \frac{72 - 87}{5/\sqrt{40}} = \frac{-15}{0.79} = -18.97 = -19$$

[In test values the sign is ignored.]

Table Z-value   The table Z-value at 1% level of significance is 2.58.

Interpretation   As the calculated Z-value of 19 is greater than the table value of 2.58, the null hypothesis is rejected.

Inference   The mean reduction in weight of 15 kg consequent to brisk walk is not a chance factor. It is inferred that continuous brisk walk helps in reducing body weight.

To Test the Significance of Difference between Means of Two Large Samples

Example 1

A social worker desires to find out whether there is any significant difference in daily wages between the plantation workers in Valparai (plantation zone in Coimbatore district of Tamil Nadu) and Idukki in Kerala. The data collected are given below:

Plantation zone	Sample size	Sample mean (₹)	Population variance
Valparai	80	82	125
Idukki	70	85	136

Test the difference at 5% level of significance.

Solution

Null hypothesis (Ho)   There is no significant difference in daily wages of the workers in Valparai and in Idukki, i.e., the wages are equal $\mu_1 = \mu_2$. As the samples are large (>30), it is assumed $\mu_1 = \bar{X}_1$ and $\mu_2 = \bar{X}_2$.

Alternative hypothesis (Ha)   There is difference in daily wages, i.e., they are not equal $(\mu_1 \neq \mu_2)$.

Given data $\bar{x}_1 = 82,\ \bar{x}_2 = 85,\ n_1 = 80,\ n_2 = 70,\ \sigma_1^2 = 125,\ \sigma_2^2 = 136$

Test criterion   Here two sample means are compared for significance of difference. As the standard deviations of the populations are known and the samples are large, Z-test is used.

$$Z = \frac{\bar{x}_1 - \bar{x}_2}{\sqrt{\dfrac{\sigma x_1^2}{n_1} + \dfrac{\sigma x_2^2}{n_2}}} = \frac{82 - 85}{\sqrt{\dfrac{125}{80} + \dfrac{136}{70}}} = \frac{-3}{\sqrt{1.56 + 1.94}} = \frac{-3}{1.87} = -1.60 = 1.60 \text{ (sign is ignored)}$$

Table Z-value   The table Z-value at 5% level of significance is 1.96.

Interpretation   As the calculated Z-value of 1.60 is less than the table value of 1.96, the N.H. is accepted.

Inference   Though the average daily wage of Idukki workers is ₹85 and that of Valparai workers is ₹82, statistically there is no significant difference. The numerical difference is only a chance factor.

Example 2

Intelligence test given to one group of girls and another group of boys showed the following results:

Gender	Number of students tested	Standard deviation	Mean intelligence score
Girls	50	10	75
Boys	100	12	70

Is the difference in the mean scores statistically different at 1% level of significance?

Solution

Null hypothesis (Ho)   There is no difference in the intelligence test scores of girls and boys, i.e., they are equal $(\mu_1 = \mu_2)$.

Alternative hypothesis (Ha)   There is difference, i.e., they are not equal $(\mu_1 \neq \mu_2)$.

Given data $\bar{x}_1 = 75, \bar{x}_2 = 70; n_1 = 50, n_2 = 100; \sigma_1 = 10, \sigma_2 = 12.$

Test criterion   Here, two sample means are compared for significance of difference. As the S.D.s of the population are known and the samples are large in size (>30), Z-test is used.

$$Z = \frac{\bar{x}_1 - \bar{x}_2}{\sqrt{\dfrac{\sigma x_1^2}{n_1} + \dfrac{\sigma x_2^2}{n_2}}} = \frac{75 - 70}{\sqrt{\dfrac{(10)^2}{50} + \dfrac{(12)^2}{100}}} = \frac{5}{\sqrt{3.44}} = \frac{5}{1.855} = 2.695$$

Table Z-value   The table Z-value at 1% level of significance is 2.58.

Interpretation   As the calculated Z-value (2.695) is greater than the table Z-value of 2.58, the N.H. is rejected and alternative hypothesis is accepted.

Inference   There is significant difference between the intelligence scores of girls and boys. The girls, in the particular test, appear to be more intelligent than boys.

TO TEST THE SIGNIFICANCE OF DIFFERENCE BETWEEN POPULATION PROPORTION AND SAMPLE PROPORTION

Example 1

The public complained that the VIP free passes at Palani temple rope-way is 20%, but the officials contested that this figure was high and conducted a survey to verify the generalization. In the survey, they found that out of 500 persons checked, 85 were holding VIP passes. Test at 5% level of significance, whether the officials are right in claiming that the percentage of travellers with VIP passes is less than 20.

Solution

Null hypothesis (Ho)   There is no difference in the population proportion (VIP pass travelling)

i.e., *Ho*: p = 20% or 0.2

Alternative hypothesis (Ha)   There is difference in the population proportion (*Ha*: $p \neq 0.20$).

Given data $p = 0.20$, [therefore $q = (1 - p) = 0.8$], $n = 500$

$\hat{p}$ (sample proportion) is $\dfrac{85}{500} = 0.17$

Test criterion   Here, as the population proportion is to be compared with the sample proportion, Z-test is used.

Calculated Z-value

$$Z = \frac{\hat{p} - p}{\sqrt{\dfrac{p \cdot q}{n}}} = \frac{0.17 - 0.20}{\sqrt{\dfrac{0.2 \times 0.8}{500}}} = \frac{-0.03}{0.0179} = 1.68$$

Table Z-value   The table Z-value at 5% level of significance is 1.96.

Interpretation   As the calculated Z-value of 1.68 is less than the table Z-value of 1.96 at 5% level of significance, the N.H. is accepted.

Inference   Though the officials reported a proportion of 0.17 (85/500) of travellers with VIP passes, it is not significantly different from the generalized proportion of 0.20. The difference observed was due to chance factor.

Example 2

A coin is tossed 100 times under identical conditions independently yielding 30 heads and 70 tails. Test at 1% level of significance whether or not the coin is unbiased.

Solution

Null hypothesis (Ho)   The coin is unbiased (i.e., proportions of heads and tails while tossing will be equal, i.e.,

$$p = q = \frac{50}{100} = 0.5$$

Alternative hypothesis (Ha)   The coin is biased, i.e., $p \neq 0.5$

Given data $p = 0.5;\ \hat{p} = \dfrac{30}{100} = 0.3;\ n = 100$

Test criterion   Here, as the population proportion is to be compared with sample proportion, Z-test is used.

Calculated Z-value

$$Z = \frac{\hat{p} - p}{\sqrt{\dfrac{p \cdot q}{n}}} = \frac{0.3 - 0.5}{\sqrt{\dfrac{0.5 \times 0.5}{100}}} = -\frac{0.2}{0.05} = -4 = 4$$

Interpretation   As the calculated Z-value of 4 is greater than the table Z-value of 2.58 at 1% level, the N.H. is rejected and A.H. is accepted.

Inference   If the coin is not biased, head should turn up about 50% of times tossed (a proportion of 0.5). In the trial head turned only 30 times out of 100 times tossed (i.e., a proportion of 0.3). The difference in proportions (0.5 and 0.3) is significantly different. That is, the coin is biased against the head.

To Test the Significance of
Difference between Two Sample Proportions

Example 1

In a study it is found out that 252 among 450 girl students go in for latest dress other than churidhars and 242 among 620 boys go after ultra-modern dress. Find out at 1% level, who is more inclined towards modern dress, the boys or the girls?

Solution

Null hypothesis (Ho)   There is no difference between girls and boys in going in for modern dress, i.e., the groups are equally inclined towards modern dress $p_1 = p_2 (\hat{p}_1 = \hat{p}_2)$

Alternative hypothesis (Ha)   There is difference, i.e., $p_1 \neq p_2 (\hat{p}_1 \neq \hat{p}_2)$

Given data

$$\hat{p}_1 = \frac{252}{450} = 0.56 \qquad \hat{p}_2 = \frac{242}{620} = 0.39$$

n_1 (sample size of girls) = 450; n_2 (sample size of boys) = 620

$\hat{p}_1$ = Proportion of girls in the sample going in for latest dress

$\hat{p}_2$ = Proportion of boys in the sample going in for ultra-modern dress

Test criterion   As the proportions of two samples are to be compared, Z-test is used

Calculated Z-value

$$Z = \frac{\hat{p}_1 - \hat{p}_2}{\sqrt{\dfrac{\hat{p}_1 \cdot \hat{q}_1}{n_1} + \dfrac{\hat{p}_2 \cdot \hat{q}_2}{n_2}}} = \frac{0.56 - 0.39}{\sqrt{\dfrac{(0.56)(0.44)}{450} + \dfrac{(0.39)(0.61)}{620}}} = \frac{0.17}{\sqrt{0.00055 + 0.00038}} = \frac{0.17}{0.03} = 5.67$$

Interpretation   As the calculated Z-value of 5.67 is greater than the table value of 2.58 at 1% level, the N.H. is rejected and A.H. is accepted.

Inference   There is significant difference between girls and boys in going in for modern dress. Girls appear to be more inclined towards modern dress than boys.

Example 2

500 units from a factory are inspected and 12 are found to be defective and out of 800 units in another factory the same number (12) of units is found to be defective. Can it be concluded at 5% level of significance that production at the second factory is better than the first?

Solution

Null hypothesis (Ho)   There is no difference in the proportion of defective units between the first and second factory, i.e., $p_1 = p_2 = 0.5$.

Alternative hypothesis (Ha)   There is difference $(p_1 \neq p_2)$.

Given data

$\hat{p}_1$ = (Proportion of defects in the sample in the 1st factory) = 12 /500 = 0.024

$\hat{p}_2$ = (Proportion of defects in the sample in the 2nd factory) = 12/800 = 0.015

n_1 (sample size of the 1st factory) = 500 and n_2 (sample size of the 2nd factory) = 800

Test criterion   As two sample proportions are to be compared here Z-test is used.

Calculated Z-value

$$Z = \frac{\hat{p}_1 - \hat{p}_2}{\sqrt{\dfrac{\hat{p}_1 \cdot \hat{q}_1}{n_1} + \dfrac{\hat{p}_2 \cdot \hat{q}_2}{n_2}}} = \frac{0.024 - 0.015}{\sqrt{\dfrac{(0.024)(0.976)}{500} + \dfrac{(0.015)(0.985)}{800}}}$$

$$= \frac{0.009}{\sqrt{0.0000468 + 0.0000184}} = \frac{0.009}{0.0080746} = 1.12$$

Interpretation   As the calculated Z-value of 1.12 is less than the table Z-value of 1.96 at 5% level, the N.H. is accepted.

Inference   There is no significant difference in the proportions of defective items between the two factories, though it appears that proportion of defects is less in second factory.

t-TEST

TO TEST THE SIGNIFICANCE OF DIFFERENCE BETWEEN POPULATION MEAN AND SAMPLE MEAN WHEN SAMPLE SIZE IS SMALL AND POPULATION VARIANCE IS NOT KNOWN

Example 1

Prices of shares (in ₹) of a company on different days in a month were found to be 66, 65, 69, 70, 69, 71, 70, 63, 64 and 68. Test whether the actual mean differs from the assumed mean of 65.

Solution

Null hypothesis (Ho)   The monthly mean price of the shares (₹65) does not differ from the 10 day average, i.e., $\mu = \bar{x}$

Alternative hypothesis (Ha)   There is difference $\mu \neq \bar{x}$

Given data $\mu =$ ₹65; $\bar{x} = \dfrac{66+65+69+70+69+71+70+63+64+68}{10} = 67.5$

$$n = 10$$

Test criterion   As population mean is to be compared with sample mean and the sample happens to be small (<30), t-test is used.

Calculated t-value $t = \dfrac{\bar{x} - \mu}{s/\sqrt{n}} = \dfrac{67.5 - 65}{2.8/\sqrt{10}} = 2.81$

$$s = \sqrt{\dfrac{\sum(x - \bar{x})^2}{n-1}}$$

$$= \sqrt{\dfrac{\begin{matrix}(66-67.5)^2 + (65-67.5)^2 + (69-67.5)^2 + (70-67.5)^2 + (69-67.5)^2 \\ +(71-67.5)^2 + (70-67.5)^2 + (63-67.5)^2 + (64-67.5)^2 + (68-67.5)^2\end{matrix}}{10-1}}$$

$$= 2.8$$

Table t-value   To find out table t-values, two aspects are to be confirmed.

  i. *Degrees of freedom (df)*   In the case of single sample, the $df = (n-1)$ and in the case of two samples, $df = (n_1 + n_2) - 2$

ii. *One-tailed or two-tailed* Whether one has to look for the *t*-value under one-tailed or two-tailed depends on the alternative hypothesis.

If the A.H. is $\mu_1 \neq \mu_2$ (there is difference), values under two-tailed are seen.

If the A.H. is $\mu_1 < \mu_2$ or $\mu_1 > \mu_2$ (greater than or less than), values under one-tailed are seen.

In the present case *df* $(n - 1) = 9$. Table *t*-value for 9 *df* at 5% level of significance is 2.262 [Two-tailed test as the A.H. is "not equal to"]

Interpretation As the calculated value is less than the table value N.H. is accepted.

Inference Though there is numerical difference, the difference is not significant. That is, the mean price of shares is ₹ 65 only.

Example 2

The cool drinks stall at Singanallur in Coimbatore had a mean sale of 510 bottles of cool drinks per day. After the inauguration of the new bus stand the sale per day for the first seven days were 501, 519, 512, 513, 505, 526 and 508. Test at 10% level of significance whether there was any increase in the sale of cool drinks in the stall after inauguration of the bus stand.

Solution

Null hypothesis (Ho) There is no difference in the mean sale of cool drinks before or after opening up of the bus stand, i.e., $\mu_1 = \mu_2 (\mu = \bar{x})$

Alternative hypothesis (Ha) There is an increase in sales after opening up of the bus stand. $(\bar{x} > \mu)$

Given data $\mu = 510, n = 7$

$$\bar{x} = \frac{501 + 519 + 512 + 513 + 505 + 526 + 508}{7} = 512$$

Test criteria As population mean is to be compared with a sample mean (where the sample is small (i.e., < 30) *t*-test is used.

Calculated t-value $\quad t = \dfrac{\bar{x} - \mu}{s / \sqrt{n}}$

$$s = \sqrt{\frac{\sum(x-\bar{x})^2}{n-1}}$$

$$= \sqrt{\frac{\begin{array}{l}(501-512)^2 + (519-512)^2 + (512-512)^2 + (513-512)^2 + \\ (505-512)^2 + (526-512)^2 + (508-512)^2\end{array}}{7-1}}$$

$$= 8.49$$

$$t = \frac{512-510}{8.49/\sqrt{7}} = \frac{2}{8.49/2.65} = \frac{2}{3.2} = 0.625$$

Table t-value   Table t-value for 6 df ($n-1$) at 10% level of significance is 1.44 (value under one-tailed is noted, as the A.H. is $\bar{x} > \mu$, i.e., greater than context).

Interpretation   As the calculated t-value (0.625) is less than the table t-value (1.44), the N.H. is accepted.

Inference   There is no significant increase in the average sale of cool drinks after opening up of the bus stand. Though there is an increase of sales for one week, the difference is not significant.

TO TEST THE SIGNIFICANCE OF DIFFERENCE BETWEEN TWO SMALL SAMPLES

Example 1

An agricultural scientist tested the effect of two fertilizers, A and B, on the yield of tomato. He applied fertilizer A in 5 plots and B in another 5 plots. The following were the yields from the 10 plots.

Fertilizer	Yield in kg / plot					
	1st plot	2nd plot	3rd plot	4th plot	5th plot	Mean
Fertilizer A	9	10	13	11	7	10
Fertilizer B	15	10	14	15	11	13

Test at 5% level of significance whether there is any difference in the effects of the two fertilizers.

Solution

Null hypothesis (Ho)   There is no difference in the effects of the fertilizers A and B on the yield of tomato

i.e., $\mu_1 = \mu_2 (\bar{x}_1 = \bar{x}_2)$

Alternative hypothesis (Ha)   There is difference.

Given data $n_1 = 5$; $n_2 = 5$ and yield in all the 10 plots.

Test criterion   As the means of two small samples are to be compared t-test is used.

Calculated t-value

$$t = \frac{\bar{x} - \bar{y}}{S\sqrt{\dfrac{1}{n_1} + \dfrac{1}{n_2}}}$$

where

$$S = \sqrt{\frac{(n_1 - 1)s_1^2 + (n_2 - 1)s_2^2}{n_1 + n_2 - 2}}$$

$$s_1^2 = \frac{\sum(x - \bar{x}_1)^2}{n - 1} = \frac{(9-10)^2 + (10-10)^2 + (13-10)^2 + (11-10)^2 + (7-10)^2}{5 - 1} = 5$$

$$s_2^2 = \frac{\sum(x - \bar{x}_2)^2}{n - 1} = \frac{(15-13)^2 + (10-13)^2 + (14-13)^2 + (15-13)^2 + (11-13)^2}{5 - 1} = 5.5$$

$$S = \sqrt{\frac{(4 \times 5) + (4 \times 5.5)}{(5 + 5) - 2}} = 2.29; \quad t = \frac{10 - 13}{2.29\sqrt{\dfrac{1}{5} + \dfrac{1}{5}}} = \frac{3}{1.45} = 2.07$$

Table value   Table t-value for 8 df $(n_1 + n_2 - 2)$ at 5% level of significance is 2.306 (value under two-tailed test as A.H. is $\mu_1 \neq \mu_2$).

Interpretation   As the calculated value is less than table t-value (2.306), the N.H. is accepted.

Inference   There is no significant difference in the effects of the two fertilizers. The difference observed is due to extraneous factors.

Example 2

Two salesmen A and B were working in a district. From a sample survey conducted by the Head Office, the following results were obtained.

Salesmen	A	B
No. of sales made	20	18
Average sales (in thousand ₹)	170	205
Standard deviation (in thousand ₹)	20	25

Test at 1% level of significance whether the sales closed by salesman B is higher than that of salesman A.

Solution

Null hypothesis (Ho)   There is no difference in the sales closed by both the salesmen, i.e., $\mu_1 = \mu_2 (\bar{x}_1 = \bar{x}_2)$

Alternative hypothesis (Ha)   Sales made by salesman B is higher than that of salesman A, i.e., $\mu_2 > \mu_1 (\bar{x}_2 > \bar{x}_1)$

Given data $n_1 = 20; n_2 = 18$ $\bar{x}_1 = 170$ $\bar{x}_2 = 205$ $s_1 = 20$ and $s_2 = 25$.

Test criterion   As the means of two small samples are to be compared t-test is used.

Calculated t-value $$t = \frac{\bar{x}_1 - \bar{x}_2}{s\sqrt{\dfrac{1}{n_1} + \dfrac{1}{n_2}}}$$

$$s = \sqrt{\frac{(n_1 - 1)s_1^2 + (n_2 - 1)s_2^2}{n_1 + n_2 - 2}} = \sqrt{\frac{19(20)^2 + 17(25)^2}{(20 + 18) - 2}} = 22.5$$

$$t = \frac{170 - 205}{22.5\sqrt{\dfrac{1}{20} + \dfrac{1}{18}}} = -\frac{35}{7.31} = -4.79 = 4.79 \text{ (sign is ignored)}$$

Table t-value   Table t-value for 36 df $(n_1 + n_2 - 2)$ at 1% level of significance lies between 2.423 and 2.457 (values under one-tailed probability level as the A.H. is $\bar{x}_1 < \bar{x}_2$).

Interpretation   As the calculated value (4.79) is higher than the table value (2.423 – 2.457) the N.H. is rejected and A.H. is accepted.

Inference   The sales made by salesman B is significantly higher than the sales made by salesman A.

PAIRED *t*-TEST

To test the significance of difference of the means with dependent samples (To test the significance of difference of means in the same sample before and after the treatment)

Paired *t*-test is a way for comparing two related samples of small size. The assumption that the two populations are normal holds good here also. For a paired *t*-test, observations are collected in matched pairs, i.e., observations from the same sample unit before and after treatment.

Example 1

A particular food drink manufacturer claims that the drink improves the memory power of children. A nutritionist desires to test the claim. He finds out the memory power of 10 children before they take the drink. Then he checks the memory of the same 10 children after making them drink the food drink continuously for one month. The data are given in the following table.

	Student No.									
	1	2	3	4	5	6	7	8	9	10
Memory power score before the intake of the drink	15	18	20	17	16	14	21	19	13	22
Memory power score after the intake of the drink	14	16	21	10	15	18	19	16	14	20

Find out at 5% level of significance whether the drink improves the memory power or not.

Solution

Null hypothesis (Ho)   The health drink has no effect on memory power.

Alternative hypothesis (Ha)   There is difference in memory power caused by the health drink.

Given data $n = 10$ and memory power scores before and after in the same sample

Test criterion   As the effect is to be compared on the same sample paired *t*-test is used.

Pairing of memory scores of children

Student No.	Memory score before taking the health drink	Memory score after taking the health drink	Difference (d)	d^2
1	15	14	−1	1
2	18	16	−2	4
3	20	21	+1	1
4	17	10	−7	49
5	16	15	−1	1
6	14	18	+4	16
7	21	19	−2	4
8	19	16	−3	9
9	13	14	+1	1
10	22	20	−2	4
			$\Sigma d = -12$	$\Sigma d^2 = 90$

$$t = \frac{\bar{d}\sqrt{n}}{s}$$

$$\bar{d} = \frac{\sum d}{n} = \frac{-12}{10} = -1.2$$

$$s = \sqrt{\frac{\sum d^2 - n(\bar{d})^2}{n-1}} = \sqrt{\frac{90 - (10 \times 1.44)}{9}} = \sqrt{\frac{90 - 14.4}{9}} = 2.898$$

$$t = \frac{(-1.2)(\sqrt{10})}{2.898} = \frac{-3.795}{2.898} = -1.309 = 1.309$$

Table t-value   Table t-value for 9 df ($n - 1$) at 5% level of significance is 2.262 (value under two-tailed probability as the A.H. is $\mu_1 \neq \mu_2$).

Interpretation   As the calculated t-value of 1.309 is less than the table t-value of 2.262 the N.H. is accepted.

Inference   The health drink does not bring in any change in the memory power.

Example 2

A new training programme was introduced in an organization and ten workers were selected to test the efficacy of the training programme. The productivity of individual workers was measured before and after the training and the results are given in the following table. Test at 5% level of significance whether the training has helped in improving the productivity?

	Worker No.									
	1	2	3	4	5	6	7	8	9	10
Productivity score before training	80	76	92	60	70	56	74	56	70	56
Productivity score after training	84	70	96	80	80	52	84	72	80	50

Solution

Null hypothesis (Ho)   The training programme has no influence on the productivity of the workers, i.e., $\mu_1 = \mu_2 (\overline{X}_1 = \overline{X}_2)$.

Alternative hypothesis (Ha)   The training programme improves the productivity, i.e., $\mu_2 > \mu_1 (\overline{X}_2 > \overline{X}_1)$.

Given data $n = 10$; Productivity scores before and after the training programme.

Test criterion   As the effect is to be compared on the same sample, paired t-test is employed.

Pairing of productivity scores of workers

Worker	Productivity before training	Productivity after training	Difference (d)	d^2
1	80	84	4	16
2	76	70	−6	36
3	92	96	4	16
4	60	80	20	400
5	70	80	10	100
6	56	52	−4	16
7	74	84	10	100
8	56	72	16	256
9	70	80	10	100
10	56	50	−6	36
			$\Sigma d = 58$	$\Sigma d^2 = 1076$

$$\overline{d} = \frac{58}{10} = 5.8$$

$$s = \sqrt{\frac{\sum d^2 - n(\overline{d})^2}{n-1}} = \sqrt{\frac{1076 - 10(5.8)^2}{10-1}} = \sqrt{\frac{739.6}{9}} = 9.07$$

Calculated t-value

$$t = \frac{\overline{d}\sqrt{n}}{s} = \frac{5.8\sqrt{10}}{9.07} = \frac{5.8 \times 3.162}{9.07} = 2.02$$

Table t-value   Table t-value for 9 df ($n - 1$) at 5% level of significance is 1.833 (value under one-tailed as A.H. is "greater than" context).

Interpretation   As the calculated t-value (2.02) is greater than the table t-value (1.833), the N.H. is rejected and A.H. is accepted.

Inference   The training programme has improved the productivity of the workers significantly.

CHI-SQUARE AS A PARAMETRIC TEST

To find out the significance of difference between population variance and sample variance:

Example 1

The purchase manager in a star hotel, while placing order for apples for a party, stipulates that the size of the apples must be uniform and the standard deviation should not vary more than 15 g. The supplier delivers 1000 apples. To verify whether the apples are uniform in weight, he takes a sample of 10 apples and finds that the S.D. is 18 g. Test at 10% level of significance whether the apples are delivered as per the stipulation.

Solution

Null hypothesis (Ho)   There is no difference in population variance and sample variance, i.e., variance of population is equal to sample variance [$\sigma^2 = s^2$]

Alternative hypothesis (Ha)   There is difference.

Given data   Population S.D. (σ) = 15 g, S.D. (s) of sample = 18 g [Therefore $\sigma^2 = 225$ and $s^2 = 324$] $n = 10$, $df = (n - 1) = 9$

Test criterion   As population variance is to be compared with sample variance, χ^2-test as a parametric test is used.

Calculated χ^2 *-value* $\quad \chi^2 = \dfrac{s^2(n-1)}{\sigma^2} = \dfrac{324(10-1)}{225} = 12.96$

Table χ^2*-value* Table χ^2 for 9 *df* at 10% level of significance is 14.68.

Interpretation As the calculated χ^2-value (12.96) is less than the table χ^2-value (14.68), the N.H. is accepted.

Inference There is no significant difference in the variances between the population and sample. The manager can accept the lot as difference in variances between his expectation and the sample is only due to chance factor.

Example 2

For the Republic Day Parade, NCC cadets of almost uniform heights are required. The authorities stipulate that the S.D. should not be more than 3.0 cm. They took a sample of 10 cadets from a college and their heights are shown below:

Cadet No.	1	2	3	4	5	6	7	8	9	10
Height(cm)	173	165	169	173	166	164	176	172	168	174

Will the authorities accept the cadets from the college? Test at 5% level of significance.

Solution

Null hypothesis (Ho) There is no difference in the desired variance of population and sample variance.

Alternative hypothesis (Ha) There is difference.

Given data $\sigma = 3$ cm, i.e., $\sigma^2 = 9$; $n = 10$; heights of 10 units in the sample.

Test criterion As population variance is to be compared with sample variance, χ^2 as a parametric test is used.

Calculated χ^2*-value*

$$\chi^2 = \frac{s^2(n-1)}{\sigma^2}$$

$$\bar{x} = \frac{173+165+169+173+166+164+176+172+168+174}{10} = 170$$

$$s^2 = \frac{\sum(x - \bar{x})^2}{n-1}$$

$$= \frac{\begin{matrix}(173-170)^2 + (165-170)^2 + (169-170)^2 + (173-170)^2 + (166-170)^2 + \\ (164-170)^2 + (176-170)^2 + (172-170)^2 + (168-170)^2 + (174-170)^2\end{matrix}}{9}$$

$$= \frac{156}{9} = 17.33$$

Calculated χ^2-value $\chi^2 = \frac{17.33(10-1)}{9} = 17.33$

Table χ^2-value   The table χ^2-value for 9 *df* at 5% is 16.919.

Interpretation   As the calculated value (17.33) is greater than the table value (16.919), the N.H. is rejected and A.H. is accepted.

Inference   The variance of the sample is greater than the desired population variance. Hence, the authorities will not accept the cadets from the particular college.

F-TEST

To test the significance of difference between variances of two samples.

Example 1

The production of dolls by 2 units of self-help groups per day are given below.

Self-help Group 1	20	16	26	27	23	22	18	24	25	19	
Self-help Group 2	27	33	42	35	32	34	38	28	41	43	30	37

Find out at 5% level of significance whether the variances in production between the two groups are same.

Solution

Null hypothesis (Ho)   The variances in production of dolls between the two self-help groups are same.

Alternative hypothesis (Ha)   There is difference.

Given data   Production per day for the Group 1 for 10 days

Production per day for the Group 2 for 12 days

Test criterion   As variances of two samples are to be compared, *F*-test is used.

$$F = \frac{\text{Larger mean square}}{\text{Smaller mean square}}$$

Differences in production of dolls of self-help group

Self-help group 1			Self-help group 2		
Production per day	Difference from mean	Mean square	Production per day	Difference from mean	Mean square
x	$(x - \bar{x})$	$(x - \bar{x})^2$	y	$(y - \bar{y})$	$(y - \bar{y})^2$
20	−2	4	27	−8	64
16	−6	36	33	−2	4
26	4	16	42	7	49
27	5	25	35	0	0
23	1	1	32	−3	9
22	0	0	34	−1	1
18	−4	16	38	3	9
24	2	4	28	−7	49
25	3	9	41	6	36
19	−3	9	43	8	64
			30	−5	25
			37	2	4
$\sum x = 220$		$\sum(x - \bar{x})^2 = 120$	$\sum y = 420$		$\sum(y - \bar{y})^2 = 314$
$\bar{x} = 22$			$(\bar{y} = 35)$		

$$s_1^2 = \frac{120}{10-1} = 13.33 \qquad s_2^2 = \frac{314}{12-1} = 28.55$$

$$F = \frac{28.55}{13.33} = 2.14$$

Table F-value

In *F*-tables, column *df* is denoted as v_1 and row *df* as v_2.

v_1 refers to the *df* in respect of larger variance

v_2 refers to the *df* in respect of smaller variance

In the present case the *df* of sample with larger variance is 11 and the *df* of the sample with smaller variance is 9.

Table *F*-value for *df* 11 and 9 at 5% level of significance lies between 3.07 and 3.14.

Interpretation   As the calculated value (2.14) is less than the table value, the N.H. is accepted and A.H. is rejected.

Inference   There is no significant difference in the variances of production between the two self-help groups. The difference seen is only due to chance factor.

Example 2

Fertilizers A and B resulted in the yields of tomato listed in the following table. Find out whether the variances are different at 5% level of significance.

	Yield in kg/plot					
	Plot 1	Plot 2	Plot 3	Plot 4	Plot 5	Mean
Fertilizer A	9	10	13	11	7	10
Fertilizer B	15	10	14	15	11	13

Null hypothesis (Ho)   The variances between the effects of two fertilizers are same, i.e., $\sigma s_1^2 = \sigma s_2^2$

Alternative hypothesis (Ha)   There is difference in the variances $\sigma s_1^2 \neq \sigma s_2^2$

Test criterion   As two sample variances are to be compared *F*-test is used.

$$F = \frac{\text{Larger mean square}}{\text{Smaller mean square}}$$

$$\sigma s_1^2 = \frac{(9-10)^2 + (10-10)^2 + (13-10)^2 + (11-10)^2 + (7-10)^2}{(5-1)} = 5.00$$

$$\sigma s_2^2 = \frac{(15-13)^2 + (10-13)^2 + (14-13)^2 + (15-13)^2 + (11-13)^2}{5-1} = 5.5$$

$$F = \frac{5.5}{5} = 1.1 \; n_1 = 5; \; n_2 = 5 \; df = 4 \text{ (for both)}$$

Table F-value　　Table *F*-value for *df* 4 and 4 at 5% level of significance is 6.39.

Interpretation　　As the calculated value is less than the table value, the N.H. is accepted.

Inference　　The variances in yields of tomato due to the fertilizers do not differ significantly.

ANOVA

Analysis of variance, popularly known as ANOVA is a technique of "partitioning" the total variability observed into different sources, "known" and "unknown".

An agricultural scientist, who got a yield increase of 1.2 t/ha for chemical A, 1.9 t/ha for chemical B and 1.5 t/ha for chemical C cannot claim that chemical B is superior to A and C because the yield obtained cannot be solely due to the chemical alone. There are other factors such as soil fertility of the plots, soil, water, ambient temperature, humidity, etc., which influence the yield. Before coming to any valid conclusion about the superiority of the particular chemical, scientist must partition the factors which influence the yield into "Known" and "Unknown". In this case the chemicals are the known factors and the soil fertility, temperature, humidity, etc. are the unknown factors. The highest increase in the yield of the plot which received chemical B need not be only due to the chemical. The other factors would have also influenced the yield. ANOVA helps to find out whether the increase is due to the "known" factor, chemical or other unknown factors.

Similarly, an MBA professor, who introduced a novel method of teaching, cannot claim that the higher scores obtained by the students taught through the novel method compared to those taught by lecture method, seminars or case studies are due to the novel method, since the higher marks obtained by the students who experienced the novel method need not solely be due to the novel method alone. "Unknown" or "extraneous" factors such as the inherent intelligence of the students of the particular group, their hard work, their memory power or their access to internet or a combination of these factors would have helped the students taught through the novel method score higher marks. ANOVA will help whether the difference in scores obtained by the various methods of teaching is significant or not.

In ANOVA, *F*-ratio is used to test the significance of differences between two or more than two sample means. As the analysis of variance was originated in agricultural research, the language is replete with such agricultural terms such as plots (referring to pieces of land) and treatments (varieties, fertilizers, chemicals, cultivation methods, irrigation, etc.). Nowadays, ANOVA is employed in every type of experimental/descriptive designs. ANOVA has become a fundamental part of planned research in judging the effects of new technology, variety, medicine, procedures and policies.

One-Way ANOVA and Two-Way ANOVA

In one-way ANOVA the data are classified according to only one criterion, i.e., only one hypothesis can be tested. In the first example given above, effect of the chemical is the criterion to be tested and the hypothesis could be whether there is any significant difference in yield increases due to the three chemicals. In the second example, method of teaching is the criterion and the hypothesis could be whether the novel method of teaching is superior to other methods or not. In two-way ANOVA, two criteria are considered simultaneously, that is, two sets of hypotheses could be tested.

One-Way ANOVA

Example 1

A nutritionist has been assigned by a health food company to find out which food is superior, A, B or C for growing children in the age group of 15 years. Fifteen boys are selected to test each of the health food (5 each). The increase in weights of the boys after five years are given in the following table. Test at 1% level of significance which is the superior drink.

	Increase in weight (kg) due to consumption of health food		
	A	B	C
Boy No 1	7	10	14
Boy No 2	5	12	16
Boy No 3	6	9	13
Boy No 4	3	8	12
Boy No 5	4	6	10
Total increase in weight	25	45	65
Mean increase	5	9	13
Mean effect (Individual mean – Group mean)	−4	0	+4

Grand total = 135

$$\text{Grand mean} = \frac{135}{15} = 9$$

Solution

Null hypothesis (Ho)   There is no significant difference in weight increase due to the food drinks, i.e., $\mu_1 = \mu_2 = \mu_3, (\overline{X}_1 = \overline{X}_2 = \overline{X}_3)$

Alternative hypothesis (Ha)   There is significant difference in weight increase.

Test criterion   As more than two means are to be compared, ANOVA is employed.

In ANOVA, the total variability is partitioned into "known factor" variability and "unknown factor" variability (extraneous factor or error).

In the instant case, health food is the "known" variable. Physical exercise, hours of sleep, main food, etc. are the "Unknown" variables.

Variability due to "unknown factors"   The variability (sum of deviations), due to extraneous factors in increasing weights in the boys who took health drink A is

$$(7-5)^2 + (5-5)^2 + (6-5)^2 + (3-5)^2 + (4-5)^2 = 10$$

Variability in the case of health drink B is $(10-9)^2 + (12-9)^2 + (9-9)^2 + (8-9)^2 + (6-9)^2 = 20$

Variability in the case of health drink C is $(14-13)^2 + (16-13)^2 + (13-13)^2 + (12-13)^2 + (10-13)^2 = 20$

Total variability observed due to extraneous factor is $10 + 20 + 20 = 50$.

Variability due to "Known factor" (health drink):

Variability due to health drink A is $= (-4)^2 \times 5 = 80$

Variability due to health drink B is $= (0)^2 \times 5 = 0$

Variability due to health drink C is $= (4)^2 \times 5 = 80$

Therefore, total variability due to known factor $= 80 + 0 + 80 = 160$

Total variability due to "Known factor" and "Unknown factor" $= 50 + 160 = 210$

This can be verified by adding the squared deviations of grand mean and individual value: $(7-9)^2 + (5-9)^2 + \ldots (12-9)^2 + (10-9)^2 = 210$.

Total variability = Variability among the health drinks + Error variability (variability due to unknown factors is called "error").

To calculate the total variability and its break-up into different components using the method of deviations is cumbersome. To overcome the said problem, computational procedure is available. The steps are:

Step 1   Compute the total for each health drink and the grand total. Thus, if T_1, T_2 and T_3 are the totals for the three drinks and T, the grand total, then $T_1 = 25; T_2 = 45, T_3 = 65$ and $T = 25 + 45 + 65 = 135$.

Step 2 Compute a Correction Factor (*CF*).

$$CF = \frac{T^2}{N} = \frac{(135)^2}{15} = 1215 \text{ where } N \text{ is the total no. of observations}$$

Step 3 Find the Total Sum of Square (SSQ_T)

It is the sum of squares of all the observations less the correction factor.

$$SSQ_T = (7)^2 + (5)^2 + \ldots (12)^2 + (10)^2 - CF = 1425 - 1215 = 210$$

Step 4 Compute the sum of squares due to differences in the health drinks (treatments). It is popularly known as "Between Group" variability.

$$SSQ_t = \frac{T_1^2}{n} + \frac{T_2^2}{n} + \frac{T_3^2}{n} - CF \text{ , where } n \text{ is the no. of observations in each drink.}$$

$$= \frac{(25)^2}{5} + \frac{(45)^2}{5} + \frac{(65)^2}{5} - CF = 1375 - 1215 = 160$$

Step 5 Error sum of squares known as "within the group variability" (SSQ_E) is found out by subtracting SSQ_t from SSQ_T as the total variability is composed of "between the group" variability and "within the group" variability.

$$SSQ_E = SSQ_T - SSQ_t = 210 - 160 = 50$$

After calculating all the sums of squares either through deviation method or the "computational steps", ANOVA table is constructed as follows:

Source of variation	df	SS (Sum of squares)	MSS (mean sum of squares)	*F*-ratio
Between groups (i.e., between the drinks)	2	160	80	19.184
Error (within the group variability)	12	50	4.17	
Total	14			

Note Degrees of freedom ($n - 1$) for "between the groups" is 2 [where "n" is the no. of groups (no. of health drinks)]. Total df ($N - 1$) is 15 where N is the total no. of observations; df for "within the group" is the difference in df between "total df" and the "df due to between the groups".

MSS Mean sum of squares is obtained by dividing the SS by the respective df.

F-ratio is obtained by dividing the MSS due to "between the group" by that of error $(80/4.17 = 19.184)$

Table F-value   Table *F*-value for *df* 2 and 12 at 1% level of significance is 6.93.

Interpretation   As the calculated *F*-ratio is greater than the table *F*, the N.H. is rejected.

Inference   There is significant difference among the three health drinks A, B and C in improving the weight of growing children. As the mean of health drink C is greater than that of A and B, it is inferred that health drink C is superior to health drink A and B.

Example 2

It is desired to find out whether there is any significant difference in the performance of three models of car A, B and C. Frequency of repairs is taken as the parameter to consider the performance. Five cars from each of the brand are chosen for the test. The frequency of repairs is given below:

	Number of repairs per year		
	Model A	Model B	Model C
Car No 1	4	7	4
Car No 2	6	4	6
Car No 3	7	3	6
Car No 4	5	6	3
Car No 5	8	5	1
Total repairs	30	25	20
Mean	6	5	4

Which car is superior? Test at 5% level of significance.

Solution

Null hypothesis (Ho)   There is no significant difference in the performance of the three models of car as measured by the no. of repairs, i.e., $\mu_1 = \mu_2 = \mu_3$ $(\bar{X}_1 = \bar{X}_2 = \bar{X}_3)$.

Alternative hypothesis (Ha)   There is difference, i.e., they are not equal $\bar{X}_1 \neq \bar{X}_2 \neq \bar{X}_3$.

Test criterion   As the no. of means is >2 ANOVA is used.

Grand total $= 30+25+20 = 75$

Grand mean = 75/15 = 5

$$CF = \frac{T^2}{N} = \frac{75^2}{15} = 375$$

Total sum of squares (SSQ_T)

$$(4^2 + 7^2 + \dots 5^2 + 1^2) - CF = 48$$

Sum of squares due to groups (SSQ_t)

$$= \frac{(30)^2}{5} + \frac{(25)^2}{5} + \frac{(20)^2}{5} - CF = 180 + 125 + 80 - 375 = 10$$

Sum of squares due to error (SSQ_E)

$$SSQ_E = SSQ_T - SSQ_t = 48 - 10 = 38$$

ANOVA for models of car

Source of variation	df	SS	MSS	F-ratio
Between groups (i.e., between the cars)	2	10	5.00	1.58
Error (within the group variability)	12	38	3.17	
Total	14	48		

Table value   Table F-ratio for df 2 and 12 at 5% level of significance is 3.88.

Interpretation   As the calculated F-ratio is less than the table F-ratio, the N.H. is accepted.

Inference   There is no significant difference in the performance of the three models of car. The insignificant difference in the number of repairs could be due to other extraneous factors such as style of driving, type of roads, mileage covered, etc.

Two-way ANOVA

In the situations considered earlier under one-way ANOVA, every observation made was subjected to only one known source, viz., health drink in the first example and type of car model in the second example. It is a one-way classification thereby meaning that there is only one experimental condition (health drink or car model). But in certain other cases the observations made would be subjected to more than one condition. For example, an agricultural scientist may want to know the varietal differences in different seasons. In this situation each plot yield is influenced by two experimental conditions, viz., varietal difference and seasonal difference. Since there are two factors, viz., variety and season, each observation (i.e., the yield per plot) is now subjected to the influence of three sources, viz., varietal effect, seasonal effect and effect due to unknown factors. Two-way ANOVA helps in partitioning the total variability into each one of these components. For a two-way data [variety and season] one-way ANOVA is applied twice, once for varieties and again for reasons.

Example 1

In a field experiment, the following data are obtained (yield in kg per plot). Test at 5% level of significance whether there is significant difference among the four varieties as well as influence due to three seasons.

Differences in yield (kg/plot) due to varieties and seasons

	Varieties				For seasons	
	V_1	V_2	V_3	V_4	Total	Mean
Season S_1	8	4	11	5	28	7
Season S_2	10	11	13	14	48	12
Season S_3	6	6	12	8	32	8
Variety total	24	21	36	27	108	
Variety mean	8	7	12	9		

Grand total : 108   Grand total : 9

Solution

Null hypothesis (Ho)   There is no significant difference among the varieties as well as the seasons.

$$V_1 = V_2 = V_3 = V_4 \text{ and } S_1 = S_2 = S_3$$

Alternative hypothesis (Ha)   There are significant differences, i.e., they are not equal $(V_1 \neq V_2 \neq V_3 \neq V_4 \text{ and } S_1 \neq S_2 \neq S_3)$

Step 1   Compute column totals (variety totals)

$$C_1 = 24; C_2 = 21; C_3 = 36; C_4 = 27$$

Compute row totals (season totals)

$$R_1 = 28; R_2 = 48; R_3 = 32$$

Grand total $= C_1 + C_2 + C_3 + C_4 = 108$ or $R_1 + R_2 + R_3 = 108$

Step 2 Compute Correction Factor (CF).

$$CF = \frac{T^2}{N} = \frac{(108)^2}{12} = 972$$

Step 3 Total sum of squares

$$SSQ_T = (8)^2 + (10)^2 + (6)^2 + \ldots (5)^2 + (14)^2 + (8)^2 - CF = 120$$

Step 4 Sum of squares between rows (seasons)

$$SSQ_R = \frac{R_1^2}{c} + \frac{R_2^2}{c} + \frac{R_3^3}{c} - CF \text{ , where } c = \text{No. of columns}$$

$$= \frac{(28)^2}{4} + \frac{(48)^2}{4} + \frac{(32)^2}{4} - 972 = 56$$

Step 5 Sum of squares between columns (varieties)

$$SSQ_c = \frac{C_1^2}{r} + \frac{C_2^2}{r} + \frac{C_3^2}{r} + \frac{C_4^2}{r} - CF \text{ Where } r \text{ is the no. of rows}$$

$$= \frac{(24)^2}{3} + \frac{(21)^2}{3} + \frac{(36)^2}{3} + \frac{(27)^2}{3} - 972 = 42$$

Step 6 Error sum of squares

$$SSQ_E = SSQ_T - SSQ_R - SSQ_c$$
$$= 120 - 56 - 42$$
$$= 22$$

ANOVA for varieties and seasons

Source of variability	df	SS	MSS	*F*-ratio
Columns (varieties)	3	42	14	3.82
Rows (seasons)	2	56	28	7.63
Error	6	22	3.67	
Total	11	120		

Table value

> *For varieties*   Table *F*-value for 3 *df* and 6 df at 5% level of significance is 4.76.

> *For seasons*   Table *F*-value for 2 *df* and 6 *df* at 5% level of significance is 5.14.

Interpretation   As the calculated *F*-value (3.82) in respect of varieties is less than the table *F*-value (4.76), the N.H. is accepted. In the case of seasons, since the calculated *F*-value (7.63) is more than the table *F*-value of 5.14, the N.H. of no difference is rejected.

Inference   From the experiment, it is inferred that there is no significant difference among the four varieties tested. But there is significant difference among the seasons. Considering the means of 3 seasons, it is concluded that season S_2 is most favourable followed by S_3 and S_1.

Example 2

The marketing department of a cell phone company appointed four sales executives A, B, C, and D and permitted them to do marketing in three territories X, Y and Z in a city. The sales of cell phones in a month are shown in the following table.

Territory	Sales by salesmen				For territories	
	A	B	C	D	Total	Mean
X	36	36	21	35	128	32
Y	28	29	31	32	120	30
Z	26	28	29	29	112	28
Total for salesmen	90	93	81	96	360	
Mean	30	31	27	32		

Grand total : 360

Grand mean : 30

Test at 5% level of significance the differences among the salesmen and territories.

Solution

Null hypothesis (Ho)   There is no significant difference among the sales of salesmen and that of territories.

Alternative hypothesis (Ha)   There are significant differences among the salesman as well as the territories.

Step 1   Compute column totals (Salesmen totals)

$$C_1 = 90;\ C_2 = 93;\ C_3 = 81;\ C_4 = 96$$

Compute row totals (Territory totals)

$$R_1 = 128;\ R_2 = 120;\ R_3 = 112$$

Grand total $= C_1 + C_2 + C_3 + C_4 = 360$

Check $= R_1 + R_2 + R_3 = 360$

Step 2   Compute the correction factor (CF).

$$CF = \frac{T^2}{N} = \frac{(360)^2}{12} = 10800$$

Step 3   Total sum of squares

$$SSQ_T = 36^2 + 36^2 + \ldots 29^2 + 29^2 - CF$$

$$= 11010 - 10800 = 210$$

Step 4   Sum of squares between rows (territories)

$$SSQ_R = \frac{R_1^2}{c} + \frac{R_2^2}{c} + \frac{R_3^2}{c} - CF = \frac{(128)^2}{4} + \frac{(120)^2}{4} + \frac{(112)^2}{4} - 10800$$

$$= 10832 - 10800 = 32$$

Step 5   Sum of squares between columns (salesmen)

$$SSQ_C = \frac{C_1^2}{r} + \frac{C_2^2}{r} + \frac{C_3^2}{r} + \frac{C_4^2}{r} - CF$$

$$= \frac{(90)^2}{3} + \frac{(93)^2}{3} + \frac{(81)^2}{3} + \frac{(96)^2}{3} - CF = 10842 - 10800 = 42$$

Step 6   Error sum of squares

$$SSQ_E = SSQ_T - SSQ_R - SSQ_C = 210 - 32 - 42 = 136$$

ANOVA for salesmen and territories

Source of variation	df	Sum of squares	MSS	F-ratio
Between columns (salesmen)	3	42	14	0.62
Between rows (territories)	2	32	16	0.71
Error	6	136	22.67	
Total	11	210		

Table value   For salesmen, Table F-value for df 3 and 6 at 5% level of significance is 4.76. For Territories, Table F-value for df 2 and 6 at 5% level of significance is 5.14.

Interpretation   As the calculated F-values in respect of both salesmen and territories are less than the respective table values, the null hypotheses of "no difference" are accepted.

Inference   There is no significant difference in the sales of mobile phone among the four salesmen. Similarly, the sales made in the 3 territories are also not significantly different. The numerical differences observed are only due to chance factors.

CORRELATION [PEARSON (PRODUCT MOMENT) CORRELATION COEFFICIENT]

✧ Correlation coefficient is a statistical measure to show the "nature" and "degree" of relationship between two measurable characteristics, viz., X and Y. "Nature" indicates whether the relationship is positive or negative. "Degree" tells about the strength of relationship.

✧ Correlation is generally denoted by the symbol r.

✧ The r may take any value from -1 to $+1$, depending upon the extent of relationship and nature of relationship between the two characteristics, X and Y.

✧ When perfect relationship exists between the two variables the correlation (r) will be unity (i.e., $+1$).

✧ When there is no correlation, r will be zero.

✧ The value will be positive when the two variables vary together in the same direction; it will be negative when they vary in the opposite direction.

When pairs of measurements (X, Y) are available for each individual,

$$r = \frac{N\Sigma XY - (\Sigma X)(\Sigma Y)}{\sqrt{\{N\Sigma X^2 - (\Sigma X)^2\}\{N\Sigma Y^2 - (\Sigma Y)^2\}}}$$

Example 1

An MBA student, specializing in marketing, desired to know the relationship, if any, between the amounts spent on advertisement and the profits of various firms in the garment industry. He collected data from 59 firms. Amounts spent on advertisements are shown as X values and the profits as Y values. Find at 5% level the significance of relationship.

Solution

Null hypothesis (Ho)   There is no relationship between the amount spent on advertisement and profit.

Alternative hypothesis (Ha)   There is relationship.

Test criterion   As relationship, if any, is to be found out between X and Y, taking into consideration the actual values of X and Y, Pearson's product moment correlation is used.

To find the nature and degree of relationship between the variables, the following steps are involved:

Step 1   Arrange the pairs of values as given in the table under column 1 and 2.

   i. Compute the sum of X values, $\sum X = 2881$.

   ii. Compute the sum of Y values, $\sum X = 1050$.

Step 2

   i. Square each X value and find their total.

$$\Sigma X^2 = 47^2 + 42^2 + \ldots + 57^2 + 52^2 = 144681$$

   ii. Square each Y value and find their total.

$$\Sigma Y^2 = 18^2 + 21^2 + \ldots + 25^2 + 9^2 = 22626$$

   iii. Find the product XY for each pair and compute their total

$$\Sigma XY = (47 \times 18) + (42 \times 21) + \ldots + (57 \times 25) + (52 \times 9) = 53751$$

Step 3   Find out the r value using the formula

$$r = \frac{N\Sigma XY - (\Sigma X)(\Sigma Y)}{\sqrt{\{N\Sigma X^2 - (\Sigma X)^2\}\{N\Sigma Y^2 \Sigma Y^2 - (\Sigma Y)^2\}}}$$

$$= \frac{(59 \times 53751) - (2881)(1050)}{\sqrt{\{(59 \times 14481) - (2881)^2\}\{(59 \times 22626) - (1050)^2\}}} = 0.63$$

Amount spent on advertisement (in thousand rupees) vs profit obtained (in lakh rupees) in garment industry

Pair No.	Amount spent on advertisement (X)	Net profit (Y)	X^2	Y^2	XY
	1	2	3	4	5
1	47	18	2209	324	846
2	42	21	1764	441	882
3	56	31	3136	961	1736
4	52	24	2704	576	1248
5	51	29	2601	841	1479
6	62	25	3844	625	1550
7	61	28	3721	748	1708
8	59	48	3481	2304	2832
9	55	25	3025	625	1375
10	57	18	3249	324	1026
11	58	22	3364	484	1276
12	44	9	1936	81	396
13	57	18	3249	324	1026
14	57	25	3249	625	1425
15	44	21	1936	441	924
16	43	4	1849	16	172
17	33	7	1089	49	231
18	29	9	841	81	261
19	37	19	1369	361	703
20	43	8	1849	64	344
21	42	7	1764	49	294
22	54	18	2916	324	972
23	45	18	2025	324	810
24	43	6	1849	36	258
25	43	12	1849	144	516
26	31	6	961	36	186
27	32	8	1024	64	256
28	33	9	1089	81	297
29	33	9	1089	81	297
30	47	8	2209	64	376
31	48	12	2304	144	576

(Contd.)

Table (Continued)

Pair No.	Amount spent on advertisement (X)	Net profit (Y)	X^2	Y^2	XY
	1	2	3	4	5
32	57	12	3249	144	684
33	51	19	2601	361	969
34	51	18	2601	324	918
35	53	20	2809	400	1060
36	51	28	2601	784	1428
37	51	22	2601	484	1122
38	54	27	2916	729	1458
39	45	17	2025	289	765
40	51	20	2601	400	1020
41	56	12	3136	144	672
42	57	25	3249	625	1425
43	36	14	1296	196	504
44	53	22	2809	484	1166
45	55	31	3025	961	1705
46	47	27	2209	729	1269
47	42	11	1764	121	462
48	60	28	3600	784	1680
49	42	18	1764	324	756
50	54	14	2916	196	756
51	55	18	3025	324	990
52	52	17	2704	289	884
53	52	9	2704	81	468
54	55	16	3025	256	880
55	48	14	2304	196	672
56	49	16	2401	256	784
57	57	19	3249	361	1083
58	57	25	3249	625	1425
59	52	9	2704	81	468
	$\Sigma X = 2881$	$\Sigma Y = 1050$	$\Sigma X^2 = 144681$	$\Sigma Y^2 = 22626$	$\Sigma XY = 53751$

Based on the *r* value itself, it cannot be concluded whether the relationship is significant or not.

t-test using the given formula is employed to find out the significance of *r* value.

$$t = \frac{r}{\sqrt{\dfrac{1-r^2}{n-2}}}$$

In the present case the calculated $t = \dfrac{0.63}{\sqrt{\dfrac{1-(0.63)^2}{59-2}}} = \dfrac{0.63}{\sqrt{\dfrac{1-0.3969}{57}}} = \dfrac{0.63}{0.10} = 6.3$

Table *t*-value for *df* 57 at 5% level of significance lies between 2.000 and 2.021.

Interpretation   As the calculated *t* (6.3) is greater than the table *t* (2.000 – 2.021) at 5%, the N.H. is rejected.

Inference   There is significant positive correlation between amounts spent on advertisement and profits. That is, higher expenditure on advertisement results in higher profits.

[Before the observed correlation is interpreted, it is necessary to make sure that it has risen due to genuine relationship between the two variables and not due to chance (extraneous) variables].

Example 2

A student-researcher specializing in finance wants to know whether there is any relationship between expenditure on employees and net profits in airline industry. He collected data from 12 airlines. The data are presented in the following table (Expenditure as *X* values and Net profits as *Y* values). Find out at 10% level of significance the relationship between expenditure on employees and net profit.

Pair No.	Expenditure on employees (in lakh rupees) (X)	Net profits (in lakh rupees) (Y)	X^2	Y^2	XY
1	57	10	3249	100	570
2	42	60	1764	3600	2520
3	40	30	1600	900	1200
4	33	41	1089	1681	1353
5	42	29	1764	841	1218
6	45	27	2025	729	1215
7	42	27	1764	729	1134
8	44	19	1936	361	836
9	40	18	1600	324	720
10	56	19	3136	361	1064
11	44	31	1936	961	1364
12	43	29	1849	841	1247
Total	$\Sigma X = 528$	$\Sigma Y = 340$	$\Sigma X^2 = 23712$	$\Sigma Y^2 = 11428$	$\Sigma XY = 14441$

$$r = \frac{N\Sigma XY - (\Sigma X)(\Sigma Y)}{\sqrt{\{N\Sigma X^2 - (\Sigma X)^2\}\{N\Sigma Y^2 - (\Sigma Y)^2\}}}$$

$$= \frac{(12 \times 14441) - (528)(340)}{\sqrt{\{(12 \times 23712) - (528)^2\}\{(12 \times 11428) - (340)^2\}}} = -0.56$$

Solution

Null hypothesis (Ho)   There is no relationship between expenditure on employees and net profits in airline industry.

Alternative hypothesis (Ha)   There is relationship.

Test criterion $t = \dfrac{r}{\sqrt{\dfrac{1-r^2}{n-2}}} = \dfrac{0.56}{\sqrt{\dfrac{1-(0.56)^2}{12-2}}} = \dfrac{0.56}{\sqrt{\dfrac{1-0.3136}{10}}} = \dfrac{0.56}{\sqrt{0.06864}} = \dfrac{0.56}{0.262} = 2.1$

Table t-value for df 10 $(n-2)$ at 10% level is 1.812.

Interpretation   N.H. is rejected as calculated value is more than the table value at 10% level.

Inference   It is inferred that higher expenditure on employees resulted in lower net profits in airlines.

NON-PARAMETRIC TESTS

CHI-SQUARE AS GOODNESS OF FIT

As a non-parametric test, Chi-square test is one of the simplest and most widely used tests.

No assumptions are made about the population being sampled. Chi-square (pronounced as Kighsquare) values (χ^2) describe the magnitude of difference between theory and observation (i.e., difference between observed values and expected values). Using χ^2-test as "test of goodness of fit" one can know whether a given difference between theory (expected values) and observation (observed values) can be attributed to chance factor or whether there is a real difference between expected and observed values. If χ^2-value is zero, it means that observed and expected values completely coincide (i.e., the theory or expectation holds good). Higher the χ^2-value, greater is the discrepancy between observed and expected values. The formula for χ^2 is $\chi^2 = \sum \dfrac{(O-E)^2}{E}$ where O = Observed value and E = Expected or theoretical value.

For interpreting the discrepancy, the calculated χ^2-value is compared with the table value of χ^2 for a given *df* at specified level of significance; *df* is $n - 1$, where n is the number of observations.

Example 1

An agricultural scientist desired to find out whether Mendelian "law of inheritance" for shape (round and wrinkle) for peas is in accordance with the ratio of 3 : 1. To verify the theory, he randomly selected a sample of 960 peas. Of these 960 peas, 704 were round and 256 were wrinkled. Do these observations conform to the expected ratio of 3 : 1 at 5% level of significance?

Solution

Based on the law, it is expected that the round peas should be 720 (3/4 × 960) and the wrinkled peas 240(1/4 × 960). But the observed values are 704 round peas and 256 wrinkled peas.

Null hypothesis (Ho)   There is no significant difference between the expected values (theoretical values) and the observed values. That is, the law of inheritance holds good.

Alternative hypothesis (Ha)   There is significant difference, that is, the law is incorrect.

Observed and expected values for peas

	Round	Wrinkled	Total
Expected	720	240	960
Observed	704	256	960

Test criterion As the observed values are to be compared with the expected values, Chi-square as a test of "goodness of fit" is used.

Calculated χ^2-value

$$\chi^2 = \sum \frac{(O-E)^2}{E} = \frac{(704-720)^2}{720} + \frac{(256-240)^2}{240} = 1.42$$

Table value Table χ^2-value for 1 df (df = no. of observations $-1 = 2 - 1$) at 5% level of significance is 3.84.

Interpretation As the calculated χ^2-value (1.43) is less than the table value (3.84), the N.H. is accepted.

Inference It is inferred that the observation of 704 round peas and 256 wrinkled peas is as per the expected values of the Mendelian law (3 : 1 ratio of round peas and wrinkled peas). The difference seen is due to chance factor. Thus observations conform to the law.

Example 2

The number of parts manufactured for a particular spare part in a factory was found to vary daily. In a sample study the following information was obtained.

Day	Mon	Tue	Wed	Thurs	Fri	Sat	Total
No. of parts manufactured	1124	1125	1110	1120	1126	1115	6720

Test at 5% level of significance whether the production depends on the day of the week.

Solution

Null hypothesis (Ho) The production does not vary with the day of the week, it is same on all days.

Alternative hypothesis (Ha)   Production varies from day to day.

Given data   Production in a day

Observed vs expected values for production (daywise)

Day	Mon	Tue	Wed	Thurs	Fri	Sat	Total
Observed	1124	1125	1110	1120	1126	1115	6720
Expected	1120	1120	1120	1120	1120	1120	6720

As per the N.H. production does not depend on the day, i.e., production is expected to be uniform on all days, i.e., 1120 per day. (Total production in a week (6720) divided by the no. of working days (6)).

Test criterion   As the observed values are to be compared with the expected values χ^2-test is used.

Calculated χ^2-value

$$\chi^2 = \sum \frac{(O-E)^2}{E} = \frac{(1124-1120)^2}{1120} + \frac{(1125-1120)^2}{1120} + \frac{(1110-1120)^2}{1120} + \frac{(1120-1120)^2}{1120}$$

$$+ \frac{(1126-1120)^2}{1120} + \frac{(1115-1120)^2}{1120} = 0.179$$

Table χ^2-value   Table value at 5 *df* (6 observations – 1) at 5% level of significance is 11.07.

Interpretation   As the calculated χ^2-value (0.179) is less than the table χ^2-value (11.07) the N.H. is accepted.

Inference   It is inferred that there is no significant difference in the day-to-day production. The difference seen is only due to chance factor.

χ^2-TEST AS A TEST OF INDEPENDENCE

Chi-square is also used to test independence of two or more variables. When individuals/items are classified simultaneously on two or more variables, the resulting table of cell frequencies is called a contingency table. χ^2-test is applied to contingency table to find out if the two or more variables are independent or associated.

Example 1

In a survey of fertilizer practices in India, each of the 323 cotton-growing fields selected for the survey was classified on the twin criteria of irrigation practice (irrigated and not irrigated) and the practice of manuring (manured and not manured) resulting in the following contingency table.

	Irrigated	Not irrigated	Total
Manured	75	35	110
Not manured	115	98	213
Total	190	133	323

Test at 5% level of significance whether irrigation and manuring are independent of each other or depend on each other.

Solution

Null hypothesis (Ho)   Irrigation and manuring are independent.

Alternative hypothesis (Ha)   Irrigation and manuring depend on each other.

Test criterion   As independence of two variables is to be tested, χ^2 as a test of independence is used.

Test values   The expected values are calculated and presented in brackets along with the observed values.

Irrigation and manuring (Observed and expected values)

	Irrigated	Not irrigated	Total
Manured	75 (64.7)	35 (45.3)	110
Not manured	115 (125.3)	98 (87.7)	213
Total	190	133	323

In a contingency table expected value in each cell is obtained by multiplying the column total with the row total and dividing the product by the grand total. For the observed value of 75 the expected value is

$$\frac{(190 \times 110)}{323} = 64.7$$

Calculated χ^2-value

$$\chi^2 = \sum \frac{(O-E)^2}{E} = \frac{(75-64.7)^2}{64.7} + \frac{(35-45.3)^2}{45.3} + \frac{(115-125.3)^2}{125.3} + \frac{(98-87.7)^2}{87.7} = 6.04$$

Table value   (In a contingency table $df = (c-1)(r-1)$ where c is the no. of columns and r is the no. of rows). Table χ^2-value for 1 $df\,[(2-1)(2-1)$ at 5% level of significance is 3.84.

Interpretation   As the calculated value (6.04) is greater than the table value (3.84), the N.H is rejected.

Inference   Irrigation and manuring are mutually related, i.e., generally irrigated fields are manured or manured fields are irrigated.

Example 2

A sample of 400 regular TV viewers was drawn from a city through convenience sampling and their preference of TV programme was enquired. The data are given below:

Category of TV viewers	Movies	News	Serials	Total
Teenagers	120	30	50	200
Adults	10	75	15	100
Old people	10	30	60	100
Total	140	135	125	400

Test at 1% level of significance whether there is any association between the different categories of people and types of TV programmes preferred.

Solution

Null hypothesis (Ho)   The different groups of people and the TV programmes viewed are independent.

Alternative hypothesis (Ha)   There is association.

Test criterion   As independence of variables is to be tested, χ^2-test is used.

Expected values are calculated and presented (in brackets) along with the observed values.

TV viewers and programs (Observed and expected values)

Categories of TV viewers	Types of TV programs			Total
	Movies	News	Serials	
Teenagers	120(70)	30(67.50)	50(62.50)	200
Adults	10(35)	75(33.75)	15(31.25)	100
Old People	10(35)	30(33.75)	60(31.25)	100
Total	140	135	125	400

Calculated χ^2-value

$$\chi^2 = \sum \frac{(O-E)^2}{E}$$

$$= \frac{(120-70)^2}{70} + \frac{(10-35)^2}{35} + \frac{(10-35)^2}{35} + \frac{(30-67.5)^2}{67.5} + \frac{(75-33.75)^2}{33.75}$$

$$+ \frac{(30-33.75)^2}{33.75} + \frac{(50-62.50)^2}{62.50} + \frac{(15-31.25)^2}{31.25} + \frac{(60-31.25)^2}{31.25}$$

$$= 180.45$$

$$df = (c-1)(r-1) = (3-1)(3-1) = 4$$

Table χ^2-value   Table χ^2-value for 4 df at 1% level of significance is 13.28.

Interpretation   As the calculated χ^2-value (180.45) is greater than the table χ^2-value (13.28), the N.H. is rejected.

Inference   There is significant association between the different categories of TV viewers and the type of TV programme. That is, teenagers prefer movies, adults news and old people serials.

PRECAUTIONS IN USING χ^2-TEST

i. The experimental data (sample observation) must be independent of each other.

ii. Sample must be drawn at random from the target population.

iii. The data must be expressed in original units for convenience of comparison, and not in percentage or ratio form.

iv. There should be not less than 5 observations (units) in any one cell (each data entry is known as a cell). For less than 5 observations in a cell, the value of χ^2 would be larger resulting in rejection of N.H. In such cases it is possible to overcome the difficulty by grouping two or more classes together to get more than 5 units in a cell.

RANK CORRELATIONS

Rank correlation is used when quantitative measure of certain factors such as leadership ability or communication skills cannot be fixed. In these cases the individuals in the group can be arranged in order, i.e., ranking is given. Spearman's rank correlation coefficient (R) is used to compare the ranks.

Example 1

In a placement interview, MBA students participated in group discussion and were ranked according to their performance. The same group of students appeared for the personal interview and were ranked. The ranks assigned are given as R_1 and R_2. Find out if there is any relationship in the ranking of students in group discussion and personal interview.

Solution

As rankings are to be compared, Spearman's rank correlation is used.

Ranking comparison—2 rankings

Student No.	Rank in group discussion (R_1)	Rank in personal interview (R_2)	$(R_1 - R_2)^2$
1	4	4	0
2	2	1	1
3	1	2	1
4	3	3	0
5	7	8	1
6	8	7	1
7	6	5	1
8	5	6	1
9	9	9	0
10	10	10	0
$N = 10$			$\Sigma D^2 = 6$

$$R = 1 - \frac{6 \sum D^2}{N^3 - N} = 1 - \frac{6 \times 6}{990} = 0.964$$

The high R value shows that there is close relationship between the performance in group discussion and that of personal interview.

Example 2

Ten MBA students appeared for personal interview in a company. The interview panel consisting of HR Manager, Marketing Manager and Finance Manager ranked the students individually and the ranks are shown below as R_1, R_2 and R_3 for the 10 students. Compare the rankings of the three managers.

Solution

As rankings are to be compared, Spearman's rank correlation is used.

Comparison of Rankings—3 Rankings

Student No.	Rank by HR Manager (R_1)	Rank by Marketing Manager (R_2)	Rank by Finance Manager (R_3)	$(R_1-R_2)^2$	$(R_2-R_3)^2$	$(R_1-R_3)^2$
1	1	3	6	4	9	25
2	6	5	4	1	1	4
3	5	8	9	9	1	16
4	10	4	8	36	16	4
5	3	7	1	16	36	4
6	2	10	2	64	64	0
7	4	2	3	4	1	1
8	9	1	10	64	81	1
9	7	6	5	1	1	4
10	8	9	7	1	4	1
				$\sum D_1^2 = 200$	$\sum D_2^2 = 214$	$\sum D_3^2 = 60$

$$\text{Correlation between } R_1 \text{ and } R_2 = 1 - \frac{6\sum D_1^2}{N^3 - N} = 1 - \frac{6\times 200}{10^3 - 10} = -0.212$$

$$\text{Correlation between } R_2 \text{ and } R_3 = 1 - \frac{6\sum D_2^2}{N^3 - N} = 1 - \frac{6\times 214}{10^3 - 10} = -0.297$$

$$\text{Correlation between } R_1 \text{ and } R_3 = 1 - \frac{6\sum D_3^2}{N^3 - N} = 1 - \frac{6\times 60}{10^3 - 10} = 0.636$$

The rank correlations show that the rankings between HR Manager and Finance Manager have higher correlation than that of HR Manager and Marketing Manager and the Marketing Manager and Finance Manager.

SIGN TEST

- ✧ It is used with matched pairs when the only information is the identification of the pair member that is larger or smaller or has more or less of some characteristics.
- ✧ Its name comes from the fact that it is based on the direction of the plus or minus signs of observations in a sample and not on their numerical magnitudes.
- ✧ It may be one-sample test or two-sample test.

One-sample sign test

Example

Eleven tele-sales girls in one year made 280, 282, 310, 273, 283, 283, 275, 300, 282, 279, and 281 successful calls. Use the sign test at 5% level of significance to test the null hypothesis that tele-sales girls make an average of 300 successful calls against the *Ha* that $\mu < 300$.

Solution

Null hypothesis (Ho) $\mu = 300$

Alternative hypothesis (Ha) $\mu < 300$

- ✧ Replace each value greater than 300 with plus sign and less than 300 with minus sign and discard the one which equals 300.
- ✧ We get $-,-,+,-,-,-,-,0,-,-,-$ signs.
- ✧ Proportion of > 300 is 1/10 and that of <300 is 9/10 (one is discarded).

Calculated Z-value $Z = \dfrac{\hat{p} - p}{\sqrt{\dfrac{p \cdot q}{n}}} = \dfrac{0.1 - 0.5}{\sqrt{\dfrac{0.5 \times 0.5}{10}}} = \dfrac{-0.4}{0.158} = -2.53$ (sign is ignored)

Table Z-value   Table Z-value at 5% level of significance is 1.96.

Interpretation   As the calculated Z-value is greater than table Z-value, N.H. is rejected.

Inference   Tele-sales girls' successful average calls is less than 300 in a year.

Two-sample sign test (sign test for paired data)   In this test each pair of values is replaced with a +ve sign if the value of the 1st sample is greater than the corresponding value of the

2nd sample and –ve sign if it is less. If two values are equal, the pair is discarded. In case of unequal sample size, extra values are discarded.

Example

The following are the numbers of cars sold by agency X and Y for 30 days.

| By X | 2032 | 1032 | 3021 | 4131 | 3631 | 3251 | 3203 | 42 |
| By Y | 0010 | 3001 | 2201 | 3110 | 2260 | 2303 | 2010 | 30 |

Using sign test, test at 5% level of significance, the N.H. that the two agencies X and Y, are equally good against A.H. that X is better.

Solution

Null hypothesis (Ho) $\mu_x = \mu_y$

Alternative hypothesis (Ha) $\mu_x > \mu_y$

Convert the pairs into signs (+ or –)

$(x - y)$: +0++ –0++ +–+0 +0++ ++–+ +–+– ++–+ ++

Total no. of +ve signs : 20; –ve signs : 6; Hence sample size is 26 (4 pairs are discarded).

Proportion of observed +ve sign is 20/26 = 0.7692 (Sales proportion for agency X); Proportion of –ve sign is 6/26 =0.2308 (Sales proportion for agency Y).

Calculated Z-value

$$Z = \frac{\hat{p}_1 - \hat{p}_2}{\sqrt{\dfrac{p \cdot q}{n}}} = \frac{0.7692 - 0.2308}{\sqrt{\dfrac{0.5 \times 0.5}{26}}} = \frac{0.5384}{0.098} = 5.49$$

Table Z-value   Table Z-value at 5% level is 1.96.

Interpretation   As calculated Z-value is greater than table Z-value, N.H. is rejected.

Inference   Agency X is better than agency Y in selling cars.

Mann–Whitney U-Test

✧ It is an alternative to t-test without the latter's limiting assumptions.

✧ When the larger of the two samples is 20 or less, special tables to interpret U are used.

✧ When the larger of the two samples exceeds 20, table Z-value is used.

✧ In calculating the U value, treat all observations in a combined fashion and rank them from smallest to largest.

✧ In case of ties, assign the rank as in other tests.

✧ After the ranking, the rank values for each sample are totalled.

Compute U as follows:

$$U = n_1 n_2 + \frac{n_1(n_1+1)}{2} - R_1 \qquad \text{or} \qquad U = n_1 n_2 + \frac{n_2(n_2+1)}{2} - R_2$$

where,

$n_1 =$ No. of units in sample 1

$n_2 =$ No. of units in sample 2

$R_1 =$ Sum of ranks in sample 1

$R_2 =$ Sum of ranks in sample 2

Use the smaller U to test the hypothesis.

Example

Sales made by MBA salesmen and Non-MBA salesmen (units sold in the first 11 months) are as follows:

MBA salesmen	Units sold per week per salesmen		
	Rank	Non-MBA salesmen	Rank
1510	15	1350	10
1550	16	1300	8.5
1890	22	1600	18
1220	6	1050	3
1370	12	1200	5
1570	17	1100	4
1800	21	1780	20
1260	7	1000	1
1300	8.5	1390	13
1360	11	1450	14
1720	19	1020	2
Total rank	$R_1 = 154.5$	$R_2 = 98.5$	

Test at 5% level of significance who is more effective. Use U-test.

Solution

Null hypothesis (Ho)   There is no difference between MBA salesmen and non-MBA salesmen.

Alternative hypothesis (Ha)   MBA salesmen are superior.

$$U_1 = 11 \times 11 + \frac{11(11+1)}{2} - 154.5 = 32.5$$

$$U_2 = 11 \times 11 + \frac{11(11+1)}{2} - 98.5 = 88.5$$

Calculated U is 32.5 [lesser U-value is taken]

Table U-value   For $n_1 = 11$ and $n_2 = 11$ at 5% level of significance (one-tailed test) U is 34.

Interpretation   As the calculated U-value is less than the table U-value, the N.H. is accepted.

Inference   There is no difference between the MBA salesmen and the non-MBA salesmen.

When $n > 20$ in one of the samples,

Calculated $Z = \dfrac{U - \mu_v}{\sigma_v}$

where, $\mu_v = \dfrac{n_1 n_2}{2}$

$$\sigma_v = \sqrt{\frac{(n_1)(n_2)(n_1 + n_2 + 1)}{12}}$$

KRUSKAL–WALLIS TEST

- ✿ It is a generalized version of U-test
- ✿ All scores in the entire pool of observations are ranked, the largest as 1st rank.

The rank sum of each sample is then calculated, with ties being distributed as in other examples.

Computed value of $H = \dfrac{12}{N(N-1)} \sum \dfrac{R^2}{n} - 3(N+1)$

where, R = Sum of ranks

$\quad\quad n$ = No. of observations in each sample

$\quad\quad N$ = Total no. of observations

Example

Using Kruskal–Wallis test at 5% level of significance, test the *Ho* that a bowler bats equally well with four types of bats. The data are as follows:

Type of bat	No. of runs in 5 games	Total of ranks
Very heavy (*A*)	21(7)27(3)12(14)7(17)16(11)	52
Heavy (*B*)	9(16)23(6)30(1)19(9)24(5)	37
Medium (*C*)	15(12)10(15)2(20)5(18)17(10)	75
Light (*D*)	26(4)3(19)28(2)20(8)14(13)	46

Solution

Null hypothesis (Ho) $A = B = C = D$

Alternative hypothesis (Ha) $A \neq B \neq C \neq D$

Rank all the values from the highest to lowest (given in the parentheses). Add them

$A = 52 \ (R_1)$

$B = 37 \ (R_2)$

$C = 75 \ (R_3)$

$D = 46 \ (R_4)$

Compute *H*.

$$H = \frac{12}{20(20+1)} \left\{ \frac{52^2}{5} + \frac{37^2}{5} + \frac{75^2}{5} + \frac{46^2}{5} \right\} - 3(20+1)$$

$$= \{0.02857 \times 2362.8\} - 63 = 4.51$$

Table *H*.

As *H* values approximate χ^2-value, find χ^2-value for 3 *df* (No. of dimensions − 1) at 5% level. It is 7.815.

Interpretation   As the calculated value is less than the table value, N.H. is accepted.

Inference   The bowler bats equally bad with all the 4 types of bats.

MULTIVARIATE ANALYSIS

The tests discussed in the "tests of significance" are concerned with one or two variables such as mean, variance, S.D., etc. That is, decisions are taken based on one or two dimensions. These tests are carried without the help of computers. But, in reality decision-making is not so simple as an array of factors is to be studied and considered. Personnel managers' problems in finding a right combination of incentives to improve the morale of the employees, the marketing managers' search for suitable promotional activities in tune with the varying tastes/preferences of the customers, the production managers' investigation for improving the productivity considering the varying quality/cost of raw materials and combination of old and new machineries, the logistics managers' work pressure to move the materials at the lowest transport cost and minimum time, the government's arduous task of classifying population as "improved" and "yet to improve" based on income, education, housing, nature of job, savings, etc., and the behavioural scientists' study to group the respondents into "cultured" and "not so cultured" cannot be studied or solved based on one or two variables. In these real-life studies, multiple variables are taken into consideration to draw reasonable conclusions. Analysis of these variables are carried out using relevant software. Manual analysis of the massive data in multivariate analysis will be a Herculean task.

In view of these complexities involved, no attempt is made here to discuss the analytical part of multivariate analysis. Only the concepts/objectives are briefly explained to help the students interpret the computed analysis and draw inferences. It is beyond the scope of this book to go into the details of multivariate analyses.

- ☼ Multivariate techniques are largely empirical (based on data) and deal with real-life situations.
- ☼ The basic objective of multivariate techniques is to transform the massive data collected into a simplified form.
- ☼ The procedures involve simultaneous analyses of data obtained on two or more variables.
- ☼ The mass observation is transformed into smaller number of composite scores reflecting as much information as possible contained in the raw data.
- ☼ Multivariate analyses are those statistical techniques which focus on structure of simultaneous relationships among two or more dimensions.

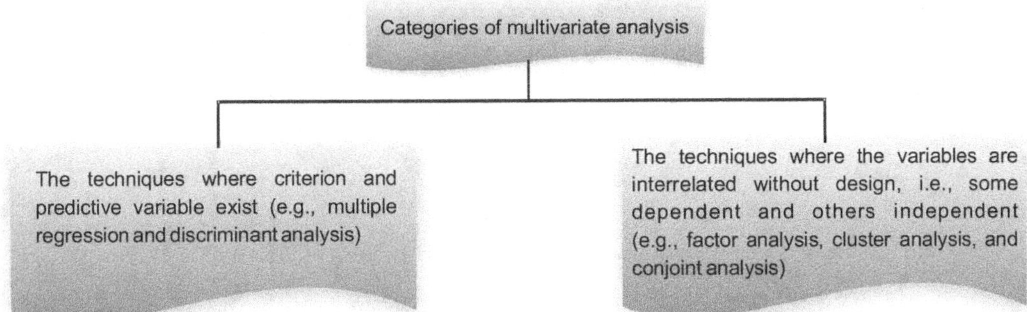

MULTIPLE REGRESSION ANALYSIS

It is a logical and mathematical extension of the bivariate regression, $y = a + bx$. In the bivariate regression (one independent variable x and another dependent variable y) a straight line is fitted through a two-dimensional phase, whereas in multiple regression a plane is filled through a multidimensional space. The output and interpretation are same as for a bivariate analysis.

$$\hat{y} = a + b_1 x_1 + b_2 x_2 + b_3 x_3 + \dots + b_i x_i \quad (\hat{y} \text{ is read as 'y hat')}$$

Where,

$\hat{y}$ = Estimated value of the criterion variable

a = Constant derived from the analysis

b_i = Coefficient associated with predictor variables such that a change of one unit in x_i, will cause a change of b_i units in $\hat{y}$ (The values for the coefficients are derived from the regression analysis)

x_i = Predictor variables that influence the criterion variable.

The primary objectives of multiple regression analysis are:

✿ To predict the level of the criterion variable (the variable in which the researcher is interested) based on certain levels of predictor variables (predictor variables are variables which influence the criterion variable)

✿ To look into the relationship between the predictor variables and criterion variables

Example

The marketing department of a company manufacturing white goods collected data on sales, promotional expenditure and no. of dealers in respect of eight zones. The data are given in the following table:

Zone	Sales (lakh ₹) (y)	Promotional expenditure (₹ in thousand) (x_1)	No. of dealers (x_2)
1	100	40	10
2	80	30	10
3	60	20	7
4	120	50	15
5	150	60	20
6	90	40	12
7	70	20	8
8	130	60	4

Based on the data the company desires to know to what extent promotional expenditure and no. of dealers influence the sale of white goods.

Solution

Here, sales is the dependant variable and promotional expenditure and no. of dealers are the independent variables.

The regression equation obtained is $y = 17.327 + 1.93\, x_1 + 2.912\, x_2$

(The calculation is not explained here)

This equation tells us to estimate the likely value of sales for a given expenditure on promotional activities and a specific number of dealers in the zone. Suppose the promotional expenditure is 80,000 and the number of dealers is 5, then it is likely to sell white goods worth of 185.617 lakhs in the particular zone as per the equation

$$\hat{y} = a + b_1 X_1 + b_2 X_2$$

$$\hat{y} = 17.327 + (1.93 \times 80) + (2.912 \times 5) = 186.287 \text{ lakhs}$$

MULTIPLE REGRESSION MEASURES OF ASSOCIATION

As in the case of bivariate regression, coefficient of determination, commonly called r^2 is calculated in multiple regression. It ranges from 0 to 1 and indicates the % of variation in the criterion variable that is explained by the entire set of predictor variables. For example, if r^2 is 28% it indicates that 28% of the variation in the criterion variable can be explained by the number of predictor variables in the equation.

Causation   The equation indicates only an association between the variables. Though it is tempting to assume that values of predictor variables cause the value of criterion variable, it must be remembered that the association is only an evidence of causation and not a proof of it. If we assume that a company bases its expenditure on advertising in electronic media on current sales, then sales is causing electronic advertising and changes in sales causes changes in advertising. A regression analysis with sales as the criterion variable and electronic advertisement as one of the predictor variables would indicate a strong association. Nevertheless, it is not justified to conclude that electronic ad causes sales.

DISCRIMINANT ANALYSIS

Quantitative relationship such as multiple regression equation is possible only when the data are measurable. If the data cannot be quantified, then techniques such as discriminant analysis are employed.

Discriminant analysis (DA) helps in classifying people or objects into two or more categories. By using DA it is possible to predict the categories or classes which are mutually exclusive. For example, it can be used to study successful salesmen and unsuccessful salesmen in order to determine the characteristics possessed by successful salesmen and not by unsuccessful salesman; or to study soft drink consumers who prefer different brands. In each of these situations, one can use DA to determine the characteristics possessed by one category of respondents and not possessed by the other category of respondents. Here, the classification will be dichotomous such as "successful" salesmen and "unsuccessful" salesmen or "synthetic drink" users and "fresh juice" users. Similarly one may wish to predict whether sales potential in a given territory will be "good" or "bad" based on certain measurements such as the personal disposable income, population density, no. of retail outlets, etc.

If only two categories are involved it is two-group discriminant analysis; if three or more categories are involved it is a multiple discriminant analysis.

Assume that a social scientist is interested in classifying the tribals in a hill station as "haves" and "have-nots" i.e., "Comfortable" living or "not-comfortable" living. The scientist may take into account the individuals' monthly earning, years of formal education, value of residence and savings. Each of these variables is given weightage, indicating its relative importance. Suppose an individual's monthly income is ₹3000, his formal education is 10 years, his residence is worth of ₹25,000 and his average saving is ₹300 per month, then it can be symbolically represented as $y = b_1(3000) + b_2(10) + b_3(25,000) + b_4(300)$ where y is a dependent variable, say, credit score or rating and b_1, b_2, b_3 and b_4 are the weights allotted to the individual independent variables. In this case, monthly income and saving may be given more weights than education and the cost of residence. A certain limit is fixed for the value of y, below which all values (individuals) will be classified as "have-nots" or "not-comfortable" and others as "haves" or "comfortable".

It may be noted that the coefficients $(b_1, b_2, b_3$ and $b_4)$ are similar to the regression coefficients. The difference is that in regression equation, the coefficient is used to predict the value of the dependent value, but in discriminant analysis the coefficients are used to classify correctly as many individuals, objects or situations as possible.

Example   A marketing agency is interested in classifying its salesmen into "successful salesmen" and "unsuccessful salesmen" based on two factors, namely, experience and education. It collects data from a number of its salesmen on their average sales, experience and education. Using procedures almost similar to those used in the regression analysis, DA performs calculations based on the available data and obtains a best linear equation for the data. The equation will be in the form $K = ax_1 + bx_2$ where x_1 and x_2 are the independent variables (in the present case x_1 is the years of selling experience and x_2 is the education; a and b are the coefficients determined in DA procedures. K, a constant (a number) is also determined in the procedure. K does not represent any of the variables. In the instant example, coefficients a and b are found to be 8 and 3 respectively (no attempt is made to describe the DA procedure as it is complex and beyond the scope of this book).

Now, the equation becomes $K = 8\,x_1 + 3\,x_2$ where x_1 is the number of years of selling experience and x_2 is the number of years of formal technical education. In the example K is found to be 22.

Using discriminating equation   The discriminating equation, generally known as "discriminator" can be used as a predictor to classify people/objects.

In the example, if a salesman has 3 years of selling experience and 5 years of formal technical education, his $K = 8(3) + 3(5) = 39$. As the calculated K-value of 39 is above the predictor K-value of 22, this salesman is placed under "successful" salesman. In the case of another salesman who has 1 year of experience and 3 years of education, his K-value will be $[8(1)+3(3)]=17$. As this value is less than the predictor value of 22 he is classified as unsuccessful salesman.

The marketing agency can use the discriminating equation in selecting prospective salesmen. By substituting the candidates' years of selling experience and years of formal technical education in the discriminating equation, the candidates' K-values are calculated and compared with the critical K-value of 22. If the candidate's K is more than the critical value, he is likely to be successful and gets selected.

In marketing management, DA can be used

- to determine early adapters of fashion
- to identify new product buyers
- to decide brand loyalty among consumers
- to differentiate between successful salesmen and unsuccessful salesmen.

Factor Analysis

Initially factor analysis was used by psychologists as a technique of indirect measurement. When human personality and intelligence are tested, a set of questions/tests is developed. It is believed that a person exposed to these questions/tests would respond on the basis of some *structure* that exists in his mind and the responses would form a certain pattern. The approach is based on the assumption that the underlying *structure* in answering the questions would be the same in the case of different respondents. The underlying *structure*, is later known as "Factor". Though factor analysis has its beginning in the field of psychology, it has since been applied to problems in different areas.

In multiple regression analysis the objective is to predict the value of a dependent variable on the basis of several independent variables. But in factor analysis there is no usual distinction between dependent and independent variables; on the other hand, it considers all the variables simultaneously.

Factor analysis aims to identify a set of dimensions that is not easily observed in a large set of variables. The analysis condenses a majority of the information in terms of relatively few new categories known as factors. The two basic objectives of using factor analysis are (i) to simplify the data by reducing the large number of variables to a set of small number of variables. (ii) to analyse the interdependence or interrelationships among a total set of variables.

It is a technique applicable when there is a systematic interdependence among a set of observed variables and the researcher is interested in finding out something more fundamental which creates a commonality.

For example, a car manufacturing company wants to come out with a new model of car with features desired by majority of the prospective buyers. It prepares a questionnaire and collects data on various features on a 5-point Likert-type questionnaire. The features included are the following.

- The car should have collapsible steering wheel.
- The colour must be flashy and gleaming.
- Cost must be reasonable.
- Seats must be fully cushioned.
- There must be power-steering.
- It should have broad wheel base.
- Spare parts must be cheap.
- There must be large leg space.

✿ Must be fitted with latest stereo sets.

✿ Must have automatic transmission system.

✿ Must give good mileage.

✿ Headlights must be powerful.

✿ Airbags must be available.

Factor analysis will be able to reduce the above attributes into four factors:

Factor 1: Economic   Price of the car, cheap spare parts and good mileage.

Factor 2: Comfort   Fully cushioned seats, power steering, large leg space and automatic transmission.

Factor 3: Safety   Collapsible steering rod, broad wheel base and safety airbags.

Factor 4: Flashy   Flashy and gleaming colours, latest stereo sets and powerful headlights.

Factor analysis will indicate high correlations among certain attributes. The different groups of attributes are identified and given appropriate names as factors. In real-life situations, there will be umpteen number of attributes making decision-making difficult. Factor analysis helps in reducing the attributes into a few manageable "factors".

Analytical procedure for factor analysis

Step 1   Generation of a correlation matrix from the original set of data, that is, correlating each pair of variables/attributes.

Step 2   Construction of a new set of variables on the basis of relationships found in the correlation matrix. Though there are a number of methods available, the "principal components technique" is the most commonly used approach. In this approach, a set of variables is transformed into a new set of factors that are uncorrelated with each other. It is to be noted that the variables within a factor are highly correlated but the 'factors' are not correlated. Each factor is defined as the best linear combination of variables in terms of explaining the variance not accounted for by the preceding factor. Additional factors may be selected until all the variance is accounted for. Generally, the procedure is stopped after a limited number of factors are drawn out.

Step 3   Appropriate names are given to the various factors.

There are several types of matrices and procedures for "rotation" of the initial results that may bring to light the relationships not previously seen and clarify the common factors underlying the data.

Factor analysis is a complicated tool whose use depends highly on the judgement of the analysis and is too technical.

Terms used in factor analysis

Factor   It is a variable or construct that is not directly observable but is developed as a linear combination of observed variables.

Factor loadings   The relationships between the observed variables and the newly produced factors are known as factor loadings. They indicate the correlation between the factors and the original values. They explain to what extent a variable in a particular factor is related to the factor. These are the correlation coefficients within the matrix that indicate the importance of the factor. These loadings range from -1.0 to 1.0.

Communalities (h^2)   Communalities are the percentage of total variance summarized by the common factors. The communalities can be found mathematically by squaring the factor loadings of a variable across all factors and then summing them. This term may be interpreted as a measure of "uniqueness". A low communality figure indicates that the variable is statistically independent and cannot be combined with other variables.

Eigen values   Eigen value is the sum of the squared factor loadings for that factor. It helps in determining the number of factors to retain in the analysis. Although a number of rules are available to decide the factors to be retained for analysis, the most commonly used is the eigen value. If the factor has an eigen value of greater than 1, it will be taken up for further interpretation.

Total variance (%)   It is a summary measure indicating how much of the total original variance of all the variables is represented by the factors.

$$\text{Total variance } CV = \frac{\text{Sum of all } h^2 \times 100}{\text{No. of variables}}$$

Factor variance (%)   It is found by squaring each factor loading in each factor, summing them and dividing the result by the number of variables. It is the amount of variation explained by each factor.

CLUSTER ANALYSIS

Cluster analysis is a means of classifying persons, objects or situations into a small number of mutually exclusive and exhaustive groups. There should be high internal homogeneity and high external heterogeneity. That is, within the cluster the units must be very similar and among the clusters the variations must be wide.

Example   Let us consider the types of purchase made by 16 persons. A two-dimensional perceptional map is drawn on the basis of data relating to (i) no. of purchases made and (ii) expenditure incurred on purchases in a given month, as follows:

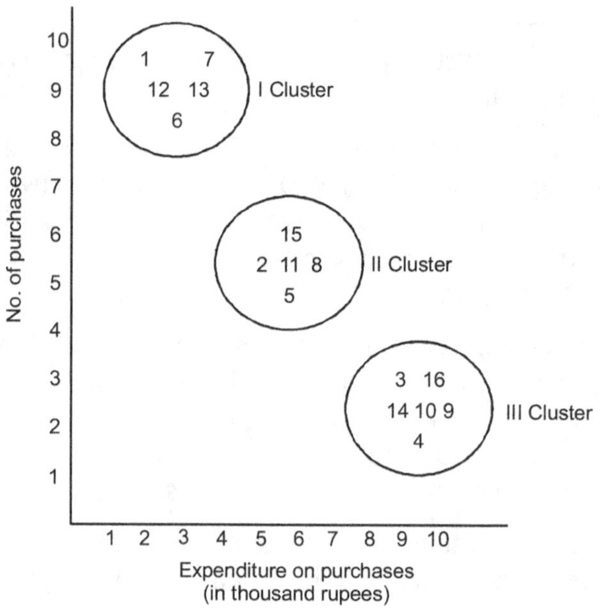

Cluster formation based on purchases vs expenditure

It will be seen that there are three distinct clusters. The cluster I comprises of five persons 1, 6, 7, 12 and 13. It shows that although these persons make many purchases, 8 to 10, they do not spend much on their purchase. It is less than 3000. The cluster II shows that the persons 2, 5, 8, 11 and 15 make moderate number of purchases (four to six) and also spend moderately (₹ 4000 to 7000). The III cluster consists of six persons 3, 4, 9, 10, 14 and 16. They have relatively less number of purchases (two to three) but spend substantially (₹ 8000 to 10,000).

It is to be noted that the points (persons) included in a cluster are close to each other and points (persons) coming under two or more clusters are at a good distance from each other. This is the essence of cluster analysis, i.e., to classify the individuals/objects on the basis of their similarity or distance from each other. Distance is an inverse measure of similarity, i.e., the shorter the distance the greater is the similarity and vice-versa.

It may be borne in mind that in reality clustering of individuals/objects will not be as simple as suggested in the example. In real-life several attributes of individuals/objects may be relevant for their classification.

Methods of cluster analysis   To understand cluster analysis procedure one must be familiar with two aspects (i) developing a measure to identify similar persons/objects and (ii) formulating a procedure to group similar persons/objects.

Different methods are employed in cluster analysis. They are classified into two major groups, viz., hierarchical and non-hierarchical methods.

Hierarchical method In this method, either the top-down or the bottom-up approach is used. In the case of the former method, all the entities (persons, objects or situations) are grouped in one cluster and divided into two sub-clusters on the basis of highest average with the cluster distance. This process is carried on until each entry is a separate cluster. In the bottom-up approach, initially there will be single-point cluster. Then the two most similar points are placed in one cluster. At each subsequent stage, the proximity matrix is recalculated to obtain the relationship of new clusters with the remaining entities. This process is continued until all single-point clusters are grouped into one large cluster.

Non-hierarchical methods Here, the "typical" entity of each cluster is defined and then most similar entities are allocated to the cluster. This method assumes that the investigator has a prior idea of what types of clusters exist. Such methods may not work out in new investigations or unfamiliar entities. In essence, the non-hierarchical methods take a fixed number of clusters ensuring that the cluster means are significantly different. This is accomplished by an ANOVA-type test.

Of these two methods, though the hierarchical method is simpler, it is more unstable and unreliable. On the other hand, the non-hierarchical method is more reliable but it is extremely difficult to interpret the series of clusters generated.

How many clusters to be generated?

The number of clusters is fixed by the researcher based on:

- The relevant theory or practice
- Cluster criterion
- Cluster pattern generated

Application of cluster analysis Cluster analysis may be used in:

- Market segmentation
- Buyer behaviour (identifying homogenous groups of buyers)
- Development of potential new products.

CONJOINT ANALYSIS

Conjoint analysis is a measure of the combined effect of two or more attributes of a product or service that are important from the view point of the consumer. When a company desires to know the most desirable attributes or their combinations for a new product or an innovative service, application of conjoint analysis will be appropriate.

The application of conjoint analysis involves three steps:

Step 1   Identification of the relevant product or service attributes.

Step 2   Collection of adequate data

Step 3   Estimation of part-worth utility function

To identify product attributes many approaches are available:

- ✿ Interviewing a number of consumers directly.
- ✿ Holding consumer focus group interviews
- ✿ Ascertaining the attributes from knowledgeable persons such as product managers, retailers or critical customers.

In the case of service such as a new public transportation system, the respondents are informed of various combination of features under consideration and are asked to indicate their 1st preference of combinations, 2nd preference, 3rd preference and so on. Conjoint analysis uses such preference data to identify the most desirable features to be included in the new product or service.

Types of data collection for conjoint analysis

"Trade-off" approach   This approach involves the consideration of only two attributes at a time to be considered by the respondents. They are asked to indicate "the more preferred" between the two attributes. It is similar to "paired comparison" method of ranking.

"Full-profile" approach   This involves consideration of all the attributes at a time. The respondents are asked to rank all the attributes. In this method, as all the attributes are considered simultaneously, the description of the concept is more realistic than that of the "trade-off" method. Here, the respondents are required to make only fewer judgements than in the case of "trade-off" method. A major limitation of the "full-profile" method is that the task of judging becomes more and more complicated when the number of attributes increases.

Salient features of conjoint analysis

- ✿ Conjoint analysis applies a complex form of ANOVA to the preference data obtained from each respondent.
- ✿ This analysis calculates a value (or utility) for each feature. Features with the highest values are considered as most important to the respondents.
- ✿ It is applied to categorical variables, which reflect different features or characteristics of the product or service under consideration.

In one way, it is similar to cluster analysis and factor analysis in the sense that all these methods try to identify the interdependence which exists among a number of variables/attributes. On the other hand it differs from cluster and factor analyses as it is applied only to categorical variables.

Usefulness of conjoint analysis Almost all industrial products and consumer durables consist of various combinations of features. All the combinations cannot be included due to the cost factor. At the same time, not all the features are of equal importance to consumers. Consequently, the manufacturers of such products always try to identify the combination of features that appeals to the customers. These appealing features can then be included in the design of the new products.

Though research based on conjoint analysis is gaining importance, of late, it is not still used frequently as other multivariate analyses.

CANONICAL CORRELATION

This is a technique used to determine the degree of linear association between two sets of variables, each consisting of several variables. It is an extension of multiple regression that focuses on the relationship between two sets of interval-scaled variables.

Suppose a marketing manager desires to know the relationship between shopping behaviour and personality traits of customers he/she can use canonical correlation technique.

$$Z = a_1 x_1 + a_2 x_2 + a_3 x_3 + \ldots a_n x_n$$
$$W = b_1 y_1 + b_2 y_2 + b_3 y_3 + \ldots b_n y_n$$

Where, Z is the total shopping behaviour and W is the total personality. While $x_1, x_2, x_3, \ldots x_n$ are the various components of shopping behaviour, $y_1, y_2, y_3, \ldots y_n$ are the different personality traits. $a_1, a_2, a_3 \ldots a_n$ and $b_1, b_2, b_3, \ldots b_n$ are the constants obtained through preliminary survey.

As indicated elsewhere, no attempt is made to explain the calculation parts of multivariate analysis in the text. Any good book on statistical analysis may be referred to.

SPSS (STATISTICAL PACKAGE FOR THE SOCIAL SCIENCES)

Before the advent of fast and all-purpose computers the statisticians used to struggle with manually operated calculators to do even the complicated statistical analyses. Now complicated calculations are made easy with new software. Presently researchers employ specific software for various statistical problems. Statistical Package for the Social Sciences, commonly known as SPSS is one of the statistical programs in the market, which was originally written for mainframe computers and designed to be used in the social sciences. Nowadays this interesting package is used by researchers in most of the disciplines. It is a powerful software for automated analysis of data. SPSS can be used for entering and formatting data, running the analysis, drawing different kinds of diagrams and interpreting data. SPSS is used effectively for teaching of statistics in colleges as well.

No attempt has been made here to explain SPSS as it is beyond the scope of this book.

REVIEW QUESTIONS

1. Differentiate between parametric and non-parametric tests.
2. What are the steps in tests of significance?
3. When Z and t-tests are used?
4. What is Chi-square test?
5. What is F-test?
6. What is ANOVA?
7. What is correlation?
8. What is rank correlation?
9. Discuss multiple regression analysis.
10. What is discriminant analysis?
11. What is the importance of factor analysis?
12. Distinguish between cluster analysis, conjoint analysis and canonical correlation.

10

APPLICATION OF ANOVA AND CHI-SQUARE TESTS IN PROJECT WORK

How ANOVA and chi-square tests could be used in project work are explained in this chapter through examples.

APPLICATION OF ANOVA

Example 1

Title   A study on the emotional intelligence of employees in XYZ company, Coimbatore.

Questionnaire   The questionnaire typically consists of two parts.

Part I elicits personal details of respondents. The personal information generally obtained from respondents in an organization are gender, age group, department or section, educational background, salary, number of years of experience, etc.

Part II contains questions to judge the emotional intelligence of the respondents. As emotional intelligence comprises five important components, viz., self-awareness, self-management, social awareness, social relationship and self-motivation, the student has included five questions under each sub-head. The total number of questions is 25 (5×5). The questions are in the form of positive statements. The respondents numbering 100 are requested to encircle the appropriate score on the 4-point Likert-type scale which indicates the opinion/attitude. Strongly Agree carries a score of 4, Agree, 3, Disagree, 2 and Strongly Disagree, 1. (Some statements are to be answered as Always, Frequently, Sometimes and Rarely).

The total score marked by each respondent is calculated as follows:

If a respondent responded as below the total score marked by him/her will be 64: (It is obtained simply by adding all the encircled scores).

Responses to statement

Statement or question		Strongly agree	Agree	Strongly disagree	Disagree
1	–	(4)	3	2	1
2	–	(4)	3	2	1
3	–	4	(3)	2	1
4	–	4	3	2	(1)
5	–	4	(3)	2	1
6	–	4	3	(2)	1
7	–	4	(3)	2	1
8	–	(4)	3	2	1
9	–	4	3	(2)	1
10	(–)	(4)	3	2	1
11	–	4	(3)	2	1
12	–	4	(3)	2	1
13	–	4	3	(2)	1
14	–	4	3	(2)	1
15	–	4	(3)	2	1
16	–	(4)	3	2	1
17	–	4	3	(2)	1
18	–	4	(3)	2	1
19	–	4	3	2	(1)
20	–	4	3	2	(1)
21	–	4	(3)	2	1
22	–	4	3	(2)	1
23	–	4	3	(2)	1
24	–	4	3	(2)	1
25	–	4	3	2	(1)

Scoring of responses

Production Dept.	Administration Dept.	Marketing Dept.
55	30	65
53	35	70
48	38	72
61	28	58
67	36	45
43	43	53
57	53	72
65	22	43
49	25	60
48	45	61
51	40	64
66	41	59
44	43	67
57	28	69
58	30	72
51	52	75
38	41	55
39	49	59
45	29	60
63	32	55
65		75
45		72
39		59
40		60
71		61
72		63
31		59
33		48
38		60
54		69

(Contd.)

Scoring of responses (Continued)

Production Dept.	Administration Dept.	Marketing Dept.
59		
48		
56		
54		
58		
47		
49		
43		
40		
49		
52		
47		
48		
65		
62		
45		
39		
53		
50		
40		
Total = 2550	Total = 740	Total = 1860
$n_1 = 50$	$n_2 = 20$	$n_3 = 30$
Mean = 51	Mean = 37	Mean = 62

Aim   To test whether the E.I. of the employees in the three departments, viz., Production, Administration and Marketing is different or same.

(Test at 5% level of significance.)

Null hypothesis (Ho)   There is no significant difference in the emotional intelligence of employees in Production, Administration and Marketing departments.

Alternative hypothesis (Ha)   There is difference.

Test criterion   One-way ANOVA as means of three groups are to be compared based on one dimension (emotional intelligence).

Analysis

Step 1   Compute the total scores of the employees in each Dept. and the grand total. If T_1, T_2 and T_3 are the total scores of employees in Production, Marketing and Administration Departments and T, the grand total, then

$$T_1 = 2550,\ T_2 = 740\ \text{and}\ T_3 = 1860\ \text{and}$$

$$T = 2550 + 740 + 1860 = 5150$$

Step 2   Compute the Correction Factor (CF).

$$CF = \frac{T^2}{N} = \frac{(5150)^2}{100} = 265225 \quad \text{(where N is the total number of respondents)}$$

Step 3   Find the Total Sum of Squares (SSQ_T). It is the sum of squares of all the observations less the correction factor.

$$SSQ_T = (55)^2 + (53)^2 + \ldots (60)^2 + (69)^2 - 265225$$

$$= 281110 - 265225 = 15885$$

Step 4   Compute the sum of squares "due to the differences" in the three departments. It is popularly known as "between group" variables.

$$SSQ_t = \frac{T_1^2}{n_1} + \frac{T_2^2}{n_2} + \frac{T_3^2}{n_3} - CF$$

where,

SSQ_t = Sum of square of treatments,

T_1 = Total score of the individuals in Production Department.

T_2 = Total score of the individuals in Administration Department.

T_3 = Total score of the individuals in Marketing Department.

n_1 = No. of employees in Production Department.

n_2 = No. of employees in Administration Department.

n_3 = No. of employees in Marketing Department.

$$\frac{(2550)^2}{50} + \frac{(1860)^2}{30} + \frac{(740)^2}{20} - 265225 = 7525$$

Step 5   Error Sum of Squares (SSQ_E), known as "within the group" variability is found out by subtracting SSQ_t from SSQ_T as the total variability is composed of "between the group" variability and "within the group" variability.

$$SSQ_E = 15885 - 7525 = 8360$$

Step 6   Construct ANOVA table.

ANOVA

Sources of variation	df	SS	MSS	F-ratio	Table F-value
Between groups	2	7525	3762.5	43.65	3.10
Within groups (Error)	97	8360	86.2		
Total	99	15885			

Total df is $(n - 1)$ where N is the total number of observations. In the instant case it is $100 - 1$, i.e., 99.

df for "between the groups" is $n - 1$ where n is the number of groups $(3 - 1 = 2)$

df for "within the groups" is total df less the df for "between the groups" $(99 - 2 = 97)$

MSS   Mean Sum of Squares is obtained by dividing the SS by the respective df.

$$\left(\frac{7525}{2} = 3762.5 \text{ and } \frac{8630}{97} = 86.2 \right)$$

F-ratio   It is obtained by dividing the MSS of "between the groups" by that of "within the groups."

$$\left(\frac{3762.5}{86.2} = 43.65 \right)$$

Table F-value   Table F-ratio for df 2 and 97 at 5% level of significance. (3.10)

Interpretation   As the calculated *F*-ratio (43.65) is greater than the table value (3.10), the N.H. is rejected.

Inference   There is significant difference in the EI of the employees in the three departments, (Production, Administration and Marketing). The employees in **Marketing Department have the highest EI** (Mean = 62) followed by the employees in the Production Department (Mean =51). The employees in the Administration Department have the lowest EI (Mean = 37).

As in the case of different Departments, significance of difference in the employees in the different age groups (<30, 31–45, >45 years), various levels of salary (< ₹10,000, 10,000–20,000 and >20,000), varying levels of experience (<5 yr, 6–10 yr and > 10 yr), etc. can be found out. In all these cases the number of employees in each group (age groupwise, experiencewise, salary slabwise, etc.) are sorted out with the corresponding total scores of the individuals in each group. Further analysis is done as detailed in the example.

Example 2

Topic   A study on the opinion of the dealers in TN on the sale of washing machines of ABC Co.

Questionnaire   The questionnaire consists of two parts. Part I covers the details of the dealers. Part II is concerned with the opinion of the dealers on the sales activities.

Part I includes information such as location of the dealership, annual turnover, experience of the dealer, number of employees, etc.

Part II consists of 20 questions, 4 each under the sub-headings, viz., promotional activities undertaken by the company profit margins, credit facilities, training, after-sales service and delivery. The questions are in the form of positive statements on 5-point Likert-type scale (Depending on the statement, the choices are Strongly Agree, Agree, No Idea, Disagree and Strongly Disagree or Always, Frequently, Sometimes, Rarely and Never with scores 5, 4, 3, 2 and 1 respectively).

As in the case of the earlier example, individual scores of the dealers are found out. As it is a 5-point scale (with a maximum score of 5 and minimum of 1 for each statement, and the number of questions being 20, the maximum score to be marked by an individual dealer will be 100 (20 × 5) and minimum 20 (20 × 1).

It is assumed that the student is interested to know whether there is any significant difference in the opinions among the dealers situated in various cities in Tamil Nadu.

Hypothetical opinion scores of the dealers are given below. (The student has collected the opinion from eight dealers in Chennai, six in Coimbatore, five in Madurai and four each from Salem and Trichy).

Scores of responses

City	Chennai	Coimbatore	Madurai	Salem	Trichy
	65	63	59	64	63
	68	67	58	67	61
	73	64	68	60	51
	61	56	64	65	69
Scores	60	63	61		
	59	65			
	70				
	64				
Total	520	378	310	256	244
	$n_1 = 8$	$n_2 = 6$	$n_3 = 5$	$n_4 = 4$	$n_5 = 4$
Mean	65	63	62	64	61

Aim   To find out if there is any significant difference in the opinion of dealers on ABC company.

Null hypothesis (Ho)   There is no significant difference in the opinions of the dealers in the various cities.

Alternative hypothesis (Ha)   There is significant difference.

Analysis

Test criterion   As more than two means are to be compared on the basis of a simple dimension, one-way ANOVA is used.

Step 1   Compute the total scores of the dealers in each city and the grand total

T_1, T_2, T_3, T_4, and T_5 are the total scores of the dealers and T is the grand total,

$T_1 = 520, T_2 = 378, T_3 = 310, T_4 = 256, T_5 = 244$ and $T = 1708$

Step 2   Compute the correction Factor (*CF*).

$$CF = \frac{T^2}{N} = \frac{(1708)^2}{27} = \frac{2917264}{27} = 108047$$

where T is the grand total and N is the total number of observations.

Step 3   Find the total sum of squares (SSQ_T). It is the sum of squares of all the observations less the correction factor.

$$SSQ_T = (65)^2 + (68)^2 + \ldots (51)^2 + (69)^2 - 108047 = 108608 - 108047 = 561$$

Step 4   Compute the sum of squares "due to the differences" in the five cities. It is known as "between the groups" variability (SSQ_t).

$$SSQ_t = \frac{T_1^2}{n_1} + \frac{T_2^2}{n_2} + \frac{T_3^2}{n_3} + \frac{T_4^2}{n_4} + \frac{T_5^2}{n_5} - CF$$

T_1 = Total score of the dealers in Chennai

T_2 = Total score of the dealers in Coimbatore

T_3 = Total score of the dealers in Madurai

T_4 = Total score of the dealers in Salem

T_5 = Total score of the dealers in Trichy

($n_1, n_2, n_3, n_4,$ and n_5, are the number of dealers in Chennai, Coimbatore, Madurai, Salem, and Trichy, respectively.)

$$= \frac{(520)^2}{8} + \frac{(378)^2}{6} + \frac{(310)^2}{5} + \frac{(256)^2}{4} + \frac{(244)^2}{4} - 108047$$
$$= (33800 + 23814 + 19220 + 16384 + 14884) - 108047$$
$$= 108102 - 108047 = 55$$

Step 5   Error Sum of Square (SSQ_E), known as variability "within the groups" is found out by subtracting SSQ_t from SSQ_T.

$$SSQ_E = SSQ_T - SSQ_t = 561 - 55 = 506$$

Step 6   Construct ANOVA table.

ANOVA

Sources of variation	df	SS	MSS	*F*-ratio	Table *F*-value
Between groups	4	55	13.75	0.598	2.82
Within groups (Error)	22	506	23		
Total	26	561			

Total df is 27 (Total number of observations is one); df for "between the group" is 4 (Total number of groups, i.e., cities is one)

df for "within the groups" is total $df - df$ for "between the groups".

Interpretation   As the calculated F-ratio is smaller than the table F-value at 5% level of significance the N.H. is accepted.

Inference   Though there are differences in the opinions expressed by various dealers in different cities, the differences are not statistically significant.

In the above two examples the differences in the total scores are taken into account. If necessary, the sub-total scores of sub-headings alone in the questionnaire can also be considered to find out the following:

- Significance of differences of opinion of employees based on various age groups, gender, or levels of salary on self-awareness, self-motivation, self-management or social relationship.

- Significance of differences of opinions among the dealers (based on turnover, experience or number of employees employed) on the company's promotional activities, after-sales service, margin or training programmes.

APPLICATION OF CHI-SQUARE AS A TEST OF INDEPENDENCE

As discussed in Chapter 9, Chi-square as a test of independence throws light whether one variable depends on the other variable, i.e., whether a variable is independent of other variable.

Example 1

Title   A study on the quality of work life in a company.

Questionnaire   A questionnaire is formulated with two parts.

Part I covers personal details such as gender, age (<30, 31–50, >50), educational qualification, department, experience, compensation, etc.

Part II consists of 30 questions, 5 each under the 6 dimensions, viz., Management's Attitude, Interpersonal Relationship, Training and Development Programme, Performance Appraisal, Compensation and Grievance Redressal mechanism. Opinions are collected on a 5-point Likert-type scale (Strongly Agree, Agree, No idea, Disagree and Strongly Disagree or Always, Frequently, Sometimes, Rarely and Never). As explained elsewhere, individual scores are obtained for each dimension and the total scores are calculated. For each dimension the maximum score will be $25(5 \times 5)$

and the minimum 5(5 × 1). In the case of individual's total score, maximum will be 150(30 × 5) and minimum will be 30(30 × 1).

Now, for example, the student is interested to know whether there is any association between age group of employees and the opinion score, i.e., whether the opinion score on quality of worklife decreases or increases with age.

Aim   To find out the relationship, if any, between age and opinion of QWL or to know whether opinion on QWL is independent of age of employees.

Null hypothesis (Ho)   There is no association between age group and opinion score.

Alternative hypothesis (Ha)   There is association.

Test criterion   Chi-square as a test of independence is employed.

Analysis

Step 1   Compute the total opinion score for each employee (by assigning 5 points to Strongly Agree/Always, 4 to Agree/Frequently, 3 to No idea/Sometimes, 2 to Disagree/Rarely and 1 to Strongly Disagree/Never.)

Step 2   Classify the individual scores as Low, Medium, and High (<50: Low; 51–100: Medium and 101–150: High) For example, classification depends on scores which may vary from project to project.

Step 3   Find out how many individuals scored low in the age group of <30 years, 31–50 and >51. Similarly find out how many individuals scored low, medium or high in the 3 age groups.

[In the present example it is assumed that the number of respondents in the age group of <30 yr is 50, 31–50 is 82 and >51 yr is 68 (Total number of respondents 200).]

The following is the classification of age groups vs opinion score.

Age groups and opinion on QWL

Age group	Opinion score (Observed values)			Total
	Low	Medium	High	
< 30 years	12	14	24	50
31–50 years	26	26	30	82
> 50 years	34	20	14	68
	72	60	68	200

Step 4   The expected value for each observed value (each cell) is calculated by multiplying the row total with column total and dividing by grand total (e.g., for the observed value of 12, the expected value is $\dfrac{50 \times 72}{200} = 18$).

Step 5   The observed values with the expected values in brackets are presented in a contingency table as shown below.

Age groups vs opinion (Expected values)

Age group	Opinion score (Expected)			Total
	Low	Medium	High	
< 30 years	12(18)	14(15)	24(17)	50
31–50 years	26(29.5)	26(24.6)	30(27.9)	82
> 50 years	34(24.5)	20(20.4)	14(23.1)	68
	72	60	68	200

Step 6   Calculate chi-square using the formula

$$\chi^2 = \sum \frac{(O - E)^2}{E}$$

$$= \frac{(12-18)^2}{18} + \frac{(14-15)^2}{15} + \frac{(24-17)^2}{17} + \frac{(26-29.5)^2}{29.5} + \frac{(26-24.6)^2}{24.6} + \frac{(30-27.9)^2}{27.9}$$

$$+ \frac{(34-24.5)^2}{24.5} + \frac{(20-20.4)^2}{20.4} + \frac{(14-23.1)^2}{23.1}$$

$$= 12.88$$

Step 7   Find out df.

$df = (c - 1)(r - 1)$ where c = number of columns; r = number of rows: $(3 - 1)(3 - 1) = 4$

Step 8   Find out the Table χ^2-value.

Table χ^2-value   Table χ^2-value for 4 df at 5% level of significance is 9.488.

Interpretation   As the calculated χ^2-value (12.87) is higher than that of the table value (9.488), the N.H is rejected.

Inference   There is significant association between age groups and opinion on the QWL in the company. Further, from the classification of original data, it is inferred that higher the age group, lower is the opinion level on QWL.

On the above line, the association between salary level, experience or compensation and the overall opinion on the QWL, management's attitude, interpersonal relationship or T and D programme can be found out.

Example 2

Title   A study on the satisfaction level of customers of an authorized car service station.

The questionnaire consisted of two parts, the first part covering the details of the customers such as gender, age group, occupation, educational background, annual income, etc., and the second part consists of 20 questions, 4 each under the headings such as behaviour courtesies of the employees, quality of spare parts/service, billing, cost of repairs and location/ambience. Scoring is to be done on a 5-point Likert-type scale as explained elsewhere. As a part of the study the student is interested to know whether there is any association between income level of the customers and the satisfaction level. The satisfaction level is classified as "satisfied" and "not satisfied". As the number of questions is 20 with a 5-point scaling, the maximum score to be obtained will be 100 (20 × 5). Scores <50 are classified as "not satisfied" and >50 as "satisfied".

The observations made are given below.

Levels of income vs opinion on service

Customers with annual income of	Opinion on the service		Total
	Not satisfied	Satisfied	
< ₹2 lakhs	10(18.7)	25(16.3)	35
₹2 to 5 lakhs	20(24)	25(21)	45
> ₹5 lakhs	50(37.3)	20(32.7)	70
	80	70	150

(Figures within parentheses are the expected values.)

Aim   To find out whether there is any association between income of customers and their satisfaction level in the service of the dealer.

Null hypothesis (Ho)   There is no association between income of the customers and their opinion on the service.

Alternative hypothesis (Ha)   There is association.

$$\chi^2 = \sum \frac{(O-E)^2}{E}$$

$$= \frac{(10-18.7)^2}{18.7} + \frac{(25-16.3)^2}{16.3} + \frac{(20-24)^2}{24} + \frac{(25-21)^2}{21} + \frac{(50-37.3)^2}{37.3} + \frac{(20-32.7)^2}{32.7}$$

$$= 19.38$$

$$df = (c-1)(r-1) = (2-1)(3-1) = 2$$

Table chi-square value for 2 df at 5% level of significance is 5.99.

Interpretation   As the calculated χ^2-value (19.38) is greater than that of the table value (5.99) the N.H. is rejected.

Inference   There is significant association between the opinion on the service and the income level of the respondents. It is inferred that people in the higher income bracket are less satisfied than the lower income group people.

Similarly, the association between age group or educational background and the overall opinion on the service provided, courtesy extended or quality of spare parts, billing, cost or location/ambience can be found out.

Alternative method of classifying data for Chi-square analysis

In the above two examples the opinions, viz., SA, A, No idea, DA and SDA are assigned points 5, 4, 3, 2 and 1 respectively and the total score is classified as low, medium and high or low and high or "satisfied" or "not satisfied" among the various groups.

In the alternative method, instead of assigning points, the numbers of the view/opinion as such are taken for analysis. Here, the number of SA, A, No Idea, DA and SDA of each respondent is found out. And the total number of each opinion is calculated under different groups.

In the example "A study on the QWL in company X" the number of questions in the questionnaire is 20 and the number of respondents is 200. Hence, there will be a total of 4000 opinions. These 4000 opinions are classified under different groups.

Suppose in the age group of <30 years the number of respondents are 50, then the number of opinions will be 1000 (50 × 20).

In the 31–50 years group if the number of respondents is 82 then the number of opinions will be 1640 (82 × 20).

In the >50 years group, if the number of respondents is 68 then the number of opinions will be 1360 (68 × 20).

The hypothetical classification is given below.

Age group vs opinion on QWL

Age group	Opinions					Total
	SA	A	No idea	DA	SDA	
< 30 years	400(215)	250(187.5)	150(190)	100(192.5)	100(215)	1000
31–50 years	350(352.6)	340(307.5)	360(311.6)	290(315.7)	300(352.6)	1640
> 50 years	110(292.4)	160(255)	250(258.4)	380(261.8)	460(292.4)	1360
	860	750	760	770	860	4000

(The expected values are calculated and presented within parentheses.)

$$\chi^2 = \sum \frac{(O-E)^2}{E}$$

$$= \frac{(400-21.5)^2}{21.5} + \frac{(250-187.5)^2}{187.5} + \frac{(150-190)^2}{190} + \frac{(100-192.5)^2}{192.5} + \frac{(100-215)^2}{21.5}$$

$$+ \frac{(350-352.6)^2}{352.6} + \frac{(340-307.5)^2}{307.5} + \frac{(360-311.6)^2}{311.6} + \frac{(290-315.7)^2}{315.7} + \frac{(300-352.6)^2}{352.6}$$

$$+ \frac{(110-292.4)^2}{292.4} + \frac{(250-258.4)^2}{258.4} + \frac{(380-261.8)^2}{261.8} + \frac{(460-292.4)^2}{292.4}$$

$$= 614.3$$

$$df = (c-1)(r-1) = (5-1)(3-1) = 8$$

Table χ^2-value for 5 *df* at 5% level of significance is 15.5.

Interpretation   As the calculated chi-square value (614.3) is greater than that of the table value (15.5) the N.H. is rejected.

Inference   It is inferred that there is significant difference in the opinion of the employees of different age groups on the QWL. Further, as the number of "DA" and "SDA" is more in the case of the age group of >50 years, it could be inferred that older employees are least satisfied with the QWL in the company.

APPLICATION OF CHI-SQUARE AS A TEST OF GOODNESS OF FIT

Goodness of fit test helps to find out whether the observed values are as expected or not. Assume that in a study a questionnaire is prepared with 20 questions/statements to be responded on a 5-point Likert-type scale (as SA, A, No idea, DA and SDA or Always, Frequently, Sometimes, Rarely or Never).

Each question/statement can be tested for goodness of fit. One of the statements may be "The performance appraisal system is not biased". To this statement assume that, out of 100 respondents, 20 would have marked "SA", 18 "A", 17 "No idea", 23 "DA" and 22 "SDA". If the N.H. states that there is no difference in the opinion of the respondents, then the expected values will be 20 (100/5) each under the opinion SA, S, No idea, DA and SDA.

Performance appraisal—observed values and expected values

	SA	A	No idea	DA	SDA
Observed	20	18	17	23	22
Expected	20	20	20	20	20

$$\chi^2 = \sum \frac{(O-E)^2}{E}$$

$$= \frac{(20-20)^2}{20} + \frac{(18-20)^2}{20} + \frac{(17-20)^2}{20} + \frac{(23-20)^2}{20} + \frac{(22-20)^2}{20}$$

$$= 0 + \frac{4}{20} + \frac{9}{20} + \frac{9}{20} + \frac{4}{20}$$

$$= 0.2 + 0.45 + 0.45 + 0.2 = 1.3$$

Table χ^2-value for 4 *df* (number of pairs – 1) at 5% significance is 9.5.

Interpretation   As the calculated value is less than the table value, the N.H. of "no difference of opinion" is accepted.

Inference   It is inferred that the performance appraisal system is neither biased nor unbiased, i.e., there is no clear-cut opinion.

Suppose the observed values are as follows :

SA: 40, A : 30, No idea: 10, DA: 15, SDA : 5

Then

$$\chi^2 = \sum \frac{(O-E)^2}{E}$$

$$= \frac{(40-20)^2}{20} + \frac{(30-20)^2}{20} + \frac{(10-20)^2}{20} + \frac{(15-20)^2}{20} + \frac{(5-20)^2}{20}$$

$$= 20 + 5 + 5 + 1.25 + 11.25$$

$$= 42.50$$

Interpretation   As the calculated value (42.50) is greater than the table value (9.5), the N.H. of " number difference of opinion" is rejected.

Inference   There is significant difference in the opinion of the respondents on the performance appraisal system and it is inferred that the performance appraisal system is not biased as majority of the employees Strongly Agreed/Agreed with the statement.

Suppose the observed values are as follows :

SA :10, A : 15, No idea : 10, DA : 35, SDA : 30

Then

$$\chi^2 = \frac{(10-20)^2}{20} + \frac{(15-20)^2}{20} + \frac{(10-20)^2}{20} + \frac{(35-20)^2}{20} + \frac{(30-20)^2}{20}$$
$$= 5 + 1.25 + 5 + 11.25 + 5 = 27.50$$

Interpretation   As the calculated value (27.50) is greater than the table value (9.5), the N.H. of no difference of opinion is rejected.

Inference   There is significant difference in the opinion of the respondents and it is inferred that the performance appraisal system is biased.

REVIEW QUESTIONS

1. Discuss the steps in ANOVA.
2. Differentiate chi-square as a test of independence from chi-square as a test of goodness of it?

11

INTERPRETATION AND REPORT PREPARATION

INTERPRETATION

It refers to the task of drawing inferences from the collected facts after an analytical and/or experimental study. It is a search for broader meaning of research findings and has two important aspects:

i. The effort to establish continuity in research through linking the results of a given study with those of another.

ii. The establishment of some explanatory concepts.

In one sense, it is concerned with relationships within the collected data, partially overlapping analysis. It also extends beyond the data of the study to include the results of other research, theory, etc. Thus, interpretation is the device through which the factors that seem to explain what has been observed by the researcher in the course of the study can be better understood and it also provides a theoretical conception which can serve as a guide for further research.

NEED FOR INTERPRETATION

It is through interpretation that the researcher can understand the abstract principle that works beneath his/her findings. Through this researchers can link up their findings with those of other studies having the same abstract principle and thereby can predict about the concrete world of events. Fresh enquiries can test these predictions later on. This way the continuity in research can be maintained.

Interpretation leads to the establishment of explanatory concepts than can serve as a guide for further research studies; it opens new avenues of intellectual adventure and stimulates the quest for more knowledge.

Researchers can better appreciate only through interpretation why their findings are what they are and can make others understand the real significance of their research findings.

The interpretation of the findings of an exploratory research study often results into hypothesis for experimental research and as such interpretation is involved in the transition from exploratory to experimental research.

GUIDELINES FOR INTERPRETATION

Interpretation requires great skill and dexterity. It is an art that one learns through practice and experience. Some guidelines for interpretation are as follows:

- Researchers must give reasonable explanation of the relation and must interpret relationship in terms of the underlying processes. This is the technique of how generalization should be done and concept be formulated.
- Extraneous information, if collected during the study, must be considered while interpreting the final results.
- It is advisable to get frank and honest opinions of experts.
- All relevant factors must be considered before generalization.

PRECAUTIONS IN INTERPRETATION

- Researchers must invariably satisfy themselves that (i) the data are appropriate, trustworthy and adequate (ii) the data reflect good homogeneity and (iii) proper statistical analysis has been applied.
- They must remain cautious about the errors that can possibly arise in the process of interpretation. They should be well-equipped with the knowledge of correct use of statistical measures of drawing inferences concerning the study.
- As the task of interpretation is very much intertwined with analysis and cannot be distinctly separated, it must be taken as a special aspect of analysis.
- Their task is not only to make sensitive observations but also to identify the factors which were not known initially. Broad generalization should be avoided because the coverage is restricted to a particular time, a particular area or particular condition.
- There should be constant interaction between initial hypothesis, empirical observation and theoretical conceptions. It is here that opportunities for originality and creativity lie.

REPORT WRITING

The importance of report writing in research needs no emphasis. A research is said to be incomplete unless it is presented in a report format. Any research will be appreciated only when it is made known to others through research report. The exotic dishes in a dinner are appreciated by the guests when the host (homemaker) lays the table neatly, explains the dishes and serves in a meticulous way. Similarly the efforts of the researcher and the fruits of the research will be appreciated only when it is presented as a report in a logical sequence incorporating all the relevant details.

Meaning A research report is a formal statement of the details of the research process and its results. It gives an account of the problem(s) studied, objectives, methodology, findings and conclusions of the research study.

PURPOSE OR FUNCTIONS OF A RESEARCH REPORT

✿ To communicate the methodology and results of the study to the targeted audience.

✿ To enable the person(s) concerned to determine the validity of the results/conclusion and judge the quality of the research project as well and as the ability and competence of the researcher to do research.

✿ To provide as a base for formulating policies and strategies in the relevant areas.

✿ To provide additional knowledge to tackle certain problems/issues.

✿ To serve as a basic reference for future study.

CHARACTERISTICS OF A GOOD RESEARCH REPORT

Not only must the report be narrative, must also be an authoritative document on the outcome. There should be no ambiguity.

✿ It must be specific and accurate and there is no question of beating around the bush.

✿ It must be written with the targeted audience in mind.

✿ It must be non-persuasive. That is, extra caution is needed while advocating a particular course of action based on the finding.

✿ It must be simple, logical and understandable.

TYPES OF REPORT

Based on the degree of formality, physical form, scope, style, size, etc., reports may be classified as technical report, interim report, summary report, research abstract and research article.

TECHNICAL REPORT (THESIS, DISSERTATION, SUMMER PROJECT)

- It is a comprehensive and full report on the research process and its outcome.
- Though it is mainly meant for the academic community, it is also useful to the industry in many instances.
- It is essentially technical in nature/scope and presented in technical language.
- It follows a specified format/pattern/style.
- It is a formal long report covering all aspects of the research process, viz., defining problem, statement of problem, objectives, review of literature, methodology (the research design, data collection and analysis), findings, suggestions and conclusions.

INTERIM REPORT

In the case of a long-term project, there will be appreciable time lag from initiation/data collection to submission of the final report. If it happens to be a sponsored project, the sponsor may lose track of the project. To convince the authority concerned that the research is alive and is in progress, interim reports are presented periodically. Work carried out so far and work to be done are detailed in the interim report. Sometimes preliminary inference and trend will be indicated.

Interim reports give indications to the society at large that a particular line of work is in progress so that repetition could be avoided. In certain cases the decision as to who has initiated the work would be based on interim reports.

SUMMARY REPORT OR POPULAR REPORT

- It is a short report consisting of a few pages.
- It is prepared in such a way that it is suitable for publication in daily newspapers or magazine.
- It is meant for general public.
- It is devoid of technical jargon.
- The findings must be of some common interest to the public in general.
- It is written in a simple language mostly supported by pictorial charts.
- Only the important findings are narrated in a lucid style.

RESEARCH ABSTRACTS

Abstracts are brief summaries of technical report/theses/dissertation circulated for a quick review before a detailed examination is made. Sometimes, it is prepared for publication in abstract journals. The objectives, methodology and findings are presented in a brief format.

RESEARCH ARTICLES

Short-term projects may be published as research articles in professional journals in specific formats. The long-term projects can also be split into different parts and published as separate research articles. Though the style of presentation may differ from journal to journal, in general, the research articles will have introduction, methodology, results and discussion, conclusion and references.

FORMAT OF RESEARCH REPORT/PROJECT REPORT

A research report will have well-defined sections/chapters arranged in logical sequence. Though there may be a little variation in the order, chapterization or details furnished depending on the research guide, area of research or institute, a general format is discussed below:

A. PREFATORY ITEMS

- Title page
- Researcher's or student's declaration
- Certificate by the Research Supervisor/Head of the Department/Institute.
- Acknowledgement
- Table of Contents
- List of Tables
- List of Graphs/Charts/Figures/Plates

B. BODY OF THE REPORT

Chapter I   Introduction

1.1 Introduction to the study/concept/theory/models

1.2 Introduction to the organization/industry/situation

1.3 Need or significance of the study

1.4 Statement of the problem

1.5 Scope of the study

1.6 Objectives of the study

1.7 Hypotheses to be tested

Chapter II   Review of Literature

2.1 Tools/Methods used in similar studies

2.2 Findings and conclusions of earlier studies

2.3 Lacunae of available literature

Chapter III   Research Methodology

3.1 Nature of the research design

3.2 Sources of data

3.3 Sampling design and sample size

3.4 Techniques/Tools of data collection, methodology of data collection and period of data collection.

3.5 Pretesting of tools

3.6 Data analysis (statistical tools and other techniques employed)

3.7 Limitations of the study

Chapter IV Analysis and Interpretation or Results and Discussion

Tables, charts, interpretation and inferences

Chapter V Summary and Conclusion

5.1 Summary

5.2 Findings

5.3 Suggestions

5.4 Conclusion

5.5 Future line of work

C. Terminal Items

- ✪ References
- ✪ Bibliography
- ✪ Appendices
- ✪ Annexures

BRIEF DESCRIPTION OF THE VARIOUS ITEMS OF A REPORT

Title Page

It is the first page in a research report. The same contents may be printed on the wrapper or cover. This page contains (i) The title of the study in bold letters (ii) Type of study and the purpose (iii) Name of the student-author followed by the name of the guide or principal investigator and co-investigators (iv) Name of the Institute (v) Month and Year of submission.

***Example* 1**   Project Report submitted by an MBA student

A STUDY ON THE EMOTIONAL INTELLIGENCE OF EXECUTIVES IN ROOTS INDUSTRY Ltd., COIMBATORE

Project report submitted in partial fulfilment of the requirements for the award of degree of Master of Business Administration of Bharathiar University

By

Ms. A. Sathya Shree

Under the guidance of

Dr. S.T. Sukumaran

Senior Professor

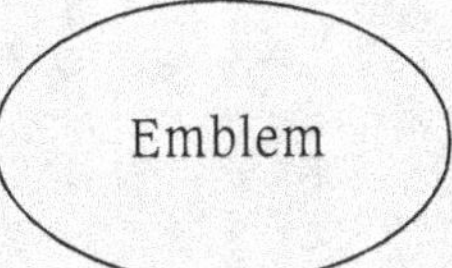

MNR School of Management Sciences

Coimbatore – 641 086.

May, 2010

***Example* 2**   A research report submitted by a faculty member to the AICTE

HRD PRACTICES IN THE TEXTILE INDUSTRY IN COIMBATORE—A CRITICAL ANALYSIS

AICTE-Sponsored major research project

Research Report Submitted by

Dr. T. Gunaseelan, Ph.D.
Principal Investigator
and
Dr. R. Lakshmanan, Ph.D.
Co-Investigator

Emblem

TNT School of Management Sciences (Autonomous)
Coimbatore – 641 076.
June, 2010

RESEARCH DECLARATION

In the case of a student submitting a project report to fulfil the requirements of a Degree/Diploma, he/she is required to make a declaration.

Example

Declaration

I, Ms. A Sathyashree, hereby declare that the project report entitled "A Study On The Emotional Intelligence of Executives in Roots Industry Ltd., Coimbatore" is a record of original research done by me under the guidance of Dr. S.T. Sukumaran Ph.D. to fulfil the requirement for the award of the Degree of MBA of Bharathiar University. This report has not been submitted for the award of any degree, diploma or any title elsewhere.

Date: Signature of the student

Place: Name of the student

CERTIFICATE OF AUTHENTICITY

Similar to student's declaration, the Research Supervisor certifies the authenticity of the report endorsed by the Head of the Dept./Director/Principal.

Example

Certificate

This is to certify that the project report, "A study on the Emotional Intelligence of Executives in Root Industry Ltd., Coimbatore" is a record of original research conducted by Ms. Sathyashree to fulfil the requirements for the award of degree of MBA of Bharathiar University.

Signature of the HOD/Director   Signature of the Guide

Designation   Name of the Designation of the Guide

Signature of the Principal/Head of Institute

Place:

Date:

ACKNOWLEDGEMENT

In the case of a researcher other than a student, the author acknowledges the help/ encouragement received, in the Preface of the report along with a brief background of the study.

In the case of a student's project research, he/she acknowledges the help/support/ encouragement received from all the individuals. They should thank the project guide, HOD, Principal, faculty members and others.

The acknowledgement page intended to express one's gratitude. Every individual who has rendered any type of help should be mentioned with gratitude and it is written in a simple language without causing any embarrassment to any source.

TABLE OF CONTENTS

The contents of the report are presented in the table of contents. Chapter titles along with page numbers are given.

CONTENTS

Chapter		Title	Page No.
		List of Tables	
		List of Graphs / Charts / Figures	
I		Introduction	
	1.1	Introduction to the study/concept/theory/model	
	1.2	Introduction to the company/industry/situation	
	1.3	Significance of the study/Need for the study	
	1.4	Statement of the problem	
	1.5	Scope of the study	
	1.6	Objectives	
	1.7	Hypotheses, if any	
II		Review of Literature	
III		Research Methodology	
	3.1	Research design	

List of Tables/Charts/Figures/Plates are presented separately with relevant titles and page numbers.

INTRODUCTION

The introduction chapter covers many important sub-topics.

Introduction to study   The concept, theory, meaning, definition, models, etc., related to the topic under study are discussed in detail. The authors of the concepts, theories, etc., can also be referred to.

Introduction to the organization, industry or situation   All relevant information such as mission, vision, objectives, products/services offered, turnover, hierarchy, etc., of the organization are presented. In the case of industry, appropriate details are furnished. If it is a study on any situation, the frequency of occurrences, people involved, monetary implications, etc., are presented.

Need or significance of the problem   It is detailed here in what way, why or how the problem is important.

Example

> **Topic: Influence of emotional intelligence of supervisors to solve industrial dispute in garment industry.**
>
> It is generally expected that the supervisors must be intelligent and knowledgeable to get the work done at shop-floor level. Though the job is getting done, there will be always a simmering of unrest among the workers. Many a time, this leads to industrial dispute. According to Golman general intelligence alone is not adequate to maintain a good industrial relation. He insists that Emotional Intelligence is of paramount importance in personnel management. It is observed that while many garment factories in Tirupur are facing high industrial disputes, there are a few companies which are able to manage the migrant labour force without any major issues. As the research done on emotional intelligence of the supervisors in garment factories is meager, this study has been taken up to find out the relationship, if any, between the E.I. of supervisors and industrial dispute.
>
> As export is of vital importance to our economy and the industrial dispute is a major constraint in export business, this study assumes significance.

Statement of problem   In the example cited above it is mentioned that the study on E.I. of people is significant in the export industry like the garment industry in Tirupur. The general problem observed is high industrial dispute/turnover of workers. Though there are many causes for industrial disputes, this study is focused on the influence of E.I. of supervisors on workers' turnover/industrial dispute in garment industry. The study specifically tries to find out to what extent the E.I. of supervisors influences industrial disputes in garment industry.

Scope of the study   The scope covers the geographical area, targeted population, specific activities, period of study, etc. Results expected are also discussed here.

Example

In the above example, the scope of the study covers the garment companies in Tirupur. The targeted population is the supervisors who handle the migrant labour force. The activities include their method of handling the industrial disputes as well as their presence of mind (Emotional Intelligence) in preventing such disputes. The results expected are that the supervisors who handle the labour problems are endowed with higher E.I. and there is a positive relationship between E.I. and reduction in industrial disputes.

Objectives of the study   The primary objective will be more or less the topic of the study itself. The secondary objectives (4 or 5) will focus on the important components related to the primary objective.

Example

> **Primary objective**
>
> To study the relationship, if any, between emotional intelligence of supervisors and industrial disputes in the garment industry in Tirupur.
>
> **Secondary objectives**
>
> - To find out the frequency and extent of industrial disputes in the garment industry.
> - To study the E.I. of the supervisors in the factories.
> - To understand the dominant component of E.I. of the supervisors which influences the resolving of disputes.
> - To know the action taken by the management in improving the E.I. of their employees.

Hypotheses   In the case of exploratory research or case study there is no need for hypotheses but in other designs such as descriptive, diagnostic (analytical) and experimental designs, hypotheses are identified and verified with relevant statistical tools.

Example

i. *Ho*   There is no difference in industrial disputes in garment industry and that of other industries.

   Ha   There is significant difference.

ii. *Ho*   There is no difference in the E.I. of supervisors in garment industry and that of other industries.

   Ha   There is significant difference.

iii. *Ho*   There is no significant difference among the various components of E.I. of garment factory supervisors.

   Ha   There is significant difference.

iv. *Ho*   There is no relationship between E.I. of supervisors and the occurrence of industrial dispute in garment industry.

   Ha   There is a relationship.

Review of Literature

It is an account of the studies conducted by others as well as the researcher on similar or related topics. Review of the earlier reports gives an insight into the problem. The research can select or fine-tune the techniques of data collection and analysis. The errors committed by other fellow researchers may be avoided or corrected in the work. It gives an idea on the current state of knowledge in the particular field. What has been done and what are the gaps/lacunae are narrated to show how the present study is going to fill up the gap.

- It is written in chronological order, i.e., starting from the earliest possible reference to the present study.
- Invariably name(s) of the author(s) along with the year of study are mentioned.
- Only the last name(s) is (are) mentioned.
- Titles such as Dr., Prof., Mr., Ms., Shree, Shrimathi, etc. are avoided.
- In the case of more than two authors only the first author is mentioned followed by the words *et al.*
- There is no hard and fast rule on the number of references. In a novel or entirely new area, there may not be any references at all. In popular studies, reference will be plenty. The researcher should meticulously select only the relevant references depending on the area of research. An MBA project may have 20–30 references. All the studies referred to are detailed under "references". For review of literature, any accessible material such as journals. books, reports, project reports, theses, etc. may be referred to.

Research Methodology

Research design In addition to indicating the nature of research design, whether it is explorative, descriptive, diagnostic or experimental, the reason for choosing the particular design is elaborated.

Sources of data It is clearly indicated whether the data are primary or secondary in the case of secondary data, the sources of data are indicated as footnotes below the tables.

Sampling design The type of sampling technique used is mentioned and the reason for selecting a particular sampling technique is explained.

Data collection The tools or techniques (questionnaire, schedule, observation or interview) used, procedure of collection and period of data collection are described.

Data analysis The statistical tools used in analysing the data (t-test, chi-square, correlation, ANOVA or multivariate techniques) are briefly explained with relevant reference.

Limitations of the study The difficulties or problems encountered by the researcher at various stages of the research process starting from defining the problem to final conclusion are mentioned as limitations.

Examples

- As it is a novel/new line of work, available literature is almost nil.
- The respondents were reluctant to divulge the relevant information.
- The responses are mostly imaginary.
- The nature and availability of the sampling technique limited the scope of better representation of the population.
- The management did not extend support.
- The time or fund allotted is not sufficient to conduct a detailed investigation.

ANALYSIS AND INTERPRETATION/RESULT AND DISCUSSION

The summary of data and the results of the statistical analysis are presented in tables. Interpretation is made based on the raw data or the statistical analysis. Based on the interpretations, inferences are drawn for each table/sub-topic.

Summary   A brief summary containing the need for the study, the objectives, methodology of data collection and statistical analysis employed, etc. are presented.

Findings   The findings are presented as "important findings" and "other findings". The interpretations/inferences following the tables/analyses are taken as findings.

Suggestions   Relevant suggestions based on the findings are outlined taking into consideration the general theoretical background and experience/knowledge of the researcher. It must be noted that suggestions are based on the findings and the findings are related to the objectives.

Conclusion   While findings are specific to the study under reference, conclusion is a generalization based on the findings. Conclusion is the overall opinion of the researcher on the topic.

Future line of work   The researcher would have envisaged certain objectives to study in an investigation. Due to certain limitations, he would not have covered those aspects. The areas which are not considered may be included under future line of work. Further, in the course of investigation, the researcher would have come across an interesting or important phenomenon. He would not have attempted to study these new areas as they would have been beyond the scope of his/her study. These items could also be the future line of work.

REFERENCES

All the works/studies/reports referred to in the "Introduction, "Review of literature", "Methodology" and "Discussion" are mentioned under references. The references are arranged in alphabetical order of the authors. Though there could be a slight variation in writing the references, a general format is given below:

If the reference is taken from a journal the sequence is: Name or names of the authors (The last names are mentioned first, followed by middle/last names or initials), year of publication of the journal, title of the paper/article, name of the journal (in italics) volume no., issue no. (within brackets) and pages (starting and ending page).

Examples

Pareek, Udai, 1997, Partnership in HR functions, *Indian Journal of Industrial Relations,* 32(3): 345-353.

Singh, Rahul, S. and Shetty, Y.K., 1970, A comparative study of personnal management practices. *Ind. J. Social Work,* 31(2):101-104.

Yamini, U., Joseph Raj, M., and Arunraj, M., 1999, Linkages between emotional leadership and industrial disputes. *Industrial and Labour Relations Review*, 49(4):635-657.

In the case of any reference from book, the sequence is: name(s) of author(s) (last names coming first), year, title of the book (in italics), place of publication, name of the publisher and total pages of the book.

Examples

Bass, B.M., 1969, *Training in Industry*: The Management of Learning, London: Tavistock Publications, p. 249.

Blum, M.L and Nylor, J.C., 1968, *Industrial Psychology*, New York: Harper and Row, p. 180.

If it is an edited book, the name(s) of author(s) and editor(s) is (are) mentioned as given in the following example.

Ramesh, K. and Kiran, K. (1996). Potential appraisal-pitfalls. *Human Resource Development* (B.Morthy, Ed.). New Delhi: Ram Publishers. pp:105–108.

In books published by an institute but not edited, the format for giving the reference is shown in the following example.

Example

Mathew, R. (2004). Career Planning in IT Industry.

In *Opportunities in Indian IT Industries,* Orax Technology, Nasik. pp. 87–95.

For references from reports in newspapers, the following is the format.

Example

Rahul, M.“Will the budget achieve its objectives?”, *The Economic Times*, 8th of March 1998.

If the references are from a report/compilations, without any specific authors, such as a publication from an organization, Dept. or Govt., Anonymous (abbreviated as Anon) is mentioned in the place of author(s).

Anonymous, 1997, *Copyright Act of India*, Ministry of Law, Govt. of India, New Delhi, pp. 22–28.

Website references are preferably avoided. Only the details are mentioned with an asterisk mark indicating that original is not seen.

References from project report/dissertation/thesis:

Thamayanthi, Y., 2009, *Influence of liberalization policy of the Govt. on the small scale industry in Tamil Nadu*, Ph.D thesis/M.Phil Thesis/MBA project submitted to the School of Management Studies, Anna University of Technology, Coimbatore. p. 472.

BIBLIOGRAPHY

Some researchers do not differentiate bibliography from references. But in fact "references" is different from "bibliography". While references are the works/reports specific to the study and referred to in the body of the report, bibliography is the list of books, journals, reports, etc. which the researcher has gone through to understand the concept, theory, methodology, etc., before starting the research work. They do not find a place in the body of the report. The materials mentioned in the bibliography would have helped the researcher to have more knowledge on the topic or to write the report.

APPENDICES

The materials/information which are closely related or essential to the study but could not be incorporated in the body of the report would appear as appendices as Appendix A, Appendix B, etc. The materials which are usually put in the appendices are original data, long tables, long quotations, supportive laws/Acts, illustrations, extensive computations, questionnaires/schedules/forms used in collecting data, transcripts of interviews, etc.

ANNEXURES

Materials which are not essential but help in appreciating the report such as copies of advertisement materials, product details, list of sister concerns, location map, publications, etc. may be included as annexures. They are arranged as Annexure I, Annexure II, etc.

PAGE NUMBERING

- Prefatory pages are not page-numbered.
- Body of the report is page-numbered in Arabic numerals (1,2,3,...)

- The terminal items are page-numbered in lower-case Roman numerals (i, ii, iii,…)
- The page where a chapter starts is not numbered though it is included in counting the number of pages.

RECAP OF SALIENT POINTS IN EXECUTING A RESEARCH PROJECT

- There must be a research problem and it is spelt out in clear terms.
- The title of the project will indicate the primary objective.
- The various dimensions of the project form the secondary objectives.
- The questionnaire/schedule is divided into many sub-titles as the number of secondary objectives (apart from the introductory part to collect information about the respondents).
- The answers to the questions/statements in the sub-titles will answer the secondary objectives.
- A combination of all the answers in the questionnaire by the respondents will answer the primary objective.
- The findings should answer the objectives, and the suggestions are based on the findings. The sequence is objectives–findings–suggestions.

PRESENTATION OF RESEARCH REPORT

- Adequate care is taken to see that there are no spelling or grammatical errors.
- The report is given in a logical sequence as explained elsewhere.
- The way the research report is presented should enhance its readability.
- It must be comprehensive, i.e., it should not omit any important aspects.
- The tone, i.e., the language used must not hurt any section of the society. Even the unpleasant findings must be presented diplomatically. Harsh language should never be used.
- Final proof of the report must be read again and again to avoid any errors.
- The title of the report must be able to convey what the report is all about.

REVIEW QUESTIONS

1. What is the need for interpretation?
2. What are the techniques of interpretation?
3. What are the precautions observed in interpretation?
4. What is report writing?
5. What are the functions or purpose of research report?
6. Discuss the characteristics of a good report.
7. What are the various types of research?
8. Discuss the layout/format of a research report.
9. What does the table of contents in a research report contain?

APPENDIX I

AREAS OF STANDARD NORMAL DISTRIBUTION

	0.00	0.01	0.02	0.03	0.04	0.05	0.06	0.07	0.08	0.09
0.0	0.0000	0.0040	0.0080	0.0120	0.0160	0.0199	0.0239	0.0279	0.0319	0.0359
0.1	0.0398	0.0438	0.0478	0.0517	0.0557	0.0596	0.0636	0.0675	0.0714	0.0753
0.2	0.0793	0.0832	0.0871	0.0910	0.0948	0.0987	0.1026	0.1064	0.1103	0.1141
0.3	0.1179	0.1217	0.1255	0.1293	0.1331	0.1368	0.1406	0.1443	0.1480	0.1517
0.4	0.1554	0.1591	0.1628	0.1664	0.1700	0.1736	0.1772	0.1808	0.1844	0.1879
0.5	0.1915	0.1950	0.1985	0.2019	0.2054	0.2088	0.2123	0.2157	0.2190	0.2224
0.6	0.2257	0.2291	0.2324	0.2357	0.2389	0.2422	0.2454	0.2486	0.2517	0.2549
0.7	0.2580	0.2611	0.2642	0.2673	0.2704	0.2734	0.2764	0.2794	0.2823	0.2852
0.8	0.2881	0.2910	0.2939	0.2967	0.2995	0.3023	0.3051	0.3078	0.3106	0.3133
0.9	0.3159	0.3186	0.3212	0.3238	0.3264	0.3289	0.3315	0.3340	0.3365	0.3389
1.0	0.3413	0.3438	0.3461	0.3485	0.3508	0.3531	03554	0.3577	0.3599	0.3621
1.1	0.3643	0.3665	0.3686	0.3708	0.3729	0.3749	0.3770	0.3790	0.3810	0.3830
1.2	0.3849	0.3869	0.3888	0.3907	0.3925	0.3944	0.3962	0.3980	0.3997	0.4015
1.3	0.4032	0.4049	0.4066	0.4082	0.4099	0.4115	0.4131	0.4147	0.4162	0.4177
1.4	0.4192	0.4207	0.4222	0.4236	0.4251	0.4265	0.4279	0.4292	0.4306	0.4319
1.5	0.4332	0.4345	0.4357	0.4370	0.4382	0.4394	0.4406	0.4418	0.4429	0.4441
1.6	0.4452	0.4463	0.4474	0.4484	0.4495	0.4505	0.4515	0.4525	0.4535	0.4545
1.7	0.4554	0.4564	0.4573	0.4582	0.4591	0.4599	0.4608	0.4616	0.4625	0.4633
1.8	0.4641	0.4649	0.4656	0.4664	0.4671	0.4678	0.4686	0.4693	0.4699	0.4706
1.9	0.4713	0.4719	0.4726	0.4732	0.4738	0.4744	0.4750	0.4756	0.4761	0.4767
2.0	0.4772	0.4778	0.4783	0.4788	0.4793	0.4798	0.4803	0.4808	0.4812	0.4817
2.1	0.4821	0.4826	0.4830	0.4834	0.4838	0.4842	0.4846	0.4850	0.4854	0.4857
2.2	0.4861	0.4864	0.4868	0.4871	0.4875	0.4878	0.4881	0.4884	0.4887	0.4890
2.3	0.4893	0.4896	0.4898	0.4901	0.4904	0.4906	0.4909	0.4911	0.4913	0.4916
2.4	0.4918	0.4920	0.4922	0.4925	0.4927	0.4929	0.4931	0.4932	0.4934	0.4936
2.5	0.4938	0.4940	0.4941	0.4943	0.4945	0.4946	0.4948	0.4949	0.4951	0.4952
2.6	0.4953	0.4955	0.4956	0.4957	0.4959	0.4960	0.4961	0.4962	0.4963	0.4964
2.7	0.4965	0.4966	0.4967	0.4968	0.4969	0.4970	0.4971	0.4972	0.4973	0.4974
2.8	0.4974	0.4975	0.4976	0.4977	0.4977	0.4978	0.4979	0.4979	0.4980	0.4981
2.9	0.4981	0.4982	0.4982	0.4983	0.4984	0.4984	0.4985	0.4985	0.4986	0.4986
3.0	0.4987	0.4987	0.4987	0.4988	0.4988	0.4989	0.4989	0.4989	0.4990	0.4990

CRITICAL VALUES OF *t* FOR GIVEN PROBABILITY LEVELS

Levels of significance for one-tailed test					
df	0.10	0.50	0.025	0.01	0.005	0.001
Levels of significance for one-tailed test					
df	0.20	0.10	0.05	0.02	0.01	0.002
1.	3.078	6.314	12.706	31.821	63.657	318.313
2.	1.886	2.920	4.303	6.965	9.925	22.327
3.	1.638	2.353	3.182	4.541	5.841	10.215
4.	1.533	2.132	2.776	3.747	4.604	7.173
5.	1.476	2.015	2.571	3.365	4.032	5.893
6.	1.440	1.943	2.447	3.143	3.707	5.208
7.	1.415	1.895	2.365	2.998	3.499	4.782
8.	1.397	1.860	2.306	2.896	3.355	4.499
9.	1.383	1.833	2.262	2.821	3.250	4.296
10.	1.372	1.812	2.228	2.764	3.169	4.143
11.	1.363	1.796	2.201	2.718	3.106	4.024
12.	1.356	1.782	2.179	2.681	3.055	3.929
13.	1.350	1.771	2.160	2.650	3.012	3.852
14.	1.345	1.761	2.145	2.624	2.977	3.787
15.	1.341	1.753	2.131	2.602	2.947	3.733
16.	1.337	1.746	2.120	2.583	2.921	3.686
17.	1.333	1.740	2.110	2.567	2.898	3.646
18.	1.330	1.734	2.101	2.552	2.878	3.610
19.	1.328	1.729	2.093	2.539	2.861	3.579
20.	1.325	1.725	2.086	2.528	2.845	3.552
21.	1.323	1.721	2.080	2.518	2.831	3.527
22.	1.321	1.717	2.074	2.508	2.819	3.505
23.	1.319	1.714	2.069	2.500	2.807	3.485
24.	1.318	1.711	2.064	2.492	2.797	3.467
25.	1.316	1.708	2.060	2.485	2.787	3.450
26.	1.315	1.706	2.056	2.479	2.779	3.435
27.	1.314	1.703	2.052	2.473	2.771	3.421
28.	1.313	1.701	2.048	2.467	2.763	3.408
29.	1.311	1.699	2.045	2.462	2.756	3.396
30.	1.310	1.697	2.042	2.457	2.750	3.385
31.	1.309	1.696	2.040	2.453	2.744	3.375
32.	1.309	1.694	2.037	2.449	2.738	3.365

(Contd.)

Levels of significance for one-tailed test						
df	0.10	0.50	0.025	0.01	0.005	0.001
Levels of significance for one-tailed test						
df	0.20	0.10	0.05	0.02	0.01	0.002
33.	1.308	1.692	2.035	2.445	2.733	3.356
34.	1.307	1.691	2.032	2.441	2.728	3.348
35.	1.306	1.690	2.030	2.438	2.724	3.340
36.	1.306	1.688	2.028	2.434	2.719	3.333
37.	1.305	1.687	2.026	2.431	2.715	3.326
38.	1.304	1.686	2.024	2.429	2.712	3.319
39.	1.304	1.685	2.023	2.426	2.708	3.313
40.	1.303	1.684	2.021	2.423	2.704	3.307
41.	1.303	1.683	2.020	2.421	2.701	3.301
42.	1.302	1.682	2.018	2.418	2.698	3.296
43.	1.302	1.681	2.017	2.416	2.695	3.291
44.	1.301	1.680	2.015	2.414	2.692	3.286
45.	1.301	1.679	2.014	2.412	2.690	3.281
46.	1.300	1.679	2.013	2.410	2.687	3.277
47.	1.300	1.678	2.012	2.408	2.685	3.273
48.	1.299	1.677	2.011	2.407	2.682	3.269
49.	1.299	1.677	2.010	2.405	2.680	3.265
50.	1.299	1.676	2.009	2.403	2.678	3.261
51.	1.298	1.675	2.008	2.402	2.676	3.258
52.	1.298	1.675	2.007	2.400	2.674	3.255
53.	1.298	1.674	2.006	2.399	2.672	3.251
54.	1.297	1.674	2.005	2.397	2.670	3.248
55.	1.297	1.673	2.004	2.396	2.668	3.245
56.	1.297	1.673	2.003	2.395	2.667	3.242
57.	1.297	1.672	2.002	2.394	2.665	3.239
58.	1.296	1.672	2.002	2.392	2.663	3.237
59.	1.296	1.671	2.001	2.391	2.662	3.234
60.	1.296	1.671	2.000	2.390	2.660	3.232
61.	1.296	1.670	2.000	2.389	2.659	3.229
62.	1.295	1.670	1.999	2.388	2.657	3.227
63.	1.295	1.669	1.998	2.387	2.656	3.225
64.	1.295	1.669	1.998	2.386	2.655	3.223
65.	1.295	1.669	1.997	2.385	2.654	3.220
66.	1.295	1.668	1.997	2.384	2.652	3.218

(Contd.)

Levels of significance for one-tailed test					
df	0.10	0.50	0.025	0.01	0.005	0.001

Levels of significance for one-tailed test					
df	0.20	0.10	0.05	0.02	0.01	0.002
67.	1.294	1.668	1.996	2.383	2.651	3.216
68.	1.294	1.668	1.995	2.382	2.650	3.214
69.	1.294	1.667	1.995	2.382	2.649	3.213
70.	1.294	1.667	1.994	2.381	2.648	3.211
71.	1.294	1.667	1.994	2.380	2.647	3.209
72.	1.293	1.666	1.993	2.379	2.646	3.207
73.	1.293	1.666	1.993	2.379	2.645	3.206
74.	1.293	1.666	1.993	2.378	2.644	3.204
75.	1.293	1.665	1.992	2.377	2.643	3.202
76.	1.293	1.665	1.992	2.376	2.642	3.201
77.	1.293	1.665	1.991	2.376	2.641	3.199
78.	1.292	1.665	1.991	2.375	2.640	3.198
79.	1.292	1.664	1.990	2.374	2.640	3.197
80.	1.292	1.664	1.990	2.374	2.639	3.195
81.	1.292	1.664	1.990	2.373	2.638	3.194
82.	1.292	1.664	1.989	2.373	2.637	3.193
83.	1.292	1.663	1.989	2.372	2.636	3.191
84.	1.292	1.663	1.989	2.372	2.636	3.190
85.	1.292	1.663	1.988	2.371	2.635	3.189
86.	1.291	1.663	1.988	2.370	2.634	3.188
87.	1.291	1.663	1.988	2.370	2.634	3.187
88.	1.291	1.662	1.987	2.369	2.633	3.185
89.	1.291	1.662	1.987	2.369	2.632	3.184
90.	1.291	1.662	1.987	2.368	2.632	3.183
91.	1.291	1.662	1.986	2.368	2.631	3.182
92.	1.291	1.662	1.986	2.368	2.630	3.181
93.	1.291	1.661	1.986	2.367	2.630	3.180
94.	1.291	1.661	1.986	2.367	2.629	3.179
95.	1.291	1.661	1.985	2.366	2.629	3.178
96.	1.290	1.661	1.985	2.366	2.628	3.177
97.	1.290	1.661	1.985	2.365	2.627	3.176
98.	1.290	1.661	1.984	2.365	2.627	3.175
99.	1.290	1.660	1.984	2.365	2.626	3.175
100.	1.290	1.660	1.984	2.364	2.626	3.174
∞	1.282	1.645	1.960	2.326	2.576	3.090

CRITICAL VALUES OF THE CHI-SQUARE DISTRIBUTION

df	0.10	0.05	0.025	0.01	0.001
1.	2.706	3.841	5.024	6.635	10.828
2.	4.605	5.991	7.378	9.210	13.816
3.	6.251	7.815	9.348	11.345	16.266
4.	7.779	9.488	11.143	13.277	18.467
5.	9.236	11.070	12.833	15.086	20.515
6.	10.645	12.592	14.449	16.812	22.458
7.	12.017	14.067	16.013	18.475	24.322
8.	13.362	15.507	17.535	20.090	26.125
9.	14.684	16.919	19.023	21.666	27.877
10.	15.987	18.307	20.483	23.209	29.588
11.	17.275	19.675	21.920	24.725	31.264
12.	18.549	21.026	23.337	26.217	32.910
13.	19.812	22.362	24.736	27.688	34.528
14.	21.064	23.685	26.119	29.141	36.123
15.	22.307	24.996	27.488	30.578	37.697
16.	23.542	26.296	28.845	32.000	39.252
17.	24.769	27.587	30.191	33.409	40.790
18.	25.989	28.869	31.526	34.805	42.312
19.	27.204	30.144	32.852	36.191	43.820
20.	28.412	31.410	34.170	37.566	45.315
21.	29.615	32.671	35.479	38.932	46.797
22.	30.813	33.924	36.781	40.289	48.268
23.	32.007	35.172	38.076	41.638	49.728
24.	33.196	36.415	39.364	42.980	51.179
25.	34.382	37.652	40.646	44.314	52.620
26.	35.563	38.885	41.923	45.642	54.052
27.	36.741	40.113	43.195	46.963	55.476
28.	37.916	41.337	44.461	48.278	56.892
29.	39.087	42.557	45.722	49.588	58.301
30.	40.256	43.773	46.979	50.892	59.703
31.	41.422	44.985	48.232	52.191	61.098

(Contd.)

df	0.10	0.05	0.025	0.01	0.001
32.	42.585	46.194	49.480	53.486	62.487
33.	43.745	47.400	50.725	54.776	63.870
34.	44.903	48.602	51.966	56.061	65.247
35.	46.059	49.802	53.203	57.342	66.619
36.	47.212	50.998	54.437	58.619	67.985
37.	48.363	52.192	55.668	59.893	69.347
38.	49.513	53.384	56.896	61.162	70.703
39.	50.660	54.572	58.120	62.428	72.055
40.	51.805	55.758	59.342	63.691	73.402
41.	52.949	56.942	60.561	64.950	74.745
42.	54.090	58.124	61.777	66.206	76.084
43.	55.230	59.304	62.990	67.459	77.419
44.	56.369	60.481	64.201	68.710	78.750
45.	57.505	61.656	65.410	69.957	80.077
46.	58.641	62.830	66.617	71.201	81.400
47.	59.774	64.001	67.821	72.443	82.720
48.	60.907	65.171	69.023	73.683	84.037
49.	62.038	66.339	70.222	74.919	85.351
50.	63.167	67.505	71.420	76.154	86.661
51.	64.295	68.669	72.616	77.386	87.968
52.	65.422	69.832	73.810	78.616	89.272
53.	66.548	70.993	75.002	79.843	90.573
54.	67.673	72.153	76.192	81.069	91.872
55.	68.796	73.311	77.380	82.292	93.168
56.	69.919	74.468	78.567	83.513	94.461
57.	71.040	75.624	79.752	84.733	95.751
58.	72.160	76.778	80.936	85.950	97.039
59.	73.279	77.931	82.117	87.166	98.324
60.	74.397	79.082	83.298	88.379	99.607
61.	75.514	80.232	84.476	89.591	100.888
62.	76.630	81.381	85.654	90.802	102.166
63.	77.745	82.529	86.830	92.010	103.442
64.	78.860	83.675	88.004	93.217	104.716
65.	79.973	84.821	89.177	94.422	105.988
66.	81.085	85.965	90.349	95.626	107.258

(Contd.)

df	0.10	0.05	0.025	0.01	0.001
67.	82.197	87.108	91.519	96.828	108.526
68.	83.308	88.250	92.689	98.028	109.791
69.	84.418	89.391	93.856	99.228	111.055
70.	85.527	90.531	95.023	100.425	112.317
71.	86.635	91.670	96.189	101.621	113.577
72.	87.743	92.808	97.353	102.816	114.835
73.	88.850	93.945	98.516	104.010	116.092
74.	89.956	95.081	99.678	105.202	117.346
75.	91.061	96.217	100.839	106.393	118.599
76.	92.166	97.351	101.999	107.583	119.850
77.	93.270	98.484	103.158	108.771	121.100
78.	94.374	99.617	104.316	109.958	122.348
79.	95.476	100.749	105.473	111.144	123.594
80.	96.578	101.879	106.629	112.329	124.839
81.	97.680	103.010	107.783	113.512	126.083
82.	98.780	104.139	108.937	114.695	127.324
83.	99.880	105.267	110.090	115.876	128.565
84.	100.980	106.395	111.242	117.057	129.804
85.	102.079	107.522	112.393	118.236	131.041
86.	103.177	108.648	113.544	119.414	132.277
87.	104.275	109.773	114.693	120.591	133.512
88.	105.372	110.898	115.841	121.767	134.746
89.	106.469	112.022	116.989	122.942	135.978
90.	107.565	113.145	118.136	124.116	137.208
91.	108.661	114.268	119.282	125.289	138.438
92.	109.756	115.390	120.427	126.462	139.666
93.	110.850	116.511	121.571	127.633	140.893
94.	111.944	117.632	122.715	128.803	142.119
95.	113.038	118.752	123.858	129.973	143.344
96.	114.131	119.871	125.000	131.141	144.567
97.	115.223	120.990	126.141	132.309	145.789
98.	116.315	122.108	127.282	133.476	147.010
99.	117.407	123.225	128.422	134.642	148.230
100.	118.498	124.342	129.561	135.807	149.449

VALUES OF *F* (VARIANCE RATIO) 1 PER CENT POINTS

v_1/v_2	1	2	3	4	5	6	8	12	24	INF
1	161.44	199.50	215.70	224.58	230.16	233.98	238.88	243.90	249.05	254.3144
2	18.512	19.000	19.164	19.246	19.396	19.329	19.371	19.412	19.454	19.4957
3	10.128	9.5521	9.2766	9.1172	9.0135	8.9406	8.8452	8.7446	8.6385	8.5264
4	7.7086	6.9443	6.5914	6.3882	6.2561	6.1631	6.0410	5.9117	5.7744	5.6281
5	6.6079	5.7861	5.4095	5.1922	5.0503	4.9503	4.8183	4.6777	4.5272	4.3650
6	5.9874	5.1433	4.7571	4.5337	4.3874	4.2839	4.1468	3.9999	3.8415	3.6689
7	5.5914	4.7374	4.3468	4.1203	3.9715	3.8660	3.7257	3.5747	3.4105	3.2298
8	5.3177	4.4590	4.0662	3.8379	3.6875	3.5806	3.4381	3.2839	3.1152	2.9276
9	5.1174	4.2565	3.8625	3.6331	3.4817	3.3738	3.2296	3.0729	2.9005	2.7067
10	4.9646	4.1028	3.7083	3.4780	3.3258	3.2172	3.0717	2.9130	2.7372	2.5379
11	4.8443	3.9823	3.5874	3.3567	3.2039	3.0946	2.9480	2.7876	2.6090	2.4045
12	4.7472	3.8853	3.4903	3.2592	3.1059	2.9961	2.8486	2.6866	2.5055	2.2962
13	4.6672	3.8056	3.4105	3.1791	3.0254	2.9153	2.7669	2.6037	2.4202	2.2064
14	4.6001	3.7389	3.3439	3.1122	2.9582	2.8477	2.6987	2.5342	2.3487	2.1307
15	4.5431	3.6823	3.2874	3.0556	2.9013	2.7905	2.6408	2.4753	2.2878	2.0658
16	4.4940	3.6337	3.2389	3.0069	2.8524	2.7413	2.5911	2.4247	2.2354	2.0096
17	4.4513	3.5915	3.1968	2.9647	2.8100	2.6987	2.5480	2.3807	2.1898	1.9604
18	4.4139	3.5546	3.1599	2.9277	2.7729	2.6613	2.5102	2.3421	2.1497	1.9168
19	4.3807	3.5219	3.1274	2.8951	2.7401	2.6283	2.4768	2.3080	2.1141	1.8780
20	4.3512	3.4928	3.0984	2.8661	2.7109	2.5990	2.4471	2.2776	2.0825	1.8432
21	4.3248	3.4668	3.0725	2.8401	2.6848	2.5727	2.4205	2.2504	2.0504	1.8117
22	4.3009	3.4434	3.0491	2.8167	2.6613	2.5491	2.3965	2.2258	2.0283	1.7831
23	4.2793	3.4221	3.0280	2.7955	2.6400	2.5277	2.3748	2.2036	2.0050	1.7570
24	4.2597	3.4028	3.0088	2.7763	2.6207	2.5082	2.3551	2.1834	1.9838	1.7330
25	4.2417	3.3852	2.9912	2.7587	2.6030	2.4904	2.3371	2.1649	1.9643	1.7110
26	4.2252	3.3690	2.9752	2.7426	2.5868	2.4741	2.3205	2.1479	1.9464	1.6907
27	4.2100	3.3541	2.9604	2.7278	2.5719	2.4591	2.3053	2.1323	1.9299	1.6717
28	4.1960	3.3404	2.9467	2.7141	2.5581	2.4453	2.2913	2.1179	1.9147	1.6541
29	4.1830	3.3277	2.9340	2.7014	2.5454	2.4324	2.2783	2.1045	1.9005	1.6376
30	4.1709	3.3158	2.9223	2.6896	2.5336	2.4205	2.2662	2.0921	1.8874	1.6223
40	4.0847	3.2317	2.8387	2.6060	2.4495	2.3359	2.1802	2.0035	1.7929	1.5089
60	4.0012	3.1504	2.7581	2.5252	2.3683	2.2541	2.0970	1.9174	1.7001	1.3893
120	3.9201	3.0718	2.6802	2.4472	2.2899	2.1750	2.0164	1.8337	1.6084	1.2539
Inf	3.8415	2.9957	2.6049	2.2141	2.0986	2.0096	1.94	1.75	1.52	1.00

VALUES OF *F* (VARIANCE RATIO) 1 PER CENT POINTS

v_1/v_2	1	2	3	4	5	6	8	12	24	INF
1	4052.1	4999.5	5403.3	5624.5	5763.6	5858.9	5981.0	6106.3	6234.6	6365.8
2	98.503	99.000	99.166	99.249	99.299	99.333	99.347	99.416	99.458	99.499
3	34.116	30.817	29.457	28.710	28.237	27.911	27.489	27.052	26.598	26.125
4	21.198	18.000	16.694	15.977	15.522	15.207	14.799	14.374	13.929	13.463
5	16.258	13.274	12.060	11.392	10.967	10.672	10.289	9.888	9.466	9.020
6	13.745	10.925	9.780	9.148	8.746	8.466	8.102	7.718	7.313	6.880
7	12.246	9.547	8.451	7.847	7.460	7.191	6.840	6.469	6.074	5.650
8	11.259	8.649	7.591	7.006	6.632	6.371	6.029	5.667	5.279	4.859
9	10.561	8.022	6.992	6.422	6.057	5.802	5.467	5.111	4.729	4.311
10	10.044	7.559	6.552	5.994	5.636	5.386	5.057	4.706	4.327	3.909
11	9.646	7.206	6.217	5.668	5.316	5.069	4.744	4.397	4.021	3.602
12	9.330	6.927	5.953	5.412	5.064	4.821	4.499	4.155	3.780	3.361
13	9.074	6.701	5.739	5.205	4.862	4.620	4.302	3.960	3.587	3.165
14	8.862	6.515	5.564	5.035	4.695	4.456	4.140	3.800	3.427	3.004
15	8.683	6.359	5.417	4.893	4.556	4.318	4.004	3.666	3.294	2.868
16	8.531	6.226	5.292	4.773	4.437	4.202	3.890	3.553	3.181	2.753
17	8.400	6.221	5.185	4.669	4.336	4.102	3.791	3.455	3.084	2.653
18	8.285	6.013	5.092	4.579	4.248	4.015	3.705	3.371	2.999	2.566
19	8.185	5.926	5.010	4.500	4.171	3.939	3.631	3.297	2.925	2.489
20	8.096	5.849	4.938	4.431	4.103	3.871	3.564	3.231	2.859	2.421
21	8.017	5.780	4.874	4.369	4.042	3.812	3.506	3.173	2.801	2.360
22	7.945	5.719	4.817	4.313	3.988	3.758	3.453	3.121	2.749	2.305
23	7.881	5.664	4.765	4.264	3.939	3.710	3.406	3.074	2.702	2.256
24	7.823	5.614	4.718	4.218	3.895	3.667	3.363	3.032	2.659	2.211
25	7.770	5.568	4.675	4.177	3.855	3.627	3.324	2.993	2.620	2.169
26	7.721	5.526	4.637	4.140	3.818	3.591	3.288	2.958	2.585	2.131
27	7.677	5.488	4.601	4.106	3.785	3.558	3.256	2.926	2.552	2.097
28	7.636	5.453	4.568	4.074	3.754	3.528	3.226	2.896	2.522	2.064
29	7.598	5.420	4.538	4.045	3.725	3.499	3.198	2.868	2.495	2.034
30	7.562	5.390	4.510	4.018	3.699	3.473	3.173	2.843	2.469	2.006
40	7.314	5.179	4.313	3.828	3.514	3.291	2.993	2.665	2.280	1.805
60	7.077	4.977	4.126	3.649	3.339	3.119	2.823	2.496	2.115	1.601
120	6.851	4.787	3.949	3.480	3.174	2.956	2.663	2.336	1.950	1.381
Inf	6.635	4.605	3.782	3.319	3.017	2.802	2.511	2.185	1.791	1.000

CRITICAL VALUES FOR THE MANN–WHITNEY U-TEST

LEVEL OF SIGNIFICANCE: 5% ($P = 0.05$)

Size of the smallest sample (n_1) — rows; Size of the largest sample (n_2) — columns.

n_1 \ n_2	5	6	7	8	9	10	11	12	13	14	15	16	17	18	19	20	21	22	23	24	25	26	27	28	29	30
3	0	1	1	2	2	3	3	4	4	5	5	6	6	7	7	8	8	9	9	10	10	11	11	12	13	13
4	1	2	3	4	4	5	6	7	8	9	10	11	11	12	13	14	15	16	17	17	18	19	20	21	22	23
5	2	3	5	6	7	8	9	11	12	13	14	15	17	18	19	20	22	23	24	25	27	28	29	30	32	33
6		5	6	8	10	11	13	14	16	17	19	21	22	24	25	27	29	30	32	33	35	37	38	40	42	43
7			8	10	12	14	16	18	20	22	24	26	28	30	32	34	36	38	40	42	44	46	48	50	52	54
8				13	15	17	19	22	24	26	29	31	34	36	38	41	43	45	48	50	53	55	57	60	62	65
9					17	20	23	26	28	31	34	37	39	42	45	48	50	53	56	59	62	64	67	70	73	76
10						23	26	29	33	36	39	42	45	48	52	55	58	61	64	67	71	74	77	80	83	87
11							30	33	37	40	44	47	51	55	58	62	65	69	73	76	80	83	87	90	94	98
12								37	41	45	49	53	57	61	65	69	73	77	81	85	89	93	97	101	105	109
13									45	50	54	59	63	67	72	76	80	85	89	94	98	102	107	111	116	120
14										55	59	64	67	74	78	83	88	93	98	102	107	112	118	122	127	131
15											64	70	75	80	85	90	96	101	106	111	117	122	125	132	138	143
16												75	81	86	92	98	103	109	115	120	126	132	138	143	149	154
17													87	93	99	105	111	117	123	129	135	141	147	154	160	166
18														99	106	112	119	125	132	138	145	151	158	164	171	177
19															113	119	126	133	140	147	154	161	168	175	182	189
20																127	134	141	149	156	163	171	178	186	193	200
21																	142	150	157	165	173	181	188	196	204	212
22																		158	166	174	182	191	199	207	215	223
23																			175	183	192	200	209	218	226	235
24																				192	201	210	219	228	238	247
25																					211	220	230	239	249	258
26																						230	240	250	260	270
27																							250	261	271	282
28																								272	282	293
29																									294	305
30																										317

APPENDIX II

ORGANISATIONAL CLIMATE IN THE
RESEARCH DEPARTMENT OF COFFEE BOARD

QUESTIONNAIRE

1. Personal information   :

    1.1   Designation   :

    1.2   Gender and Age   :

    1.3   Qualification   :

    1.4   No. of years of service   :

    1.5   Marital status   :

    1.6   If married, no. of children   :

    1.7   No. of school-going sons/daughters   :

    1.8   No. of college-going sons/daughters   :

    1.9   Is your spouse employed   :

    1.10 Occupation and educational background of parent(s) :

    1.11 Annual income of self and family   :

2. Attitude analysis

Several statements are given below describing the organizational climate of the Research Department of the Board. You are requested to assess each statement using a 4-point scale. You may indicate your rating by encircling the appropriate number.

1 = not at all true   3 = sometimes true

2 = rarely true   4 = mostly true

2.1 Management's approach

2.1.1 The management believes that human resources are extremely important and bestows more emphasison employees' development.   1 2 3 4

2.1.2 The management goes out of the way to make sure that the employees enjoy their work.   1 2 3 4

2.1.3 The management makes efforts to identify and utilize the potential of the employees.   1 2 3 4

2.1.4 The personnel policies of the management facilitate self-improvement and career development of the employees.   1 2 3 4

2.1.5 The capabilities of various categories of the employee are fully utilized by the management.   1 2 3 4

2.1.6 Changes in the policies and programmes are communicated to the concerned before implementation.   1 2 3 4

2.1.7 The management's future plans are made known to all to enable them prepare for the future.   1 2 3 4

2.1.8 The management makes conscientious attempts to consider the views of the employees concerned.   1 2 3 4

2.2 Senior officers' attitude

2.2.1 The senior officers give a good hearing to the ideas of the juniors and invite suggestions.   1 2 3 4

2.2.2 Projects/targets are assigned in consultation with juniors.   1 2 3 4

2.2.3 Seniors sincerely guide their juniors and prepare them for future responsibilities.   1 2 3 4

2.2.4 The subordinates lacking competence are helped by the senior officers and not left unattended.   1 2 3 4

2.2.5 Mistakes by subordinates are not taken seriously and their weaknesses are communicated in a gentle manner.   1 2 3 4

2.2.6 The seniors appreciate juniors who do good work and take special care for their improvement.   1 2 3 4

2.2.7 Developmental opportunities are pointed out to the juniors by the seniors and suitable advice is made.   1 2 3 4

2.2.8 The senior officers try to help their subordinates to solve their day-today problems.   1 2 3 4

2.3 Employees' inter-relationships

2.3.1 The various categories of employees trust each other.   1 2 3 4

2.3.2 The employees are helpful to each other and work with team spirit.   1 2 3 4

2.3.3 The employees enjoy good communication and are aware of the activities of other sections/divisions/regions.   1 2 3 4

			1	2	3	4

2.3.4 Information is passed among the employees without deliberate distortion   1   2   3   4

2.3.5 Professional jealousies do not hinder the performance of duties   1   2   3   4

2.4 Performance appraisal/Reward system

2.4.1 Performance appraisal is based on objective assessment and not based on personal favouritism.   1   2   3   4

2.4.2 Suitable mechanisms are available for rewarding meaningful contributions.   1   2   3   4

2.4.3 Promotional decisions are based on merit, qualification, experience, etc. rather then personal prejudice.   1   2   3   4

2.4.4. No anomalies exist in rewarding with promotion/better place of working.   1   2   3   4

2.4.5 The reporting officers frankly discuss with the subordinates before assessing their performance.   1   2   3   4

2.4.6 The reporting officers help the subordinates to develop through performance appraisal.   1   2   3   4

2.4.7 The existing performance appraisal system is appropriate and helps employees' development.   1   2   3   4

2.5 Training programme

2.5.1 Training needs of all the cadres are assessed periodically.   1   2   3   4

2.5.2 Employees are sponsored for training programmes, internal and external, based on actual needs.   1   2   3   4

2.5.3 In the training programme, the employees take genuine interest and try to learn.   1   2   3   4

2.5.4 After training, the employees are given opportunities to try out what they have learnt.   1   2   3   4

2.6 Working environment

2.6.1 Psychological climate in the dept. is conducive for productive/creative work.   1   2   3   4

2.6.2 There are ample chances to develop oneself by acquiring new skill/knowledge.   1   2   3   4

2.6.3 Employees are encouraged to try new ideas instead of following the already tested ones.   1   2   3   4

2.6.4 Targets/projects are well-defined and instructions/directions are unambiguous.   1   2   3   4

2.6.5 Employees are adequately delegated with authority to take decisions to solve their day-to-day problems.   1   2   3   4

2.6.6 Nature of work is so simple that it is not at all difficult to put in logical sequence.   1   2   3   4

2.6.7	Employees are free to discuss with each other any problem they face.	1	2	3	4
2.6.8	Discussion in the departmental meetings are free and open.	1	2	3	4
2.6.9	Materials/tools/know-how are easily available for work execution.	1	2	3	4
2.6.10	There is no paucity of funds and no worthwhile project is held up for want of funds.	1	2	3	4
2.6.11	Employees' grievances are handled properly and humanely.	1	2	3	4
2.6.12	Promotional avenues are encouraging compared to that of other similar organizations.	1	2	3	4
2.6.13	Delegation of authority to encourage juniors to develop their capacities to handle higher responsibilities is common.	1	2	3	4
2.6.14	Pay scales and other prequisites are quite adequate compared to that of other similar organizations.	1	2	3	4
2.6.15	Employees are given equal and adequate opportunities to participate in seminars/workshops/conferences held outside.	1	2	3	4
2.6.16	As the living conditions in all the working places are quite encouraging in respect of social contacts, children's education, etc. employees are happy to work.	1	2	3	4
2.6.17	Most of the employees feel that this organization is better than any other similar organizations.	1	2	3	4
2.6.18	Employees are reluctant to leave the department if similar positions are offered outside.	1	2	3	4

A STUDY ON DEALERS' SATISFACTION WITH RESPECT TO ABC COMPANY (MANUFACTURING WHITE GOODS)

PART–I   DETAILS OF DEALERS

1. Type of dealership
   (a) Exclusive dealership for ABC & Co.,
   (b) Multicompany dealership
2. Dealership in
   i.   TV/DVD/Home Theatre
   ii.   Refrigerator/washing machine/micro-oven/grinder/mixie
   iii. All the above white goods.
3. Area of operations: Metropolitan city/II tier city/Big town/Village

4. Location
   - (a) Commercial area
   - (b) Main road
   - (c) Shop–in–shop (in mall)

5. Annual turnover
   - (a) < ₹10 lakhs
   - (b) ₹11 lakhs – ₹20 lakhs
   - (c) > ₹20 lakhs

6. Size of establishment
   - (a) Small
   - (b) Medium
   - (c) Large

7. Total experience
   - (a) <5 years
   - (b) 6 to 10 years
   - (c) >10 years

8. Experience with ABC & Co.:
   - (a) <5 years
   - (b) 6 to 10 years
   - (c) >10 years

9. Dealer's expertise:
   - (a) Technically qualified and well-versed.
   - (b) Technically qualified but not well-versed
   - (c) Non-technical and well-versed.
   - (d) Non-technical and not well-versed

10. Gender
   - (a) Male
   - (b) Female

Part–II   Opinion of dealer on ABC Company
[Please tick (✓) Your Opinion]

A. Credit Facilities

1.	Credit given is adequate	Always	Sometimes	Rarely
2.	Procedure for extending credit	Easy	Not so easy	Difficult

3.	Credit period	Adequate	Just sufficient	Inadequate
4.	Availability of additional credit	Always	Sometimes	Rarely
5.	Commitments attached to credit facility	No commitment	Normal	Abnormal

B. Margin Available

1.	The goods sell well	Always	Sometimes	Rarely
2.	Profit margin	Good	Average	Poor
3.	Discount sales are compensated by the company	Always	Sometimes	Rarely
4.	Opportunity to improve profit margin	Good	Average	Poor
5.	Good profit in spite of poor sales	Yes	To some extent	No

C. Incentives to Improve Sales

1.	Incentives in cash are satisfactory	Agree	To some extent	Disagree
2.	Incentives in kind (Gift, free trips, etc.) are satisfactory	Agree	To some extent	Disagree
3.	Incentives are timely	Agree	To some extent	Disagree
4.	Incentives are on par with other similar companies	Agree	To some extent	Disagree
5.	Incentives are regular	Agree	To some extent	Disagree

D. After-Sales Service

1.	The service personnel are competitive.	Yes	To some extent	No
2.	After-sales service is carried out on time.	Always	To some extent	Rarely
3.	Spare parts are easily available.	Agree	To some extent	Disagree
4.	Dealer's sales personnel are also trained.	Always	Sometimes	Rarely
5.	Sales are good because of the company's prompt after-sales service.	Agree	To some extent	Disagree

E. Promotional Activities

1.	The company's print and electronic advertisements are effective in improving sales.	Always	To some extent	Rarely
2.	Promotional activities such as lucky-dip, contest, etc. are effective.	Always	To some extent	Rarely

3.	The company involves the dealers in ad campaigns.	Always	Sometimes	Rarely
4.	Ad campaigns costs are not passed on to the dealers.	Agree	To some extent	Disagree
5.	Ad campaigns are ethical.	Agree	To some extent	Disagree

ACADEMIC PERFORMANCE IN RELATION TO DEMOGRAPHIC, PERSONAL AND SOCIAL FACTORS—A STUDY OF MBA STUDENTS IN SELF-FINANCING COLLEGES

A. PERSONAL DATA

Gender	:	
Medium of study in school	:	
Type of school	:	Convent/Govt.
Degree	:	BBM/B.A/B.Sc/B.Com/Others
Percentage of marks in U.G.	:	
Parents' qualification	:	
Parents' Occupation	:	
Parents' monthly income	:	
No. of PGs/Professional degree holders in the family	:	
Nativity	:	Rural/Urban
College (UG)	:	Town/City
MBA I semester marks	:	%
MBA II semester marks	:	%

B. OPINION

I. Home/Hostel Enviornment: (Please (✓) the appropriate score) (Strongly Agree: 5, Agree: 4, Neutral: 3, Disagree: 2, Strongly Disagree: 1)

1.	Study/Hostel room is not convenient	5	4	3	2	1
2.	Disturbance from friends/relatives	5	4	3	2	1
3.	Distraction due to T.V/noise	5	4	3	2	1
4.	Mental disturbance for want of money	5	4	3	2	1
5.	Disturbance from family problems	5	4	3	2	1
6.	Disturbance due to extraneous work	5	4	3	2	1
7.	Joined against parent's wish	5	4	3	2	1
8.	Worries of ailment of self/family	5	4	3	2	1
9.	More preference to family business	5	4	3	2	1
10.	Worries due to unknown factors	5	4	3	2	1

II. Peer Influence (Please tick the appropriate score) (Always: 5, Frequently: 4, Sometimes: 3, Rarely: 2, Never: 1)

Classmates/Friends

1.	Prevent taking class notes	5	4	3	2	1
2.	Discourage clarifying of doubts	5	4	3	2	1
3.	Make fun while answering	5	4	3	2	1
4.	Compel for chatting	5	4	3	2	1
5.	Discourage going to library	5	4	3	2	1
6.	Prevent joining management meets outside	5	4	3	2	1
7.	Criticize while reading G.K. books	5	4	3	2	1
8.	Discourage participation in debates	5	4	3	2	1
9.	Prevent attending professional meets	5	4	3	2	1
10.	Make fun of contribution to magazines	5	4	3	2	1

III. Study Habits (Always: 5, Generally: 4, Frequently: 3, Sometimes: 2, Rarely: 1)

1.	Study only the easier topics	5	4	3	2	1
2.	Only superficial reading	5	4	3	2	1
3.	Not making up for missed classes	5	4	3	2	1
4.	Preparing for exam at 11th hour	5	4	3	2	1
5.	No discussion with friends	5	4	3	2	1
6.	Satisfied only with class notes	5	4	3	2	1
7.	Fail to clarify doubts then and there	5	4	3	2	1
8.	Do not read regularly	5	4	3	2	1
9.	Do not pay attention in class	5	4	3	2	1
10.	Absenting due to lack of interest	5	4	3	2	1

IV. Learning Problem (Strongly Agree: 5, Agree: 4, Neutral: 3, Disagree: 2, Strongly Disagree: 1)

1.	Dislike for certain subjects	5	4	3	2	1
2.	Problem in presentation	5	4	3	2	1
3.	Distraction due to day-dreaming	5	4	3	2	1
4.	Lose interest after few lessons	5	4	3	2	1
5.	No discussion with friends	5	4	3	2	1
6.	Satisfied only with class notes	5	4	3	2	1
7.	Fail to clarify doubts then and there	5	4	3	2	1
8.	Do not read regularly	5	4	3	2	1
9.	Do not pay attention in class	5	4	3	2	1
10.	Absenting due to lack of interest	5	4	3	2	1

V. Students' Attitude (Strongly Agree: 5, Agree: 4, Neutral: 3, Disagree: 2, Strongly disagree: 1)

1.	Enjoyment is preferable to study	5	4	3	2	1
2.	No models to follow	5	4	3	2	1
3.	Spending money/time in college is waste	5	4	3	2	1
4.	College education is just a status	5	4	3	2	1
5.	Passing is just a hit or miss case	5	4	3	2	1
6.	Should have gone for a job	5	4	3	2	1
7.	Subjects do not help in real life	5	4	3	2	1
8.	No hurry in getting the degree	5	4	3	2	1
9.	Should have joined some other course	5	4	3	2	1
10.	Joining college was a bad decision	5	4	3	2	1

GLOSSARY

Alpha error The rejection of null hypothesis which should have been accepted. It is also known as Type-I error.

Alternative hypothesis Denoted by "Ha", is opposite to Null hypothesis and states that there is difference, effect or association among variables.

Analytical research Also called as diagnostic research, it is a research design to find why a particular phenomenon has occurred or is occurring presently.

Annexures Materials which are not essential but help in appreciating the report, presented in the end pages after "Appendices".

ANOVA Analysis of Variance. It is a parametric test used to test the significance of difference of means of two or more samples.

Appendices Appendices are materials/ information which are closely related or essential to the study but could not have been incorporated in the body of the report, presented in the end pages after bibliography.

Applied research It aims at finding a solution to the current or long-pending problem.

Arbitrary scale A scale developed on ad-hoc basis depending on the researcher's own subjective selection of items.

Area sampling *See* Multistage sampling.

Basic research *See* Fundamental research.

Beta error Accepting a null hypothesis which should have been rejected. It is also known as Type-II error.

Bibliography A list of books, journals, reports, etc. which the author has gone through to understand the subject matter. It is presented in the alphabetical order of the authors in the end pages after References.

Bivariate analysis A type of analysis and hypothesis testing used in the simultaneous investigation of two variables.

Canonical correlation A statistical technique used to determine the degree of linear association between two sets of variables, each consisting of several variables.

Case study method An in-depth and thorough study of an organization, a group of people, an industry, an individual, a phenomenon, etc. over a period of time.

Census It is a collection of data/information from all the units/elements of a population.

Central tendency An error occurring when the raters are reluctant to give extreme judgement scores resulting in scores near the centre of the scale.

Chi-square test As a parametric test, it is used to test the significance of differences between population variance and sample variance and as a non-parametric test. It is used to find out the significance of differences between observed and expected values (Goodness of Fit test) and also to find out the association, if any, between two variables (Test of Independence).

Clinical interview   An interview technique concerned with broad underlying feelings, motivations or life experiences.

Closed-end questions   Standard questions with two or more alternative responses for the respondent to choose.

Cluster analysis   A statistical technique to classify persons, objects or situations into a small number of mutually exclusive and exhausted groups ensuring high internal homogeneity and high external heterogeneity.

Cluster sampling   A probability sampling technique where the units of population are divided into many groups or clusters and every cluster is considered as a sample unit. All the units in the randomly selected clusters are studied for inference.

Communalities   They are the percentage of total variance summarized by the common factors in factor analysis and found mathematically by squaring the factor loadings of a variable across all factors and summing them.

Comparative scale   A ranking scale where the respondent compares the items, objects, stimuli, etc. against a standard.

Completely randomized design   An experimental design where the treatments are allotted to the experimental plots completely at random enabling any experimental plot to receive any treatment.

Conceptual research   A qualitative research related to some abstract ideas defying clear explanations.

Conclusion-oriented research   A research where the researcher is free to choose a problem and design the research as he/she wishes according to the objectives or situation.

Conjoint analysis   A statistical technique to measure the combined effect of two or more attributes of a product or service that are important from one's point of view.

Consensus scaling (Thurstone scale)   A scale developed with questions or statements selected by a panel of judges.

Construct validity   The degree to which scores on test or measurement are accounted for by explanatory constructs of a theory.

Content validity   The extent to which a measuring instrument provides adequate coverage of the study.

Controlled observation   An observation method where the techniques are standardized with maximum control over extrinsic and intrinsic variables by adopting experimental design and recording the observations systematically.

Convenience sampling   A non-probability sampling technique where a sample is taken according to the convenience of the researcher. It is also called incidental or haphazard sampling.

Correlation   A parametric test to find out the relationship, if any, between two different sets of variables.

Criterion-related validity   It relates to the ability of a measurement to predict some outcome or estimate the existence of some current condition.

Cross-sectional research   A one-time research confined to a single period of time and the results are obtained within a short period of time.

Cumulative scale (scalogram)   A procedure to determine whether a set of items forms a one-dimensional scale.

Data processing   A process to identify variables, hypothetical relationship, if any, among the various variables and tentative research hypothesis.

Decision-oriented research   A type of research where the researcher conducts a research as per the requirements or direction of a decision-maker or authority.

Declarative question Question to which the answer is to be selected only from a series of statements given.

Deliberate sampling *See* Judgement sampling.

Depth interview An intensive and searching interview aimed at studying the respondent's opinion, emotions or convictions to elicit unconscious as well as extremely personal feelings.

Descriptive research/design A type of research design to describe the existing or past state of affairs. It is also known as Ex Post Facto analysis.

Diagnostic research *See* analytical research.

Dichotomous question Question to be answered either as 'yes' or 'no' without any choice such as "undecided", "do not know", "sometimes" or "partially".

Direct observation An observation for collection of data or information where the investigator observes the phenomenon personally when it takes place.

Discriminant analysis A statistical tool to classify people, objects, etc. into two or more categories based on several criteria.

Editing A process to detect and correct errors or omissions and mainly done to check for completeness, accuracy and uniformity.

Eigen values The sum of the squared factor loadings for a particular factor in factor analysis which helps in determining the number of factors to retain in the analysis.

Element/unit A member of the population and the subject on which information is collected or measurement is made.

Empirical research Data-based quantitative research amenable for verification.

Ethics in research Ethics refers to the moral principles and values that determine whether the actions taken are right or wrong and the outcomes are good or bad. Ethics in research is to ensure that no one is harmed or made to suffer due to the adverse consequences of the research activities.

Experience survey Interviewing people having adequate and relevant experience to secure insights into the subjects.

Experimental design A design where the researcher or experimenter is able to alter the variables of interest and observe the after-effect.

Experimentation A research to study the causal relationship between variables aiming at the effect of an independent variable on a dependent variable keeping other extraneous variables under control.

Exploratory design An unstructured design to gain familiarity with an unknown population or phenomenon.

Ex post facto design *See* descriptive design.

Factor A variable or construct in factor analysis that is not directly observable but is developed as a linear combination of observed variables.

Factor analysis A statistical tool to identify a set of dimensions that is not easily observed in a large set of variables. It is based on the systematic interdependence of the variables.

Factorial design An experimental design where the effects of more than one factor are studied simultaneously.

Factor loadings The relationship between observed variables and the newly produced factor in factor analysis.

Factor scales (Semantic differential scale) A scale based on inter-correlations of items which indicate that a common factor accounts for the relationship among items.

Factor variance The amount of variation explained by each factor in factor analysis which is found by squaring each factor loading in each factor, summing them and dividing the results by the number of the variables.

Field research Involves conducting research in actual situations by collecting data through observation, questionnaire, interview, etc. from real population.

Finite population The number of elements or units in a population is limited and accessible to the researcher for data collection. It is known as finite population.

Focused interview A semi-structured interview where the investigator attempts to focus the discussion on the actual effects of a given experience to which the respondents have been exposed.

Focus group A panel of individuals led by a trained moderator to focus or guide the group in an exchange of ideas, feelings and experience on a specific topic.

Forced ranking scale A ranking scale where the respondent ranks the attributes or objects relative to each other.

Formal research A full-fledged serious research with substantial structure of well-defined parameters.

F-test A parametric test based on *F*-distribution and used to compare the variances of two independent samples.

Fundamental research Basic or pure research. Fundamental research is concerned with throwing light on the basic aspects, theory or the intricacies of a phenomenon.

Halo effect A systematic bias the rater introduces by carrying a generalized impression from one rating to another.

Haphazard sampling *See* Convenience sampling.

Historical research The analysis and interpretation of historical records or documents (secondary data).

Hypothesis A statement, assumption, proposition, tentative answer, generalization or a shrewd guess to be verified by survey observation or experimentation.

Hypothesis testing *See* Test of Significance.

Incidental sampling *See* Convenience sampling.

Indirect observation An observation for collection of data/ information where the physical presence of the observer is not required and the recording is done by mechanical, photographic or electronic devices.

Infinite population If the researcher has no definite idea of the total number of units of a population and accessibility to all the units is not easy for data collection, it is an infinite population. It is also referred to as universe.

Interim report A short report before completion of the project on the work carried out so far and the work to be done to give indications that a particular line of work is in progress and to avoid repetition of the same type of work by others.

Interpretation A task of drawing inferences from the collected data or information after an analytical and/or experimental study.

Interval scale Placing objects or persons in order with distance relationship but without origin.

Interviewing A two-way systematic conversation between the researcher and the respondent, initiated for obtaining information relevant to a specific study.

Interview schedule A questionnaire or schedule used to collect information or data from the respondents through interviewing and recording the same by the researchers themselves.

Item analysis (Likert scale) A procedure for evaluating an object, group, institution, etc. based on how well it discriminates between those persons whose total score is high and those whose total score is low.

Judgement sampling Also known as deliberate or purposive sampling. It is a non-probability sampling technique where the researcher exercises his/her judgement in the choice of sample units and includes those units in the sample which he/she thinks are most typical of the population with regard to the characteristics under investigation.

Lab research A small group study on random behaviour, role plays and role analyses.

Latin square design (LSD) An experimental design in a two-dimensional heterogeneous population where the treatments are allotted in such a way that each of the treatments will find a place in the column as well as the row.

Leniency It is an error occurring when a respondent is an "easy-rater" or "hard-rater".

Level of significance A level of risk involved in taking a decision based on the study.

Likert scale *See* Item analysis.

Limitations of the study Difficulties or problem encountered by the researcher at various stages of the research process starting from defining the problem to final conclusion.

Local control Controlling of all factors excepting the ones under investigation in an experiment to reduce variation or exclude the effect of extraneous influence.

Longitudinal research A research extended over a longer period of time to yield any result.

Mail survey (positive/e-mail) A method of collecting data or information by mailing the questionnaire to respondents for their response.

Measurement Assignment of numerals to objects/ events according to rules or to represent amounts or degrees of a property possessed by all of the objects.

Multiple choice questions Questions to which the answers will be multiple (more than one).

Multiple regression analysis A statistical tool to find out the effects of more than one independent variable on a dependent variable.

Multi-stage sampling A probability sampling technique involving selection of units randomly in several stages.

Multivariate analysis Statistical methods that allow simultaneous investigation of more than two variables.

Nominal scale Classification of variables into several sub-classes by assigning numbers or any other symbols without any order, distance relationship and origin.

Non-parametric tests Tests used when the population is not normal (skewed population) and the parameters of the population such as mean, variance, standard deviation, etc. are not known.

Non-participant observation An observation for collection of data/information where the observer stands aloof and records his observation without actually participating in the phenomenon.

Non-probability sampling Each and every unit does not have equal chance to enter into the sample and units are included in the sample merely by chance or accident.

Non-sampling error The difference between true population value and the sample value due to sources other than sampling such as errors in observation, measurement or response.

Null hypothesis Denoted by Ho, a null hypothesis generally states that there is no difference, no effect or no association among variables.

Objectivity The willingness and ability to conduct research without any favour, fervour, hatred or partiality.

Observation A systematic viewing of a specific phenomenon in its proper setting for the purpose of gathering data for a particular study.

One-way ANOVA A statistical tool to test only one hypothesis as the data are classified according to only one criterion.

Open-ended questions Unstructured questions providing free scope to the respondents to reply with their own choice of words and ideas.

Ordinal scale Placing objects/persons in order by assigning ranks in ascending or descending order without distance relationship and origin.

Paired comparison A ranking scale where the respondent expresses attitudes/opinions unambiguously by choosing between only two objects/factors.

Paired *t*-test A parametric test based on *t*-distribution to test the significance of difference of values of means in the same sample (before and after treatment).

Parameters Characteristics of a population such as total number of units (N), mean, variance and standard deviation. *See* Statistics.

Parametric tests Tests used when the population is normal and the parameters of the population are known.

Participant observation An observation for collection of data or information where the observer is a part of the phenomenon or group which is observed and acts as both an observer and a participant.

Pilot study It is a mini-project or a "small-scale" replica of the main study. It is a miniature rehearsal of the main research.

Population Also known as universe. It is the total collection of elements or units about which some inferences are drawn.

Practicality Quality of an instrument or method which is economical, convenient and interpretable.

Pretesting of questionnaire To test the questionnaire whether it is effective in collecting the required information or data by administering the same on a small group of respondents. It is tested for validity, reliability and practicality.

Primary data Data collected directly by the researcher from the original sources afresh.

Pure research *See* Fundamental research.

Purposive sampling *See* Judgement sampling.

Qualitative research Research concerned with the quality of phenomena which are not easily measured in quantitative terms.

Quantitative research Research in which the observations are quantified and the results are expressed in terms of different units.

Quota sampling A non-probability sampling technique where quotas (proportions) are set up in the heterogeneous population and within each quota (homogenous proportion of population) sample units are selected according to the convenience or judgement of the researcher to form a composite sample.

Questionnaire A set of questions posed to the respondents in writing to collect data or information for a specific study and the responses being filled in by the respondents.

Randomization Assigning the treatments or factors to be tested to experimental units according to definite law of probability to reduce or control the variation due to extraneous factors in an experiment.

Randomized complete block design (RCBD) An experimental design in a heterogeneous population where the experimental plots are grouped into separate homogeneous blocks, and treatments are allotted at random within each block ensuring that every block will have each of the treatments.

Rank correlation A statistical tool used to find out the significance of association between ranks.

Ranking scales Also known as category scales, Ranking scales are used to give scores on object or attitude without making a direct comparison to another object or attitude.

Ratio scales The highest and ideal level of measurement containing order, distance relation and origin.

References Works or studies or reports referred to in the body of a report and presented in the alphabetical order of the authors in the end pages.

Reliability Ability of an instrument (questionnaire, interview or observation) to measure accurately with consistent results.

Replication Repetition of an experiment under identical conditions for confirmation of results in an experiment.

Research A systematic or scientific investigation to search for solutions to the existing and future problems, to establish relationship, if any, among variables or to find something new to increase the body of knowledge.

Research abstracts Brief summaries of technical report/theses/dissertations circulated for a quick review before a detailed examination is made.

Research articles Short technical reports on projects published in professional journals in specific formats.

Research design A logical and systematic plan to conduct a research study. It is a blue print detailing the objectives, methodology, techniques, sources of data, collection of data and allocation of resources/time.

Research methodology The way a research problem is systematically solved employing the relevant research methods.

Research methods The technologies a researcher employs in conducting research.

Research problem Some difficulty experienced by a researcher in the context of either a theory or practical situation which requires a solution.

Research process The methodology or well-defined procedure of conducting a research.

Research report A formal statement of the details of the research process and its results giving an account of the problem studied, objectives, methodology, findings and conclusions.

Review of literature Surveying and examining all available literature (information) concerning the research problem, right from the concept/theory through methodology to the style of presentation of a report.

Sample The portion of the population which is supposed to truly represent the population.

Sampling The process of selection of a sample (a part of the population) with a view to obtain information or draw inference about a population.

Sampling error The difference between the true population value and the sample value due to non-representativeness of the sample or the inadequacy of the sample size.

Sampling frame A list of all sampling units from which the sample is to be drawn.

Sampling technique/design The procedure adopted to draw a sample from the population.

Scaling A procedure to assign numbers (or symbols) to a property of objects to impart some of the characteristics of numbers to the properties in question.

Scalogram *See* Cumulative scale.

Scope of study A statement in a report covering the geographical area, targeted population, specific activities, period of study, etc. of a particular study.

Secondary data Data which has been already collected by others.

Semantic differential scale *See* Factor scales.

Simple random sampling A probability sampling technique in which each and every item of the population is given an equal chance of being included in the sample.

Simulation research   Studying any phenomenon through duplication of the real situations extensively using computers.

Snowball sampling   A non-probability sampling technique of "building up" a list or a sample of a special population by using an initial set of sample units or members as indicators/informants.

Statistics   They are characteristics of a sample such as total number of units, mean, variance and standard deviation. *See* Parameters.

Stratified sampling   A probability sampling technique where the heterogeneous population is divided into smaller homogeneous groups or strata. A composite sample is taken by combining the sub-samples drawn from each stratum randomly.

Structured or directive interview   An interview with a detailed, standardized schedule where the researcher puts the same questions to all the respondents in the same way and in the same order to promote measurement reliability.

Systematic sampling   A probability sampling technique which involves selection of every kth item from the list where k refers to the sampling interval and calculated by dividing the size of the population with the sample size.

Tabulation   A process of summarizing raw data into meaningful categories and presenting them for a quick understanding.

Target population   A part of the population about which the study is concentrated.

Technical report   *See* Research report.

Test of significance   A technique to find out whether or not the observed means, percentages, proportions, variances, etc. differ significantly by formulating a test criterion on which to base one's judgement whether a difference in the parameters/statistics is a chance difference due to extraneous factors or the difference is genuine.

Thurstone scale   *See* Consensus scaling.

Total variance   A summary measure (%) in factor analysis indicating how much of the total original variance of all the variables is represented by the factors.

t-test   A parametric test based on t-distribution and used to test the significance of difference in means when the sample size is small (<30 units) and population variance is not known.

Type-I error   *See* Alpha error.

Type-II error   *See* Beta error.

Two-way ANOVA   A statistical tool to test two hypotheses simultaneously as the data are classified on two dimensions/criteria.

Uncontrolled observation   A type of observation system which has no control over the extrinsic and intrinsic variables and primarily used for descriptive research.

Univariate analysis   A type of analysis that assesses the statistical significance of hypothesis about a single variable.

Universe   *See* Infinite population.

Unstructured or non-directive interview   An interview technique where the interviewee is encouraged to talk freely with a minimum of prompting or guiding, and employed to collect data in exploratory research or to gather information on sensitive topics.

Validity   The extent to which a test measures what is actually meant to be measured.

Z-test   A parametric test based on normal probability distribution to judge the significance of difference of several statistical measures, particularly mean and proportion, when the sample size is large (>30 units) and population variance is known.

BIBLIOGRAPHY

Alan Bryman and Emma Bell.(2010). *Business Research Methods*. Oxford University Press, New Delhi. p. 786.

Amir, D. Aczel and Jayavel Sounderpandian. (2008). *Complete Business Statistics*. Tata McGraw-Hill Publishing Co. Ltd., New Delhi. p. 820.

Beri, G.C. (2008). *Business Statistics*. Tata McGraw-Hill Publishing Co. Ltd., New Delhi. p.728.

Bharadwaj, R.S. (2008). *Business Statistics*. Excel Books, New Delhi. p. 773.

David, J. Luck. and Ronald, S. Rubin. (2006). *Marketing Research*. Prentice-Hall of India, New Delhi. p. 683.

David, R. Anderson, Dennis, J. Sweeney and Thomas, A. Williams. (2009). *Statistics for Business and Economics*. Cengage Learning India Pvt. Ltd., New Delhi. p. 1023.

Donald, R. Cooper and Pamela, S. Schindler. (2006). *Marketing Research–Concepts and Cases*. Tata McGraw-Hill Publishing Co. Ltd., New Delhi. p. 771.

Donald, R.Cooper and Pamela, S. Schindler (2010). *Business Research Methods*. Tata McGraw-Hill Publishing Co. Ltd., New Delhi. p. 757.

Gilbert, A.Churchill, Jr. and Dawn Iacobucci. (2008) *Marketing Research–Methodological Foundations*. Cengage Learning India Pvt. Ltd., New Delhi. p. 694.

Gupta, S.C. and Kapoor, V.K. (2009). *Fundamentals of Mathematical Statistics*. Sultan Chand and Sons, New Delhi.

Hooda, R.P. (2006). *Statistics for Business and Economics*. Macmillan, Delhi. p. 855.

Kothari, C.R. (2009). *Research Methodology-Methods and Techniques*. New Age International (P) Ltd., New Delhi. p. 401.

Richard, I. Levin and David, S. Rubin. (2009). *Statistics for Management*. PHI Learning Pvt. Ltd., New Delhi. p. 1026.

Teresa Brannick and William, K. Roche. (2001). *Business Research Methods*. Jaico Publishing House, Mumbai. p. 296.

William, G. Zikmund and Barry, J. Badin. (2007). *Essentials of Marketing Research*. Thomson South-Western, Delhi. p. 414.

William, M. and Trochim, K. (2008). *Research Methods*. Biztantra, New Delhi. p. 363.

www.ingramcontent.com/pod-product-compliance
Lightning Source LLC
Chambersburg PA
CBHW081209130726